# HOME & Garden

# 100 EASY ANNUALS

| | | |
|---|---|---|
| **Home & Garden**<br>**No. 1** | **Vice President, Editorial**<br>Becky Bell | **Senior Art Director**<br>Pat Murray |
| | **Creative Director**<br>Marissa Conner | **Electronic Publishing Specialist**<br>Ron Gad |
| | **Special Projects Editor**<br>Arthur Walker | **Contributing Writer**<br>Lynn Adams, M.S. |

**Lynn Adams** has an M.S. in botany and has written a number of gardening books on topics such as perennial flowers, herbs, and vegetables. She also is a popular lecturer and writes about gardening for magazines and newspapers. She likes to grow annual flowers for landscape color and cutting and uses her garden to test promising new varieties.

Back cover: **Derek Fell** (center)

**Heather Angel**: 20 (left), 102, 149; **Bill Beatty**:125, 171; **Crandall & Crandall**: 90, 101, 131, 140; **Derek Fell**: 6–7, 8, 10 (bottom), 12 (bottom), 14 (top), 15, 17, 20 (center), 22, 33, 38, 39 (bottom), 43 (left center), 49, 50, 61, 82–83, 95, 100, 105, 111, 112, 114, 116, 119, 126, 143, 161, 175, 178, 187; **David Liebman**: 89, 92, 142, 147, 181; **Jerry Pavia**: Table of contents (bottom right), 13, 18, 19 (top), 20 (right), 21, 30, 43 (right center), 51, 66, 84, 85, 87, 91, 93, 94, 96, 98, 104, 106, 107, 109, 110, 113, 115, 117, 120, 121, 122, 123, 124, 127, 132, 133, 134, 136, 137, 138, 139, 141, 144, 145, 146, 150, 151, 153, 154, 155, 156, 157, 159, 160, 162, 163, 165, 167, 168, 169, 170, 172, 174, 176, 177, 179, 180, 182, 183, 184, 185, 186, 188; **Positive Images**: Patricia J. Bruno: 73, 74 (bottom), 108, 128; Karen Bussolini: 19 (bottom), 118; Jerry Howard: 11, 148; Ben Phillips: Table of contents (top left), 9, 10 (top), 12 (top), 14 (bottom), 25 (bottom), 39 (top), 43 (bottom), 86, 103, 135, 164, 173; **Richard Shiell**: 97, 129, 158; **Lauren Springer**: 88, 99, 130, 152.

Illustrations: Sharon Keeton; Mike Muir.

Map illustration: Susan and Mark Carlson/Publishers' Art.

LeRoy Collins Leon Co
Public Library System
200 West Park Avenue
Tallahassee, FL 32301

# CONTENTS

## EASY ANNUAL INFORMATION     7

Learn about planting and growing all kinds of easy annuals from seed to bloom. All of the aspects of gardening are covered, including: preparing the soil, gardening in containers, garden design, and getting the most out of your annuals.

*Chapter 1*
## ANNUAL BASICS     8

Getting a good start on your annuals garden will be much smoother when you choose easy, disease-tolerant annuals. Get all of the dirt on the most versatile annuals available. This chapter is brimming with enough suggestions to inspire any gardener!

*Chapter 2*
## A POTPOURRI OF ANNUAL USES     16

Planning a successful garden can be almost as much fun as reveling in its splendor. Such considerations as color, form, texture, and scale are outlined in detail. Also, get all of the hints and tips you need to garden in containers and for drying colorful annual cuttings.

*Chapter 3*

## IDEAL CONDITIONS FOR YOUR ANNUAL GARDEN 38

Most easy annuals are a snap to get growing. However, if you provide just the right conditions, your annuals will not only survive, they will thrive! Make sure your soil is of good quality, and plant your annuals in optimal conditions. Growing characteristics for annuals, such as amount of sun, type of soil, and whether and when to fertilize, are discussed.

*Chapter 4*

## GETTING THE GARDEN GROWING 49

Now that the beginning basics have been covered, it's time to get that garden going! The basics of growing your own annuals from seed, propagation, and selecting and planting prestarted annuals are outlined. Put your plans into effect and create some annual magic!

## PLANT HARDINESS ZONE MAP 64

*Chapter 5*

## KEEPING THE GARDEN GROWING    66

Your plans have been fulfilled: The annuals are planted, watered, and eagerly growing. But you want to be sure that the garden will flourish all summer. Get the basics of additional fertilizing, watering techniques, pruning and deadheading, and dealing with weeds. Also included is a chart outlining common pests and diseases and how to handle them.

## THREE GARDEN DESIGNS    80

## ENCYCLOPEDIA OF EASY ANNUALS    83

We've chosen 100 of the easiest, most common annuals to present to you in this encyclopedia. Each featured plant is depicted in full-color and important information such as description, easy-care growing instructions, propagation techniques, uses, and related species and varieties is included. This is your guide to getting the most out of every annual you plant.

## INDEX    189

# EASY ANNUAL INFORMATION

Planning and creating an annuals garden can be a truly fulfilling experience when you have the knowledge needed for success. Annuals are some of the easiest outdoor plants and flowers to grow—especially when you know their particular requirements. And one of the beautiful aspects of growing annuals is that you have the pleasure of creating a new garden design each year. Try new arrangements and types of annuals—experimenting with annuals is a wonderful way to express your individuality.

Whether you live in the country, suburbs, or city, in a house, townhouse, or apartment, annuals can always brighten your surroundings. Put the finishing touches on your new yard or spruce up your existing space. Within the following chapters, you will find all of the instructions you will ever need to grow your own annuals garden from start to finish. Take a little time, get your hands dirty, and then sit back and bask in the splendor that you have created!

*California poppies*

## Chapter 1
# ANNUAL BASICS

**W**HAT ARE ANNUALS? Annuals are fun and flamboyant flowering and foliage plants that germinate, grow, flower, produce seed, and die—all within a single growing season. Like thoroughbreds at the racetrack, they're off to a quick start—flowering in as little as six or eight weeks after the seed germinates and providing instant color when you buy plants pre-started in a greenhouse. Their fast-paced lifestyle provides welcome contrast to trees, which may take decades to mature, and even to young perennials, which may take a couple years to fill out.

Unlike hardy perennials and trees, however, annuals are transient. It is their nature to die when their life yearly cycle is finished or when frost and winter cold cut their existence short. This opens up an endless choice of new options for you. Using fresh, new plants each spring, you can change past color schemes, height arrangements, and even subtle combinations of leaf texture.

While these generalizations provide a good working definition of annuals, the huge cast of characters we call annuals encompasses a potpourri of different kinds of performers.

True annuals in the botanical sense live only one growing season, or even less time. Their life span is genetically programmed to end after they have flowered and set seed, paving the way for a new generation of plants. Sweet alyssum, for example, which thrives in cool spring temperatures, produces

*'Carpet of Snow' sweet alyssum*

tiny, white, sweet-scented flowers in abundance. But the combination of summer's heat and the stress of seed production often finishes the plant. This is not a sad story, because when the cool, moist weather of late summer or fall arrives, seeds dropped by that first plant may sprout into another generation.

Basil, an annual of the Old World tropics, thrives during frost-free weather and begins blooming about midsummer from a late spring planting. Should the flowers be allowed to go to seed, the foliage will begin to grow skimpy and the plant will begin to fade away. You can delay that process and encourage new growth by pinching off the old flower heads before they turn to seed.

Tender perennials, which account for most of the bedding annuals we grow, include geraniums, impatiens, begonias, and ornamental peppers. They are quick-maturing tropical or subtropical plants that thrive during warm weather but die with the first heavy autumn frost. If brought indoors before this chilly final curtain, pots of geraniums, fuchsias, perillas, hibiscus, and others could continue to grow for many years.

**EASY-CARE CHARACTERISTICS** For the past several decades, most large seed companies have focused on developing annuals that

*'Busy Lizzie' impatiens*

would inspire winter-weary gardeners making spring shopping trips. They developed neat, compact, early-blooming varieties that caught the eye in a 6-pack or 4-inch pot. But it didn't take long before annual suppliers realized that presenting a pretty package in the garden center wasn't enough. People want annuals that are going to perform well in the garden long after they leave the store. Consequently, they've endowed some of the easiest-growing annual varieties with improved resistance to diseases, a naturally full form, cold and heat tolerance, and sturdy, non-flopping stems. It is wise to look for some of these qualities in annuals for your garden.

**DISEASE RESISTANCE** For an annual to provide you with outstanding performance, it has to be healthy. And there is no easier or better way to ensure good health than to plant annuals that are naturally immune to problem diseases. Also, some annual varieties can tolerate diseases better than others.

One of the most remarkable examples of disease tolerance are zinnias 'Profusion Cherry' and 'Profusion Orange.' Garden zinnias *(Zinnia elegans)*, although enthusiastic bloomers and high performers, are particu-

*Garden zinnias*

*'Summer Madness' multiflora petunias*

larly prone to powdery mildew. This disease attacks during warm, humid weather, coating the plant with ugly white pallor and causing the flowers and leaves to drop. In contrast, the closely related *Zinnia angustifolia*, which develops smaller marigold-like flowers, is immune to powdery mildew. Hybrids between these two species, such as the Profusion Series, combine the flashy flowers of garden zinnias with built-in disease tolerance from *Zinnia angustifolia*—effectively achieving the best of both worlds.

Petunias, with their bright, open-faced flowers, may develop gray mold infections that attack older flowers during wet weather and can infect the stem, killing new buds and leaves and causing a significant decline in performance. Gray mold can be particularly troublesome for grandiflora petunias. These stately annuals bear magnificent, large flowers on a limited number of stems. When several stems are taken out of action, the plants will begin to look shabby. In bright and beautiful contrast are multiflora and floribunda petunias, which bounce right back after wet weather. Their secret is bearing slightly smaller flowers on many more stems, enough to lose a few to gray mold without effecting overall performance.

**HEAT AND COLD TOLERANCE** One of the true tests of an easy-care annual comes when mild spring weather turns to the blazing heat of summer. This inevitable change can spell the end to annuals that cannot tolerate too much heat. If heat tolerance is a priority in your area, look for annuals such as melampodium, native to Mexico and Central America, that are natural heat-lovers. Or for annuals like ivy geraniums, that ordinarily suffer in hot weather, look for heat-tolerant

*'Maxim Marina' pansies*

cultivars such as 'Matador Burgundy' and 'Matador Light Pink.'

Likewise, the transition from warm, frost-free weather in fall to frosty, late autumn weather finishes off most annuals. But a few hardy annuals, such as pansies, take the change without faltering. 'Maxim Marina' is one of the most exceptionally cold-tolerant pansy cultivars. It usually even opens a few blooms in late winter whenever the snow melts—a pleasant harbinger of spring.

**SELF-BRANCHING** Until recent years, a handsome bed of annuals was achieved only with painstaking pinching, removing the tip of every main stem on every plant. This process, still necessary on chrysanthemums, slows upward growth and encourages side branch development. It transforms a naturally tall and lanky plant into a full and bushy shape with more abundant blossoms.

Thankfully, with most annuals, this is no longer necessary—and you can thank breeders for that. They have developed annuals that branch out naturally, a trait that is called self-branching. The 'Super Elfin' line of extra-compact impatiens, which grow only 10 inches high and spread even wider, is an excellent example of self-branching. You also can find basal branching (extra sprouting

*Mixed zonal geraniums*

from the base of the plant), in zonal geraniums such as 'Melody Red,' 'First Kiss,' and 'Patriot Salmon Blush,' and also in the cascading floribunda geranium 'Maureen.' In upright-growing larkspurs, the self-branching 'Imperial' develops into a particularly handsome plant.

**NATURALLY COMPACT GROWTH** Neat, low-growing annuals have been a hot commodity for the past 20 years, primarily because they look great in the spring nursery. They also need little planning to use in the garden as they can spread in low sweeps across the front of a garden, below shrubs and trees, and in large, bright, ground-hugging

bedding schemes. If you like annuals to be low, you have an excellent selection from which to choose. Melampodium, for instance, reaches only 10 to 15 inches in height and spreads even wider to make a graceful, low mound. Sunflowers, gangly annuals reaching heights as grand as 10 feet, have been reduced to knee-height with the cultivar 'Sun Spot.' And this strain bears full-sized flower heads regardless of its miniature stem. Many wonderful ground cover-type annuals such as the 'Purple Wave' and Surfinia petunias and verbena 'Imagination' grow only inches high and can spread for several feet.

*'Medallion' melampodium*

*'Brandywine' cannas*

One of the best of the tall annuals is the stately canna, a tender perennial that has a stocky main stem that may reach a height of 5 feet and bear large tropical leaves and spikes of big, bright flowers. For a sturdy-stemmed, 18-inch-tall version of the compact ageratum, with its charming blue, powder-puff flowers, look for 'Blue Horizon.' There are also taller and easy-growing versions of begonias, marigolds, and calendulas well worth considering.

**SELF-SUPPORTING STEMS AND FLOWERS**
Not everyone wants compact flowers—in fact, there has been a backlash against the huge numbers of neat, low annuals and a return to popularity for taller annuals. Long-legged flowers work well for providing height in the rear of the annual garden, filling in the gaps between newly planted perennials, or providing long-stemmed cut flowers. However, in order to qualify as an easy-growing annual, long-stemmed beauties must be sturdy enough to hold their own flowers up and not fall flat in a gale.

**SELF-SHEDDING FLOWERS** A few annuals, such as Shirley and California poppies, are self-shedding. They drop their old petals naturally so you don't have to watch them deteriorate or go outside and cut them off. You may want to remove the developing seed pods,

*California poppies*

however, so plants can put their energy back into producing more flowers and maintaining their foliage.

**CALCULATE YOUR CONDITIONS** Most annuals, with the exception of certain fussy rare wildflowers and unusual alpines, can be easy to grow if you keep one condition in mind. You need to find annuals that will thrive in the growing conditions—sun or

*Fibrous-rooted begonias*

shade and soil type—you have at home. Man-handling even the most durable petunia into a deeply shaded, root-riddled nook under a large spruce tree won't produce satisfactory results. Where conditions are marginal, annuals seldom grow or flower and, in this weakened state, fall prey to pests and dis-eases. But put the same plant into loose, rich, and fertile soil and full sun, and it can reward you with lavish blossoms for months.

Read Chapter 3 ("Ideal Conditions for Your Annual Garden" pages 38–48) to learn about your site conditions. Then pay atten-tion to the labels on annuals in the garden centers and consult details in the "Encyclo-pedia of Easy Annuals" (pages 82–88) to find a plant that matches your garden's quotient of sun or shade, light or heavy soil. Where you have full sun, globe amaranth and cosmos are ideal. For well-drained, light soil, try candy-tuft and lantana. Where the soil stays moist most of the time, caladiums, calla lilies, and fuchsias thrive.

Certain extra-easy annuals, such as fibrous-rooted begonias and ageratums, are flexible and adaptable. They can grow in a variety of good garden sites in sun or light shade. Coleus, with rainbow-colored leaves, stays more compact in full sun and needs careful atten-tion to watering. But it also thrives in shade, reaching slightly greater heights and often going for longer

*'Blue Hawaii' ageratums*

periods without extra irrigation. Beginning gardeners, still getting a feel for site conditions, can get great results when working with these easy-growing annuals.

One way to identify especially adaptable annuals is to look for All-America Selections Winners, a list

*Black-eyed Susans*

of the best new annual cultivars released every year. New annuals are grown in 33 different flower judging locations and 21 different bedding plant locations, located as far south as Disney World in Orlando, Florida, to as far north as Devon, Alberta, Canada. Winners must excel in all these locations, without regard to variations of soil type and temperature. This means that there's an excellent chance that they'll do the same for you.

Some of the truly great and easy-growing past winners for sun include 'Indian Summer' coneflower, with 6-inch-wide, golden, black-eyed Susan–type flowers on plants reaching to 3½-feet high. 'Purple Wave' petunia is a remarkable annual with brilliant purple flowers on creeping stems that spread to 5 feet across. For a unique look in a 12- to 14-inch-high annual, try 'Strata' salvia, with upright spike-shaped inflorescences with blue petals emerging from a gray background. The breakthrough mildew-tolerant zinnias, 'Profusion Cherry' and 'Profusion Orange' are also All-America Selections Winners.

## Chapter 2
# A Potpourri of Annual Uses

**V**ERSATILITY, the ability to do many things well, is valuable in the sporting arena, the workforce, around the house, as well as in the garden. When it comes to versatility, annuals are the champs. They are fast performers, speedier than any other type of plant, providing nearly instant results in any garden—new or old.

Annuals' finite, one-season-long life cycle also has advantages. If you move, you won't be reluctant to leave the annual garden behind. You can replant annuals wherever you go just as easily as you did before. This is perfect for renters, who can enjoy one bright growing season without worrying about what will happen next year.

Annuals don't need any elaborate staging. You don't even have to own a house and yard or dig in the dirt at all. Many annuals will thrive in commercial planting mixes in pots or planters on a patio or balcony. They grow without worry for winter survival—as there would be for perennials—or any need for elaborate sheltering and wintering schemes.

Annuals can be changed at a moment's notice, sprucing up a flower garden, patio, or even an entire yard for an outdoor wedding, special guest, or just for your own pleasure. A favorite time for this is fall, when other plants are fading, and pansies, annual mums, and other cool season annuals are just beginning.

If you redesign your interior decor, you can change the annual colors outdoors to match. Echoing the pink floral on your curtains with same color of pink impatiens is an elegant way to connect outdoors and indoors.

*Geraniums in planters accent walkways beautifully.*

Picking up the blue pinstripe in the couch with a blue salvia is decorating perfection brought to life.

As time changes a beautiful landscape, annuals can come to the rescue, helping keep it colorful and lush. Your mature, old-fashioned roses or rhododendrons may grow leggy and barren around the bottom. A petticoat of larkspurs or annual poppies may be just the thing to bring them back into balance. A once-young tree surrounded by sun-loving perennials may have grown so much that it has made the area into a shade garden. Move the sun-lovers to a more appropriate site and let the shade sparkle with color from impatiens, tuberous begonias, and other annuals for shade. Replace a dead shrub or perennial, which otherwise would leave a gaping hole in the garden, with annuals.

No matter whether your garden is new or old, large or small, annuals are here to serve you in many ways.

**SELECTING ANNUALS** Your annual garden will have the most impact if, as part of the planning process, you consider all that each variety has to offer. One of the most effective annual planting schemes is also the easiest. Select one favorite flower and flood an entire planting area with it. Painted with uniform

*Astutely arranged annuals invite a lingering eye.*

highlights of pink, or blue, or gold, the entire yard glows with a simple beauty. When using this approach, you don't need to decide where to plant a particular variety; you don't need to be concerned about selecting colors and textures that blend well together; and there's no need to learn the cultural requirements for more than one kind of plant.

If you want some variation in height, texture, and color, however, mix different annuals or even different varieties of the same annual in your garden. But be prepared to spend a bit more time in planning. Consider flower and leaf colors, plant height, shade or sun preference, soil requirements—so that all the annuals will have optimal growth development and look great with their neighbors.

Planning ahead is easy if you just sit down and do it, preferably before you go annual shopping. Make a note on your calendar to devote a morning in winter or early spring, before the weather is warm enough for planting, to organizing the garden. It will give you a lift and ensure that your garden meets your highest expectations in the growing season to come.

Begin by listing your favorite plants on paper first, noting their available colors and cultural requirements—the technical term for growth needs. It helps to make columns of information such as height in inches, foliage color, flower color, sun or shade, rich or light soil. Then you can scan down the column and immediately see which plants are culturally compatible and what color combinations would occur if you grouped them together in a garden. Plan to put shorter annuals toward the front of the garden and build to taller annuals in the back, adding a third

*'Angel's Earrings' fuchsia*

dimension—space—to this creative process. As you narrow down the annuals that will work well together, you can actually see a workable garden emerge before your eyes.

Next, you will need to determine availability. If you choose the most common annuals—such as marigolds, pansies, and petunias—you will probably be able to find them at most garden centers. But if you want a specific cultivar, for instance, heat-tolerant 'Angel's Earrings' fuchsia or a more unusual annual such as a Mexican zinnia, you may have to look a little harder. You can call around to local greenhouses and specialty growers and ask if they have or can order these plants. If not, you'll surely find them in a mail-order nursery or commercial seed catalogue.

Always try to discover the best plant for a given location, rather than settling for one that happens to be readily available. Above all, don't worry too much about making a bad choice. One beautiful aspect of annuals is that you get another chance every growing season!

**COLOR** The dominant decorative characteristic of annuals is their color, bringing drama and excitement to the garden. Since there are annuals of so many different colors—every hue of the rainbow—you get the pleasant responsibility of considering questions of an aesthetic nature. Will a pale pink petunia look best beside blue ageratum, or would a bright pink be better? In most cases, there are no right or wrong answers to color questions, just the task of finding the spectrum that pleases you the most.

*'Aussie Sweetie' basil*

Flower color is important, but it's not the only color annuals bring to a garden. There is the foliage to consider, too. Look for subtle but interesting variations in green; from glaucous blue-green leaves of California poppies to the light green of bush basil to the dark green of ivy geraniums.

An increasing number of annual cultivars have maroon foliage—such as red-leaved cockscomb and cannas. Others—such as ornamental cabbage and New Guinea impatiens—have foliage that is mottled, striped, or variegated with yellow or white on a green background. Some annuals are grown primarily, or even exclusively, for their foliage. Outstanding examples are silvery-gray dusty miller, purple basil and perilla, and the myriad colors of coleus.

*Ornamental peppers*

Finally, there are those annuals that are primarily treasured for their fruits and seedpods. This group includes ornamental peppers and eggplants, castor beans (which are poisonous and inedible), and purple-beaned dolichos, which resemble a decorative climbing lima bean.

# SELECTING ANNUALS BY COLOR

There is no better way to start color planning than by listing the annuals that flower in the color range you are looking for. This is by no means a complete list (many of these annuals come in several colors), but it should give you some idea of how to begin.

Because there are always new cultivars coming out in stunning new hues, you will be able to add to these color lists. Check seed and nursery catalogues for the latest in annual varieties.

**WHITE**
sweet alyssum
globe amaranth
browallia
chrysanthemum
cobbity daisies
cosmos

English daisy
forget-me-not
impatiens
moonflower
morning glory vine
pincushion flower
snow-in-summer
zinnia

**BLUE**
bachelor's button
browallia
heliotrope
larkspur
lobelia
love-in-a-mist
nierembergia

salvia
statice

**PURPLE**
annual candytuft
dianthus
foxglove
impatiens
larkspur
pansy
perilla

salvia
stock
viola

**RED**
calliopsis
canna
castor bean
cockscomb
dianthus
dracaena
fuchsia

geranium
hibiscus
lobelia
nasturtium
scarlet runner bean

**PINK**
ageratum
baby's breath
begonia
caladium
annual candytuft
cleome
coleus
gladiolus
lantana
musk mallow
nicotiana
phlox
sweet pea
vinca

**YELLOW**
tuberous begonia
black-eyed susan
blanket flower
calliopsis
dill

gladiolus
licorice plant
marigold
melampodium
petunia
California poppy
portulaca
primrose
snapdragon
strawflower

sunflower
zinnia

**ORANGE**
tuberous begonia
blanket flower
calendula
calliopsis
dahlia
lantana
marigold
portulaca
primrose
tithonia

Colors of flowers, foliage, and fruit all have their places in the annual garden. Consider the potential of each before planting to get the most satisfaction out of gardening.

**FORM** Besides color, you can paint beautiful pictures with annuals by blending different overall plant forms and flower shapes. Annual plants range from tall and skinny like cosmos to low and spreading like 'Purple Wave' petunia. Their flowers vary between tall spikes, round globes, sprays, and clusters. While grouping clumps of identical plants provides simplicity and strength, your design will be most interesting if you also develop a pleasing mixture of contrasting plant and flower forms.

The forms you choose to use will influence the atmosphere of the garden. A flower bed planted exclusively with such open, airy plants as baby's breath and asparagus fern would appear to be a floating mist. By contrast, a bed planted entirely with bold, massive plants, such as marigolds, would be heavy and solid-looking. But a blend of both creates the beauty of contrast and balance.

For an example of how you might blend colors, forms, and heights, consider this hypothetical garden. You might devote the front of the garden to large masses of fibrous-rooted, pink-flowered begonias with some purple-flowered creeping petunias filling openings between them. For the middle of the garden, try vase-shaped 'Blue Horizon' ageratums planted in clumps of seven or nine and mingled amid red, spike-flowered nicotiana and more creeping petunias at their feet. The rear of the garden could feature large sweeps of upright cosmos with pink flowers that match the begonias and occasional spike-flowered red cannas that echo the color of the nicotiana.

*Nasturtium*

**TEXTURE** As you work through annual characteristics with an increasingly focused eye, you will notice the varying qualities of annual foliage, well beyond its color alone. Annuals such as geraniums, nasturtiums, and ornamental cabbage have bold leaves—large and

*'Royal Queen' cleome*

plants, such as vining hyacinth beans with small flowers, appear demure. Small plants with huge flowers, such as 'Super Elfin' impatiens, may seem gaudy or at least attention-grabbing. Some annual species, zinnias for example, offer a wide range of flower sizes and forms on plants that are all pretty similar. You can juggle use of this full range of flower and plant size to provide interest in your garden.

When choosing plants for a garden, match the size of the garden or yard to the size of the plant for a pleasing proportion overall. Miniature plants are great to use in small spaces and where people are close enough to see them, but in a large area, they can become completely lost. On the other hand, large-growing plants, such as cleome, cosmos, and vining nasturtiums, may dominate and even smother smaller neighbors when your gardening space is limited.

rounded. Even more dramatic are the huge palmate leaves of castor bean and the shield-shaped leaves of caladium. These leaves provide design strength, but they might overwhelm some gardens if used exclusively. They can be counterbalanced with more finely textured leaves, like the feathery foliage on cosmos and parsley and the tiny rounded leaves on bush basil.

**SCALE** The proportional nature of a garden or plant often influences how well you like a particular annual or garden. Very large

**ANNUAL GARDEN DESIGN** Consider yourself lucky if you are able to create an attractive annual garden simply by planting out boxed plants or flower seeds without any plan. More often than not, this approach produces unsatisfactory results. Get organized in advance to make sure that you have everything you need, and know the best locations for all of your annuals. Try this easy six-step planning guide.

1. Start with a simple sketch, drawing a quick outline of your garden bed, noting its approximate dimensions and the amount of sun the area receives each day. Also list the names of your favorite annuals so you'll be sure to include most, if not all, of them in your plan.

2. Look up your favorite annuals and jot down the colors they come in and their growth habits. Mark down whether they prefer full sun, partial shade, or full shade. Also specify how tall they grow. Check to see if any of your favorites prefer a different amount of sun than your site has available; cross out those that prove to be unsuitable.

3. If you have very few favorites and a large space to fill, add a second list of annuals that you find attractive and that fit the conditions of your site. Use seed catalogs to help you choose. Be sure to note variety names and sources if a plant comes in more than one desirable color.

4. Use colored pencils to sketch planting sections within your bed outline. A more informal and interesting design will result if you vary the size and shape of these sections. Then decide which plants should go into each section of your plan. Remember to keep tall plants in the back and low plants up front, filling in with intermediate heights. If a bed is going to be in an area where it will be seen from all sides, the tallest plants should be in

*Open space becomes an oasis in this garden design. (See page 80 for garden description.)*

the center of the bed with low ones around the outer edges.

5. As you plan, be sure flower colors in adjacent sections vary but don't clash. Maintain a balance of color in the bed. In large beds, repeat the same variety in several sections, making the sections much larger than you would in smaller beds. Once you've decided what will go in each section, double-check to be sure that you haven't inadvertently made a mistake. If you have, it's easy to change on paper.

6. Once the plan is in its final form, you can then figure out approximately how many plants you'll need of each kind. This will help in ordering seeds for sowing or starting ahead and in buying commercial bedding plants. Caution: If you plan to buy bedding plants rather than growing from seed, remember that the variety of plants available will be limited. It might be best to visit suppliers and make a list of what colors and kinds of plants they have available before making your garden plan. That way you won't have to settle for substitutions or totally redo your garden plan.

**BEDDING OUT AND MASSING COLORS** The easiest, most straightforward way to use annuals is to select one favorite flower cultivar and flood the entire planting area with it. Certainly, the impact of all one kind and color of bloom can be very dramatic. Imagine an entire garden awash with fiery red geraniums or bold, yellow marigolds; fluorescent-pink fibrous begonias, or cooling white petunias!

Another advantage of this approach is that it eliminates the need to decide where to plant a particular variety, select colors and textures that blend together effectively, or learn the cultural requirements for more than one kind of plant. It can be a money-saving solution as well: You only need to purchase one or two

## GOOD CHOICES FOR BEDDING MASSES

Most low-growing to medium-sized annuals can be used for bedding schemes. However, among the best are those listed below that have gracefully mounded or creeping shapes and can grow together to appear like an unbroken carpet of color.

| | |
|---|---|
| ageratum | melampodium |
| sweet alyssum | nierembergia |
| China pink | petunia |
| coleus | pansy |
| forget-me-not | annual phlox |
| impatiens | portulaca |
| licorice plant | snow-in-summer |

*A formal design becomes the highlight of your yard. (See page 81 for garden description.)*

packets of seed to obtain enough plants to fill an entire planting area.

Variations of this approach are also possible. If you prefer a variety of colors, but all the same kind of plant, a checkerboard design would dramatically facilitate such a planting. The lipstick shades of impatiens work well in this kind of massing, as do geraniums.

Alternatively, some species come in an abundant variety of flower and plant sizes and make interesting subjects for a design all their own. A bed filled with marigolds, for example, could include everything from dwarf 10- to 12-inch French marigolds in front of larger flowered 2- to 3-foot-tall background clumps of American marigolds. For a carefully color-coordinated pair, try 'Queen Sophia' French marigold, with russet-red

petals edged in gold, at the feet of 20-inch-tall golden-flowered 'Gold Lady,' both of which are extremely vigorous and foolproof.

Another way to mass annuals is to keep to a single color but use several different plant varieties. The resulting garden would contain plants of different forms and heights with a variety of different flower shapes, all in varying shades of one color. A unique option for this style of massing would be a silver-gray garden.

*'Burgundy Sun' coleus*

No matter which design option you select, massed plantings are generally rather formal looking—bold and dramatic rather than homey or quaint. They're the perfect

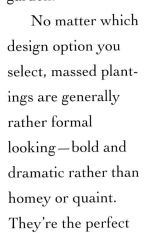

complement to a large or formal house. They also provide a clean, uncluttered look where garden space is relatively limited.

**CONTAINER GARDENING** An easy and potentially elegant option is container gardening. It is one of the most popular forms of gardening today. And, it is perfectly suited for annuals. You can plant mixed baskets, pots, planters, antiques, tubs, urns, old high-top tennis shoes—just about anything that will hold soil—with mingled annuals and tropicals. Or grow one kind of plant per pot for its singular and exceptional beauty. The potted plants become both miniature gardens and a living flower arrangement that can last for weeks or months.

You can garden in containers where other kinds of gardening are impossible, such as where there is no yard or soil available, on a rooftop, a high-rise balcony, deck, a fire escape, or even in an area that's covered with concrete. You can grow annuals in containers where the soil is predominantly composed of heavy clay or dry sand or in the small sunbeams that filter through tree canopies in an otherwise densely shaded yard.

The containers themselves can be as plain or elaborate as you wish, a reflection on your personal taste and budget. Clay or plastic pots; wood, plastic, or metal window boxes; decorator pots of ceramic, terra cotta, alabaster, or wrought iron; recycled plastic or metal pails; wire frames lined with sphagnum moss; a child's cast-off metal wagon; hanging planters; a plastic-lined bushel basket—any of these can be used. Here's a chance to use your imagination.

Bigger is usually better when it comes to growing annuals in pots. Bigger pots hold more soil and moisture, both essential facets for continued growth. And they suffer less-extreme temperature fluctuations than little pots. They also provide more space and sub-

*Both mixed and single annuals work well in pots.*

*Container gardening lets annuals go almost anywhere.*

stance for mixed plantings and allow you to flex your artistic thumb. One essential you should make sure is included in any container or pot—large or small—is bottom drainage holes. These allow excess moisture to escape so the pot won't fill with rainwater or over-abundant irrigation water, swamping the annuals inside.

Small, medium, or large (but lightweight) pots have yet another advantage; they are portable. You can move them here and there—to the back patio for a barbecue, to the front steps for a garden tour, or into the backyard for convalescence, if needed. Just remember to keep shade-loving plants in the shade to prevent an ugly case of sunburn. Sun lovers, which can tolerate shade for a few days, won't flourish if kept in the dark for much longer than that.

You can set individual planters on either side of a walk or doorway or at the corner of a patio or on a deck bench. Or, for a garden-esque effect, group pots in clusters, with smaller pots in the front and taller in the back. Try blending in houseplants brought outdoors for the summer months. Or insert pots in full bloom between shrubs or amid a perennial garden. Hang baskets and other containers from a garden fence, a low-hanging tree limb, or a porch rail. Even a small apartment balcony can be given a pastoral accent with potted annuals.

While you won't have to spend too much time caring for container plantings, they will require daily attention. Check every evening to see if the soil has dried out. When the weather is hot, dry, and windy, it doesn't hurt to check soil moisture morning and evening.

*Add depth to a backyard fence with hanging planters.*

Rub a small amount of the surface soil from each pot between your thumb and finger to test the moisture level. Be sure to check below the surface of the soil and not just on the very top of the container. Ideally, you want to rewater each planter before the soil becomes bone-dry. On the other hand, the soil should not be constantly soaking wet or the plants will drown. Therefore, it's necessary to keep track of the moisture level very conscientiously.

To be sure that water reaches all of the soil in the container, fill the planter to the rim with water, allowing it to soak in completely. If no water comes out of the drainage holes, fill again. Repeat this process until water starts to drip from the bottom of the container.

To keep the plantings looking full and to encourage abundant blooming, remove dead flower heads promptly. At the same time, check for any signs of insect or disease problems. Once every ten days to two weeks, water with a mild fertilizer solution. That's all it takes to keep container gardens in peak condition.

Container gardening can be an ideal solution for people with physical limitations that prevent them from working down at ground level. For anyone, growing annuals in containers can provide an extra dimension of gardening pleasure, both outdoors in summer and inside in winter.

### MIXED GARDENS

Annuals are harmonious plants that mix as well with ornamental trees, shrubs, perennials, herbs, and vegetables as with other annuals, brightening any dull spot. Only evergreen trees skirted in heavy shade year-round and shallow-rooted trees that fill the soil with roots and leave no soil for lesser plants are difficult companions for annuals.

*Let your creativity flow when gardening in containers.*

*Ivy-leaf geraniums, nierembergia, and calliopsis*

If most of your perennials have gone out of bloom in summer, slip in some taller annuals such as spider flowers or cannas to carry on with color. Plant ground-covering annuals such as sweet alyssum and forget-me-nots in the spaces between spring bulbs for synchronized bloom. The annuals can fill in as the bulb leaves die back. A flourish of bedding annuals can be just the thing to fill gaps left after perennials such as old-fashioned bleeding heart and poppies die back in summer and when early flowering biennials such as foxgloves and English daisies go to seed and fade away.

If your perennial bed is so packed that there is no free space in which to plant annuals, consider another approach. Place pots or boxes of annuals on small outdoor tables or stools. Tuck these display stands here and there in the border. Or, if there is a fence or wall behind the border, use it as a support

from which to hang half-baskets or window boxes full of flowering annuals.

Liven up the kitchen garden with edgings of pansies, calendulas, and other edible flowers, colorfully interplanted with red leaf lettuce and blue-leaved broccoli. If your kitchen garden becomes a little picked over by summer, add some quick-growing seeds of zinnias, dill, basil, sweet peas, and other seeds easily found on discount racks at the garden center. Since the kitchen garden is a working garden, you can feel free to add cut flowers such as dahlias, globe amaranths, and strawflowers. While in decorative gardens you can cut a few flowers but need to leave the rest on display, in this case you can cut every blossom if you wish.

*Sweet alyssum and vegetables*

When you combine annuals with vegetables, you can lay the garden out in various ways. You can plant annuals around the outer edges of the garden, hiding or disguising

the vegetable patch. Or you can plant rows of annuals here and there among the vegetables, attracting beneficial insects and pollinators to create a healthier, more environmentally friendly garden.

Another option is to make a formal geometric garden, laid out with some of the beds planted with annuals and others with vegetables. The final choice, of course, depends on your personal preferences as well as the dictates of your garden site.

Yet another place where annuals provide welcome cheer is in a spring-flowering shrub border that has settled down to mere greenery for the summer months. You can cheer it up with a big underplanting of shade-loving begonias and impatiens. You'll be amazed at how much more attractive such an area becomes when you add a generous helping of annuals.

## COTTAGE GARDENS Old-fashioned

gardens of European common folk and American colonists blended a variety of different useful plants—a hodgepodge of annuals, perennials, and shrubs. Frequently,

there were also trees, vegetables, and small fruits—strawberries, raspberries, or currants—mixed in.

It seemed that gardens, rather than being planned, more or less "happened." More likely, they evolved. As the gardener fancied something new or was given a plant by a friend, it was inserted into an available blank spot. Where yards were small and space was limited, these mixed gardens combined whatever was at hand. The end result often had an individual charm that was undeniable and delightful.

This same informal look and carefree nature is particularly appealing to modern gardeners, who may not have the time or

*Cottage gardens reflect the individual tastes of each gardener. (See page 81 for garden description.)*

desire to keep a painstakingly designed and highly manicured garden. You can enjoy the pleasure of growing and using wonderful plants—cut flowers, fragrant flowers, and edible foliage—without worrying excessively about design.

If you only have a small space for a garden, the mixed cottage garden makes especially good sense. You can squeeze in all your personal favorites, rather than limiting yourself to only a few kinds of plants—as is the case in massed garden designs.

Don't worry about what other people are doing in their gardens; your cottage garden is a reflection of your taste and preference. It exists solely to provide you pleasure. If your visitors also happen to find it enjoyable, so much the better.

Some uniquely charming cottage gardens are possible. Use spring-flowering fruit trees, such as peaches, pears, or apples, to supply partial shade to flower beds filled with combinations of different-colored annuals and perennials. Mingle clumps of your favorite vegetables, which visitors might never notice, among the flowers. You also can use more obvious and decorative vegetables that have bold foliage, such as Swiss chard and rhubarb, to complement nearby flowers and foliage textures. Feathery carrot tops, pur-

## ANNUALS FOR THE CUTTING GARDEN

| | |
|---|---|
| ageratum (long stemmed) | ornamental grass |
| | larkspur |
| globe amaranth | pot marigold |
| bachelor's button (long stemmed) | nicotiana |
| | pansy |
| calendula (long stemmed) | blue salvia |
| | scabiosa |
| canna | snapdragon |
| chrysanthemum | stock |
| cobbity daisy | sweet pea |
| cockscomb (long stemmed) | vinca |
| | zinnia |

plish beet greens, the bold and interesting foliage of parsnips, smooth, blue-green onion spikes, and tall, feathery asparagus ferns all make attractive additions to any flower bed.

If you don't want to be limited to only a few kinds and colors of flowers in your garden, consider planting a cottage garden. With the wonderful array of annuals at your disposal, it's even possible to have an entirely different and unique cottage garden every growing season.

**CUT FLOWERS** Watching flowers grow outside the window or along the walk is only part of the pleasure of cultivating annuals. If you plant some flowers for cutting, you can bring them indoors and put them in vases on the fireplace mantle, the kitchen counter, even in the bathroom and see them whenever you're nearby. You can observe the flowers up close, learning about the intricate patterns of the petals and how the colors interact with other flowers.

You might feel squeamish about cutting many blooms from your regular flower beds because you want as full and colorful a display as possible. Setting a special garden aside to supply flowers for cutting is a good solution. This can be a separate flower bed, or you can devote a row or two of your vegetable patch to a flower crop.

*Use a knife—not scissors—when taking cuttings.*

An easy way to begin is with packets of "Cutting Flower Mix" that contain a variety of flowering annuals. The mixture varies, but it will always include seeds that are easy to grow and produce nice, bouquet-type flowers. Mixes usually include some, but not all, of the following plants: marigolds, zinnias, feathered cockscomb, baby's breath, bachelor's buttons, calendulas, cosmos, asters, blanket flowers, and seedling dahlias.

The problem with buying such a mix is that you don't know in advance what colors the flowers will be. If you want to key the flower colors to the colors in your home or if you only want specific kinds of cut flowers, then you'll need to plant accordingly.

When cutting flowers for vases or arrangements, select flowers that are in bud or in early stages of bloom. Cut off and compost old flowers. They sap the plant of strength as they go to seed and often limit the production of new flowers.

For the longest possible period of enjoyment from cut flowers, pick them in the early morning when they are fresh and full of moisture. Use a sharp knife and make a slanted cut in the stem, just above the point where another flower bud or a side shoot is beginning to grow. This way, plant energy will shift to production of additional blooms.

Immediately after cutting, place the flowers in a container of water and bring them promptly indoors. Remove the leaves from the lower portion of each stem, immediately putting the flowers back into a tall container of fresh water. You can either arrange bouquets right away or keep cut flowers in a cool location to arrange later.

Each time you recut a stem, always use a sharp knife and cut on a slant. This keeps all available stem cells open to the transfer of water up into the cut flower and discourages wilting. Scissors and shears can pinch some of these water channels closed, which limits the life of cut flowers. Also, remember to remove all leaves that will be underwater once the flower is in a container. If left on, they'll rot, not only causing a terrible odor, but also diminishing flower life by clogging stem cells needed for water transfer.

Annuals are lovely in elaborate formal arrangements and in simple, informal bou-

*'Forest Fire' plumed cockscomb*

quets. It's easy to quickly make attractive bouquets if you keep these hints in mind as you pick and arrange flowers:

🌢 Select flowers in bud as well as in early full bloom

🌢 Select colors that blend well

🌢 Separate clashing colors with gray foliage or white flowers

🌢 Cut flowers at different lengths. Leave longer stems on smaller flowers; shorter stems on larger ones

🌢 Mix flowers of varying sizes and forms

🌢 Use containers that are narrower at the top than at the bottom for an easy, informal bouquet

🌢 Match container size to bouquet size

**DRYING ANNUALS** If you miss the vivacious color of annuals in the winter, then growing flowers for drying would be a good hobby for you. You can preserve a lot of dried flowers for all kinds of winter flower arranging or craft projects, or just a few for a favorite vase.

The flowers most easily dried are called everlastings. This group of flowers includes strawflowers, statice, and some cockscombs. Everlastings naturally keep their shape and color when dried. All you need to do is

hang them to dry—no special equipment or processing is necessary.

After picking, remove all the leaves and group the flowers in bunches of 6 to 8 stems. Wind an elastic band tightly around the stems. Hang the bundles upside-down in a dark but well-ventilated, dry area, like an attic or unused room. Leave enough space between bundles to allow for good air circulation. Another option is to protect the bundles by enclosing them in large paper bags. The flowers will dry in two to three weeks and are finished once the stems are snapping crisp. Store your dried flowers in completely sealed, airtight storage boxes that will keep humidity as well as insects out.

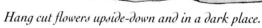

*Hang cut flowers upside-down and in a dark place.*

Some flowers are too thick and others too delicate to successfully hang dry. Instead you can dry them with a desiccant—a material that will draw moisture out of the flower and into itself. Floral desiccant is sold commercially. However, you can make it yourself by mixing equal parts of fine, dry sand and borax powder.

To use, pour an inch or more of desiccant in the bottom of a box, then lay the flowers on top. Very carefully, spoon more desiccant up and around each flower head. Once all of the flowers are mounded over, pour an additional inch or two of desiccant on top. Use a large, shallow box for long spikes of bloom, such as larkspur. For single, dense blooms, such as roses and marigolds, remove the flower stem first and replace it with a stiff wire stem. Lay the flowers flat on the surface of the desiccant, then mound more around and over them.

Drying will probably take several weeks, depending on the density of the flowers. When they're dry, carefully uncover them, gently brush away any adhering desiccant with a soft paintbrush, and store them in covered, airtight boxes in a dry place until you are ready to display them.

A third drying method is to press flowers and leaves between layers of absorbent blotting paper or paper towels. The drawback to this method is that everything comes out flat. But the flowers are wonderful to use in pictures, notepaper, or as a frame around a motto or wedding announcement, all of which would be costly handicrafts if you were to purchase

*To replace a stem with wire, first remove the old stem. Then slide a stiff wire through the center of the flower from the bottom. Make a small curve at the top of the wire and gently pull it down securely. Then, if you wish, you can wrap decorative tape around the wire.*

them at a gift shop. And you have the satisfaction of creating something on your own!

This pressing technique works best with small flowers that are not very thick, such as pansies, petunias, and baby's breath. It is also suited for parts of flowers, such as single petals of sweet peas, poppies, or cosmos. To dry, start with a piece of heavy cardboard as a base; then lay a sheet of drying paper on top. Carefully arrange flowers and leaves, making sure that there is space between them. Lay one or two more layers of drying paper on top. Arrange another layer of leaves and flowers. Keep alternating until you have a half dozen layers of plant materials. Top these with more drying paper and a final piece of cardboard.

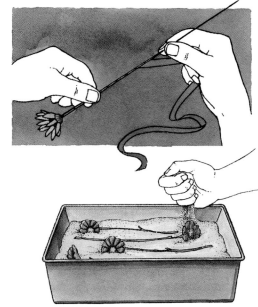

*Sprinkle the desiccant on and around the flower head.*

*When flowers are dry, use a brush to help dust the desiccant off of the head.*

*It sometimes helps to use clamps when drying flowers by pressing.*

Finally, place a heavy weight on top of the stack. Moisture will be squeezed out of the flowers into the paper. Check after a week to see how the drying is progressing. If any mold has formed, remove and replace the drying paper. After several weeks, the plant materials will be ready to use or store.

**ANNUAL VINES** Some annuals, real movers and shakers, grow as vines. They cover a lot of territory, creeping up a bare wall, fence, or trellis, winding up a tree trunk or into a shrub. When the annual vines have filled out, you know summer is in high season.

Where you need attractive year-round coverage, evergreen perennial vines are the better choice. You still can use annual vines, letting them help fill in areas that the perennials have not yet reached or making stalwart evergreens such as ivy and wintercreeper twinkle with color during summer. However, keep an eye on these annuals. As long as you are careful to prune back the annual vines if they threaten to overwhelm the perennials, the two can coexist very effectively.

Give annual vines some kind of support to climb so that they can reach for the sun instead of sprawling across the bed. Use a simple support of wire or string woven into netting or stretched vertically between the top and bottom of a constructed frame. You also can use more elegant trellises made from plastic or wood, either homemade, purchased preassembled, or as a kit. The vines will hold on to these supports by simply twisting their stems or leaf tendrils around it.

The first time you try annual vines, start with the most inexpensive and sensible choice. Run strands of sturdy twine up and down between two horizontal pieces of wood—one no higher than 6 inches from the ground; the other 6 feet or so above the ground. When the

*Give annual vines something to use for climbing.*

vine is done for the season, you can cut the twine off and throw it, vines and all, into the compost pile. To save a little start-up time, you can substitute woven polyester string netting or garden netting—both can be found at most garden shops—but these are not suitable for composting. If you plan to grow vines year after year, a more solid and permanent support, such as a wood, plastic, or metal trellis or climbing frame, is the best choice.

Whatever kind of support you choose, the most important factor to keep in mind is that vines become surprisingly heavy

*Pinch the growing tip of annual vines to stimulate growth.*

with foliage as the season progresses. The support should be solidly built and strong enough to hold up the vine's weight. A flimsy support will sag or even buckle and break partway through the season, leaving a troublesome tangle.

Annual vines require very little special care. When they first begin to vine, steer them toward the bottom of the support if they start to run along the ground rather than vertically. Once they start their climb, how-

ever, no other encouragement is needed. If you want to propagate multiple stems, pinch back the growing tip when the plants are 10 to 12 inches high.

Some annual vines only bloom during certain hours of the day. The moonflower vine, for instance, begins blooming late in the day and flowers overnight (hence its name); it has a lovely perfume and is ideal for a porch or patio that is used mostly in the evening. Morning glories, on the other hand, open early in the morning and bloom until about noontime. Most other annual vines bloom around the clock. Keep these factors in mind when you make your selections.

Annual vines are also effective when grown in window boxes or large pots on a house deck or apartment balcony. They'll twine up existing railings or any supports specifically constructed for them. With some imagination, it's possible to create an unexpected and delightful garden retreat far above ground level!

## Chapter 3
# IDEAL CONDITIONS FOR YOUR ANNUAL GARDEN

**I**T MAY BE TEMPTING to squeeze a few petunias into an old foundation planting by chipping some holes out of the ground and stuffing plants in. But rock-hard clay, riddled with roots and densely shaded by overgrown evergreens, does not make a promising location for flowers of any kind.

That barren opening on a sandy slope may seem to cry out for annuals. But barren, sun-cooked sand that is too dry for grass, ground covers, and other kinds of plants isn't likely to grow annuals either. Just because annuals are easy to grow doesn't mean that they can survive in impossible places.

To get the most out of your annuals, you need to set the stage for success. This is where preparing a healthy garden site in advance comes in. With good soil and suitable sunshine, success is practically assured. Just as

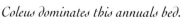

*Coleus dominates this annuals bed.*

students can breeze through classes if they do their homework and are prepared, easy-care annuals can perform without a hitch if you give them a good garden site.

Soil, the foundation of a good garden, should be loose and fertile with a good structure. Although you won't see all the growth that occurs underground, you can't miss the reflective effects of a well-developed root system in the lushness and longevity of shoots, leaves, and flowers.

Light, which provides the energy plants need to feed themselves, must be available in enough abundance to keep plants strong and healthy. How much sun will annuals need? That depends on which annuals you want to grow. Make a garden in full sun for sun-lovers. Or if your gardening area is shaded, choose between sun-loving annuals

# Annuals for Sun, Partial Shade, and Shade

If you have a sunny garden, you can choose from many annuals. As shade intensifies, your selection diminishes. If most of the yard is shady, you might still be able to enjoy sun-loving annuals by growing them in pots in any, or every, sunny opening.

### SUN

ageratum
sweet alyssum
globe amaranth
baby's breath
bachelor's button
black-eyed Susan
blanket flower
ornamental cabbage
annual candytuft
canna
castor bean
chrysanthemum
cleome
cockscomb
cosmos
dahlia
English daisy
forget-me-not
fountain grass
foxglove
geranium
gladiolus
golden ageratum

heliotrope
New Guinea
    impatiens
lantana
larkspur
lobelia
love-in-a-mist
marigold
morning glory vine
nicotiana
nierembergia
pansy
parsley
ornamental pepper
perilla
petunia
phlox

poppies
portulaca
scarlet runner bean
snapdragon
stock
strawflower
sunflower
sweet pea
tithonia
verbena
vinca
zinnia

### PARTIAL SHADE

ageratum
sweet alyssum
rose balsam
tuberous begonia
browallia
coleus
English daisy
dracaena
forget-me-not
foxglove

fuchsia
ivy-leaf geranium
impatiens
lobelia
nicotiana
pansy
parsley
primrose
viola

### SHADE

fibrous-rooted
    begonia
tuberous begonia

caladium
coleus
foxglove
impatiens

that tolerate light shade and annuals that prefer shade.

Paying attention to sun and soil requirements is the stuff that turns a black thumb into a green thumb. It is not some mysterious ability to commune with plants, but the basic knowledge of what elements plants need and the ability to provide those elements.

**LIGHT** Some people get mired in depression due to sunlight deprivation during gloomy winter weather. But plants require light to photosynthesize and make their own food, and the lack of sunlight can be deadly. Plants that love full sun may stop growing or become leggy and produce very few flowers if they're planted in a shady spot. By the same token, some plants are sensitive to too much light and will burn when placed in bright sunlight.

Instead of guesstimating sun levels, see how much sunlight is available in your chosen garden site and then determine whether you should grow annuals for full sun, partial shade, or full shade. Count the number of hours the sun strikes the bed. If it is six hours or more, the garden is in full sun. Four to six hours of sun makes for a lightly shaded or partly sunny garden. Less than four hours of sun dictates a shaded garden. Fortunately, there are annuals for all lighting conditions, except for those locations of deepest shade.

*Take soil samples from several areas in your garden bed.*

**SOIL** Soil qualities vary in every yard, and unfortunately it's hard to tell exactly what you're dealing with by solely looking at the surface. Soil may range from the extremes of constantly dry, nutrient-poor sand or 90 percent rocks held together with 10 percent soil to rich, heavy clay (which forms a slick, sticky, shoe-grabbing mass when wet, then dries to brick hardness). Fortunately, most soil conditions fall somewhere between these extremes. Still, very few people find they have the ideal "rich garden loam" to start a garden with. The first step is to determine your soil type. The way to do this is to have your soil tested. In some states, the county Cooperative Extension office will do soil tests; in others, it's necessary to use the services of a private testing lab, which can be recommended by the local Cooperative Extension office. Laboratories will send you a test kit consisting of an information sheet, which you should fill out, a packet for your soil sample, and an address to mail the kit and payment when ready.

*Once your soil samples have been collected, mix them well.*

Soil may vary slightly here and there in your yard, especially if you've already done some soil amending or if builders brought in new topsoil before planting the lawn. Therefore, take several soil samples to get a good overview of underlying conditions. When the soil is dry, dig down 4 to 6 inches deep to get soil from the prime root zone. Take a tablespoonful from each end of the bed and another from somewhere in the middle. Mix all of the samples together thoroughly in a single container to make a soil composite that will be representative of your entire garden area. Then mail the mixture to the soil lab.

Ask the lab for a complete soil test, which won't leave you guessing about any particular soil quality. You'll receive a report on the soil pH, results of a test that determines soil acidity or alkalinity. A pH between 6.0 and 7.0 is ideal and requires no adjustment. A pH below 6.0 indicates the soil is on the acidic side and may need adjusting with ground limestone. If the reading is over 7.2, the soil is too alkaline. To solve this problem, add powdered sulphur or, for quicker results, iron sulfate.

In addition to pH, you'll receive information about the nutrients in your soil. If there is a deficiency in any of these, you'll need to add the missing elements as recommended in the report.

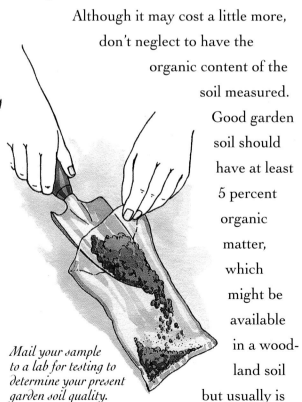

*Mail your sample to a lab for testing to determine your present garden soil quality.*

Although it may cost a little more, don't neglect to have the organic content of the soil measured. Good garden soil should have at least 5 percent organic matter, which might be available in a woodland soil but usually is

lacking in ordinary lawns. Adding an inch-deep layer of compost before planting, and every year afterward, can bring organically depleted soil back into the healthy range.

Some homesites have so little soil or the soil is so poor that it cannot—or should not—be used at all. You can garden on top of this soil, building slightly elevated planting mounds in gentle, curving shapes. Buy topsoil, preferably a premium blend that mixes good soil and organic material, from a quality soil supplier. Heap it up in the garden site, smooth it into a gracefully arching mound, and you're ready to plant. This may seem like a costly solution in the short term, but it will work much better than slowly trying to correct very difficult soil and will last

for years. You also can make more permanent and solidly structured raised beds, held in place with timbers, stones, or bricks. (See page 44.)

Another solution, especially in a small area, is to garden entirely in containers. You could install a deck or patio over the useless ground and then decorate it with container-grown plants to transform a sad eyesore into an oasis. (You'll find more details on container gardening on pages 26–28.)

**HOW TO PREPARE THE SOIL** Just as there are many ways to make wood into fine furniture, many different gardening techniques can achieve the same goal—better soil and a great garden. You can use the natural, organic approach or a fast—but often short-lived—approach using synthetic fertilizers and other chemicals. Either way, make sure you correct every shortage pinpointed by the soil test, and success will be yours. However, remember that synthesized chemical fertilizers

*Raised beds are a good solution for areas that lack suitable garden sites.*

# ANNUALS FOR DRY SOIL, AVERAGE SOIL, AND MOIST SOIL

**B**eyond providing anchorage for plants and a place for roots to grow, different types of soil provide varying levels of moisture. Soils high in coarse sand or gravel tend to be on the dry side while soils high in fine clay and organic matter remain moister. Well-drained loams, or combinations of sand, clay, and intermediate-sized particles, can be of average moistness. The following list groups annuals and their recommended soil types.

### DRY SOIL

sweet alyssum
globe amaranth
black-eyed Susan
blanket flower
calliopsis
annual candytuft
lantana
morning glory vine
nasturtium
portulaca
snow-in-summer
verbena
vinca

### AVERAGE SOIL

ageratum
sweet alyssum
globe amaranth
asparagus fern
snowstorm bacopa
fibrous-rooted
   begonia
tuberous begonia
bells of Ireland
black-eyed Susan
blanket flower

calendula
calliopsis
canna
candytuft
china pink
chrysanthemum
cleome
plumed cockscomb
cosmos

dahlia
dill
dusty miller
forget-me-not
fuchsia
geraniums
gladiolus
golden ageratum
heliotrope
impatiens
lantana

larkspur
lavatera
lobelia
love-in-a-mist
marigold
morning glory vine
musk mallow
nasturtium

nicotiana
pansy
petunia
phlox
primrose
salvia
snapdragon
snow-in-summer
sweet pea
verbena
vinca
zinnia

### MOIST SOIL

rose balsam
tuberous begonia
browallia
caladium
canna
coleus
dahlia
English daisy
forget-me-not
foxglove
fuchsia
geraniums
ornamental gourds
Chinese hibiscus
impatiens
lobelia
musk mallow
nicotiana
pansy
primrose

vinca

can be dangerous to animal life (including humans). Be sure to consider all of the options before making your final decision.

If the results of your soil test indicate a lack of certain nutrients, you should follow the recommendations for supplementing the soil. If the imbalance is slight, you can use organic fertilizers, which generally contain a low percentage of nutrients that are slowly released into the soil. Their gradual and, often, long-lasting effects may not be fast-acting or concentrated enough for immediate results. However, to avoid using too much inorganic fertilizer, a compromise can be reached. Use the quick-to-feed commercial plant foods first (in limited quantities), and then follow up in subsequent years with the natural, slow-feeding organic fertilizers.

Chemical fertilizer is commonly formulated in some combination of the three major

# MANY POSSIBILITIES FOR RAISED BEDS

Where there is much work to be done on less-than-ideal soil, building a raised bed or elevated planting area, may be the easiest solution for you. Raised beds become elegant elements of landscape, gracefully held behind retaining walls of stone, brick, or timbers. They elevate the planting area above the surroundings, ensuring good water drainage so soil won't stay soggy during extended wet weather. They also allow a generous amount of space for you to build an ideal soil.

Make simple, low-lying raised beds by raking soil up into a 4- to 6-inch-high mound (discussed on page 42) which can add some interesting gentle undulations to a flat yard. For more height and structural design strength, you can add some built raised beds. Use timbers to make square, triangular, or rectangular raised beds in formal, geometrically patterned gardens or working gardens of cut and edible flowers. Build low, dry stone retaining walls—made with staggered layers of flat rocks—for gently curving beds, elevated foundation plantings, or gardens beside stone patios or walks. Low brick retaining walls, which may require professional installation, are the perfect complement for raised beds located beside brick walks, patios, or homes. For easy maintenance, raised beds should be no wider than 4 feet or have an access path down the center so you can tend them without stepping on the soil.

*Elegant foxgloves highlight this raised bed design.*

*Once you have a spot picked out for your annuals garden, remove all of the sod from the area.*

nutrients: nitrogen, phosphorous, and potassium—N, P, K. The numbers featured on each bag represent the percentage of each of these nutrients in the mix. For example, 5-10-5 contains 5 percent nitrogen (N), 10 percent phosphorous (P), and 5 percent potassium (K). 10-10-10 contains 10 percent of each. The NPK formula is also listed on organic fertilizer labels, which usually have lower percentages of major nutrients but also may contain important trace elements such as calcium, iron, or magnesium in minute amounts.

If your garden soil lacks only one element, you can correct the deficiency with a fertilizer containing a single nutrient. Rock phosphate, for instance, is a source for phosphorus. Consult with your Cooperative Extension office

(there's one in every county) or another qualified horticulturist at a botanical garden, arboretum, or full service garden center if you feel uncertain about solving nutrient deficiency problems.

In addition to adjusting the nutrient and pH levels, you may need to alter the soil consistency, which influences moisture, oxygen, and nutrient availability. To fortify sandy soils, break up clay soils, or enrich average soils, add one or several "soil conditioners." The most commonly used conditioners are leaf mold, compost, well-rotted cow manure, and peat moss. For heavy soils, you also can add vermiculite, perlite, and sand (coarse builder's sand—*never* use beach or sandbox sand).

To properly prepare a planting bed, first remove any sod from the area, then rototill or dig the soil by hand, turning it over thor-

*Using a rototiller to turn all of the soil over in your garden area saves you from a lot of back-wrenching manual labor.*

*After rototilling, add any necessary soil conditioners.*

oughly. (Rototillers can be rented by the day, and it's often possible to hire someone to come and till by the hour, if you don't have a tiller of your own.)

If the area is rocky, remove as many stones as possible as you till. Next, spread the necessary fertilizer, soil conditioners, and pH-adjusting chemicals over the area. Till again. You should be able to till more deeply the second time; ideally, you want to loosen and improve the soil to a depth of more than 6 inches. Turn and loosen the soil by hand with a spade where the area is too small to require a rototiller or where the soil is already loose and light. You will need to follow a pH adjustment program regularly to prevent excessive acidity or alkalinity from returning.

If possible, allow the soil to stand unplanted for a week or more. Stir the soil on top (an inch or two below the surface) every three to four days with a scuffle hoe or cultivator to eradicate fast-germinating weed seeds. This will lessen your weeding chores during the rest of the season.

Now is the perfect time to install some kind of mowing strip around the garden bed. Patio squares or slate pieces laid end-to-end at ground level will keep grass and flowers from intermixing. Other options include landscape logs, poured concrete strips, or bricks laid side-by-side on a sand or concrete base. The mowing strip must be deep and wide enough so grass roots cannot tunnel underneath or travel across the top to reach the flower bed. To save yourself tedious grass

*Adding a mowing strip around your garden is a good idea.*

trimming, make the top of the strip low enough to accommodate your lawn mower.

Over time, a mowing strip will save more gardening effort, to say nothing of the gardener's patience, than any other device. It's well worth the time and money invested at the beginning!

## THE IMPORTANCE OF ORGANIC MATTER

Organic gardeners know the value of organic material, which builds so-so soils into highly productive soils and gives the entire garden a face-lift. Organic matter includes such ordinary elements as fallen leaves, grass clippings, chipped bark or wood, sawdust, animal bedding, and livestock manure.

*Use organic fertilizers when possible.*

All are derived from living things and release elements needed for growth as they decay and become part of nature's efficient recycling system.

Organic matter works several ways in the garden, which accounts for much of its effectiveness. As it decays, organic matter releases small doses of many major and minor nutrients. Livestock manure and green grass clippings are particularly rich in nitrogen. In contrast, hard and woody organic matter such as fresh wood chips, sawdust, and bark mulch consume nitrogen as they decay and can actually pull it out of the soil. You may want to add supplemental nitrogen fertilizers when working these materials into the soil.

If you add enough organic matter, it can bring about an almost magical improvement in soil consistency. The coarse organic particles—old stems, twigs, and leaves—physically break up dense soil. The degeneration process also changes dense soils chemically by releasing humic acid. This causes small clay particles to clump together, loosening the soil naturally. Organic matter can also enrich dry, sandy soils. After sand particles have shed their moisture reserves, the surface of each organic particle may still hold a coating of water that is easily released to feed thirsty plant roots.

Organic matter has yet another important function, one that many good gardeners have long suspected but which is only now receiving documentation through scientific studies. Organic matter creates a healthy subterranean environment, nurturing earthworms, mycorrhizae (an interaction of fungus with the plant's roots), and beneficial microbes that, in turn, benefit the annuals you grow. In a compost-rich soil, the beneficial microorganisms responsible for organic decay can be so plentiful that they overwhelm populations of disease-causing bacteria and fungi, limiting problems with root rot and other common diseases. This finding is revolutionizing the commercial container growing industry, as many commercial nursery gardeners have begun adding compost to their growing mixes to produce healthier plants.

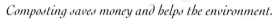
*Composting saves money and helps the environment.*

**MAKING YOUR OWN COMPOST** Compost is no longer a dirty word across America. As yard scraps are systemically banned from landfills and the value of organic matter in the garden is better understood, more homeowners are finding out-of-the-way places to recycle their own leaves and lawn clippings into compost. Here are some easy options, one of which is sure to be right for you.

🔥 Till autumn leaves into the garden in fall to boost the organic content by spring

🔥 Dig a large pit in the back of the garden, fill it with old organics, then cover with soil

🔥 Make a cold compost pile, heaping up vegetable leftovers in a pile or containing them in a neat cubicle made of snow fencing

🔥 Build a set of wood-slat compost bins open at the top and with an access door at the bottom to release the decayed material

🔥 Invest in compost making equipment—bins, barrels, and buckets—specially designed to make composting neat and efficient

🔥 Compost starters—blends of nutrients and microorganisms specially formulated to hasten decay—are also worth a try

Remember to exclude meat, fat, and any meat by-products (grease, drippings, etc.) from your compost, as these will attract animals (and develop a foul smell as they decay).

## Chapter 4
# GETTING THE GARDEN GROWING

WHEN THE WEATHER gets warm, even the most casual gardeners get the itch to go outside, work in the soil, and fill their yards with color. The prime annual starting season begins after the last spring frost, when tender and tropical annuals can thrive outdoors. It is a time of promise and potential as you decorate the yard for a festive summer season.

If you enjoy spring planting, you may decide to extend the pleasure by learning how to start your own annuals from seeds or cuttings. You might begin as early as 8 or 10 weeks before the actual planting season, nurturing little sprouts into thriving, young

*Starting annuals from seed can be very rewarding.*

starts for your garden. It's especially fulfilling to bring along these fledglings yourself and save money in the process.

The planting season is a good time to learn to be a crafty consumer and buy the best annuals: problem-free plants that are growing vigorously and ready to move into the garden. Look for telltale signs of good health—rich green leaves and healthy roots. You'll find an abundance of other tips to help you on pages 61–62.

You can experiment with different planting arrangements, massaging your sketched design into the garden. Set the plants around the garden according to the plan, but don't plant them yet. Step back and check to see if the layout is everything you envisioned. You may see places where you want to modify the spacing between plants or enlarge a grouping of annuals of your favorite color. All of this is easily accomplished during this trial run. Then the garden is all set for planting.

If you take the time to learn how to plant annuals properly so the roots can

dig right in and get established, your plants will be prepared for a long and lovely season of blooming. Proper planting techniques are easily done if you only know how.

**COOL SEASON ANNUALS** The beginning gardener is likely to wait until the last spring frost date has passed and then, like hoards of other prime time gardeners, rush to the garden center for a quick fill of color. But gardeners who've been at the game a little longer or have had a chance to wander lovely gardens earlier in spring will know that there is another season—the cool season—that can be ideal for gardening as well.

The cool season, usually arriving a month or two before the last spring frost date in northern climates, is characterized by cool but mild and not yet frost-free weather. It is an ideal time for planting hardy annuals and biennials such as pansies, Johnny jump-ups, sweet alyssum, calendula, and stock. Once hardened off (see page 57), they don't mind a little frost either. Cool season annuals are great to interplant with spring-flowering bulbs such as tulips, daffodils, and hyacinths. The annuals can bloom in harmony with the bulbs and continue the display as the bulb foliage fades away.

In fall, count on cool season annuals to come to the rescue after summer petunias and marigolds grow spent, frost nipped, and lose their summer glow. Cool season annuals thrive during the mild days and cool nights of early autumn, and especially during the brief respite of Indian summer. For the best display, plant cool season annuals in midsummer so that they will be established and in the full flush of bloom as other plants are fading.

*'Majestic Giants' pansies*

Autumn annuals, such as pink pansies and white sweet alyssum, look wonderful in combination with autumn-blooming perennials such as purple asters and white boltonia. Golden and orange calendulas also can bring out the best in autumn foliage, complementing the bronze of fading peony leaves and the vibrant reds of dogwoods.

*Calendulas*

Don't depend strictly on the calendar when planting cool season annuals. If spring weather arrives late, delay planting accordingly. But if spring arrives early, often predicted by the early appearance of flowering daffodils and tulips and the swelling of willow buds, by all means join the fun and plant your cool season annuals. Should an arctic blast threaten even these cool weather annuals, cover them with a tarp or old bushel basket for a day or two until more pleasant weather returns.

**PROPAGATING YOUR OWN ANNUALS** If you have extra time on your hands and enjoy devoting it to gardening, try starting your own plants from seeds and cuttings. Doing your own propagation allows you to grow many annuals that are unavailable from commercial greenhouses and garden centers. You also can grow large numbers of plants (some seed packets carry 50 to 100 seeds each), without spending your entire gardening budget on flats that someone else grew. Like making homemade bread, propagation can be easy once you have a modest amount of equipment and understand the step-by-step process necessary to accomplish the task.

**STARTING FROM SEED** Many annuals are easy to start from seed, either indoors or directly in the garden. In general, they aren't terribly fussy about where they grow or how they're treated. However, if you give them the extra boost of the best possible growing con-

ditions, they're bound to thrive and bloom more abundantly than they would under less ideal circumstances.

When purchasing packets of seeds, check to be sure that the seeds are fresh. The intended date for planting should be somewhere on the label. Make sure it's the current year. Second, when deciding between several sources for the same kind of seed, look at the number of seeds each company offers in its packet. A lower priced packet may contain fewer seeds—a bargain if you only want to grow a handful of plants, but not if you want dozens or intend to save extra seeds for later.

## SOME ANNUALS TO START INDOORS

These annuals do best when provided with an indoor head start to give them a jump on the growing season.

| | |
|---|---|
| ageratum | impatiens |
| globe amaranth | lobelia |
| asparagus fern | nicotiana |
| fibrous begonia | ornamental pepper |
| tuberous begonia | pansy |
| candytuft | petunia |
| cleome | salvia |
| coleus | snapdragon |
| dahlia | stock |
| dusty miller | verbena |
| geranium | vinca |

All of the large seed houses supply reliable, fresh, high-quality seed. In addition, you'll find that there are many small specialty seed companies with a marvelous selection of uncommon and choice annuals. You can also find annual seeds, especially heirloom types, through seed sharing networks, offered through gardening magazines, plant societies, and heirloom seed organizations. Most of the people who share seeds are amateurs, and the quality of seed is likely to vary dramatically.

Over time, you'll develop your own list of garden supply sources. The list below is intended to introduce a few well-known, reputable mail-order seed companies that offer a large selection of annual seeds. Start with these, then add others after trying them personally or receiving recommendations from experienced gardeners in your area.

W. Atlee Burpee & Co.
Warminster, PA 18974

Geo. W. Park Seed Co., Inc.
1 Parkton Ave.
Greenwood, SC 29647-0001

Seed Saver's Exchange
3076 North Winn Road
Decorah, IA 52101

Shepherd's Garden Seeds
30 Irene Street
Torrington, CT 06790-6658

Stokes Seeds Inc.
P.O. Box 548
Buffalo, NY 14240-0548

Thompson and Morgan, Inc.
P.O. Box 1308
Jackson, NJ 08527-0308

The most essential ingredient for successful seed starting is adequate light. It's possible to start seeds on the sill of a sun-filled window, but plants often stretch out toward the light source and become leggy. Set up a three-sided white or silver reflector shield behind the plant trays to reflect light back onto the plants to help combat this problem.

Where there is not enough light available naturally—a common problem in climates where winter clouds fill the sky for days on end—raise seedlings under fluorescent lights. To provide maximum light from all sides, surround the area under the lights with a white or silver-painted reflector or sheets of aluminum foil with the shiny side pointed toward the seedlings.

Along with light, many annuals—especially those that originated in tropical climates—need warm soil for quick germination. If the air temperature in the chosen growing area is colder than 70°F, supply bottom heat by installing a heating cable under the growing medium. You can find heating cables at many full-service garden centers and also in gardening supply catalogues.

*Raise young seedlings near a sunny window.*

Water is a third requirement for plant growth and seed starting. If you set seed trays and young potted plants on a rimmed watering tray, you can water them from the bottom. Top watering can batter plants down, as well as increase the possibility of fungus problems.

When bottom watering, be wary of over-watering. Water shouldn't continuously stand in the watering tray. Pour water to a ¼-inch depth into the tray. Leave it for five to ten minutes. At the end of that time, observe how much water is left in the tray. Also, roll a small pinch of the planting soil between thumb and finger to test for moisture. What you want is soil that feels wet but has very little or no water remaining in the tray.

Test the soil moisture once each day by rolling a small amount between your fingers. Water again when the soil feels more dry than wet. It's impossible to predict how many days will be needed between waterings. However, you'll soon be able to make a fairly accurate estimation of how often to water your plants.

Instead of using regular soil to start your seedlings, you can buy special seed starting mix. These mixes are usually a blend of peat moss, vermiculite, and sometimes perlite. These ingredients combine to make a well-aerated mix—much lighter than true soil—ideal for seed sprouting and the establishment of young seedlings. Seed starting mixes also are sterile and free of diseases, another important plus for your seedling nursery. Moisten the mix, firm it gently into sterile containers, then sow the seeds.

Seeds can be started in a variety of containers: Milk or egg cartons with holes punched in their bottoms or low on their sides, plastic or wooden boxes, clay or plastic pots, peat pots, or special seed starter cubes and trays are all equally acceptable. Virtually anything that will hold soil and allow easy passage of water through drainage holes in the bottom will work.

*Plant two seeds in each pot or section of a starter tray.*

Containers designed to hold a single plant are the best choice for large plants that tend to crowd each other out in six-packs; for plants that don't like to have their roots disturbed by transplanting; and for climbing vines. Fortunately, most annuals will thrive in almost any container.

Sow seeds individually in single pots. Plant two seeds in each, removing the weaker

*Broadcast seeds when sowing many of a single type.*

of the two seedlings when they grow their first real leaves (the very first leaves to unfold from a new seedling are called the seed leaves; the second set of leaves are their first real leaves).

When sowing a packet of seeds in a box or larger pot, you can either broadcast the seeds sparingly over the surface in a scatter pattern or plant them in rows. If you only want a few plants of each kind, rows make more sense; when larger numbers of plants are desired, broadcasting is faster. If the seeds are very small, don't cover them with additional planting mix after sowing; medium to large seeds should have a layer of planting mix sprinkled on top. Lightly press the surface of the planting mix after sowing.

Be sure to label each planting in some way. Write in permanent ink (so that it won't wash off in water at least for a month or two) on plastic labels, spoons, wooden tags, or

whatever else is handy. You can also chart the planting plan on a separate piece of paper. From a practical perspective, the labeling system you use doesn't matter as long as you have one.

After sowing and labeling, cover the containers with clear plastic wrap, which will hold in moisture like a miniature greenhouse. Check daily for the first telltale hint of greenery poking up, then move the seedlings into bright light. Germination time varies widely. Ideally, you should start the slower growers earlier than those that germinate rapidly in order to have them all at the same stage when planting time arrives. Study the descriptions of each plant to know when to get each of them started.

Probably the worst enemy of successful seed starting is a problem known as "damping off." It strikes within two weeks of germina-

*Sow each type of annual in a row of its own.*

tion when seedlings are very young. When it hits, the plants simply lay down and die, usually in less than a day's time. Damping off is a fungus infection that can best be avoided by making certain that both the soil and containers in which seeds are planted are sterile. Planting seeds sparsely and thinning out overcrowded seedlings will minimize or eliminate problems. Check young seedlings at morning and evening for any sign of a problem, which can be corrected with a fungicide or, if none is available, a mild vinegar solution.

Prepared seed starter mixes usually have plant nutrients in them that feed the seedlings. If you make your own homemade starter, you'll need to fertilize in some way. The easiest method is to add a water soluble fertilizer at a very weak rate to the regular

waterings. (For details on various organic and inorganic fertilizers, see pages 67–68.)

If seedlings are not planted in individual pots, you'll need to transplant them when their first or second set of true leaves appear. This first transplanting is usually referred to as "pricking off." Move seedlings into small individual peat pots, planting cubes, or partitioned growing boxes. They will remain in these containers until planting time.

Fill the boxes with commercial, peat-based growing mix. Gently lift out and separate the young plants, holding them by their seed leaves. Then place the seedling in the new container so the soil line will be at the same level on the stem as it was in the seed tray. Gently firm the soil around the plant roots, bringing it to within ¼ inch of the container rim. Water from the top with a weak fertilizer

*Heated soil, an aluminum reflector, and a grow lamp on a timer ensure that these seedlings started indoors receive controlled, thoughtful care.*

solution. Place these pricked-off plants back by the window or under growlamps to continue their growth.

After a short while, plants should grow to be stocky and strong, but they will need some toughening up before heading outdoors. This process is referred to as "hardening off." It'll keep the plants from suffering shock, or trauma, when they are planted outside.

Carry the plants outdoors each day for a few hours, bringing them back inside overnight. Start them out in shade and gradually increase their exposure to sun. Give them a couple days under a tree or on the north side of your home. Then move sun-loving annuals into the sun for an hour or two, bringing them back into the shade afterwards. Gradually increase the length of time they're outdoors and in the sun. After a week, they usually are ready to remain outdoors.

Although starting your own seedlings takes a bit of time and effort, it can be a very enjoyable activity. The annuals you grow are wholly yours, from beginning to end. The sensation of being the complete author of your vibrant summer garden is truly fulfilling. And best of all, you can have as many plants as you want of exactly the species and varieties you prefer.

*For a unique design, use a stick to mark planting rows.*

**DIRECTLY SOWING SEEDS** If you want an easy and inexpensive way to grow annuals, sowing seeds directly into the garden is the natural solution. Once the ground is warm and the planting bed properly prepared, it's amazing how quickly most annuals sprout and grow to the flowering stage.

There are some plants that grow better when planted directly in the garden rather than started ahead as boxed plants. For example, both Shirley poppies and zinnias have difficulty surviving transplanting. You'll also find that trailing and vining plants can't be started very much ahead of planting time or they become hopelessly tangled. As a result, most vines don't gain enough of a head start to make the extra effort worthwhile.

There are several ways to approach direct seeding. For a somewhat structured but still informal cottage garden look, use a stick to

## SOME ANNUALS TO BE DIRECTLY SOWN OUTDOORS

These are some annuals that are either fast starting or dislike root disturbance.

| | |
|---|---|
| sweet alyssum | nasturtium |
| blanket flower | ornamental kale |
| castor bean | California poppy |
| cosmos | portulaca |
| forget-me-not | scabiosa |
| marigold | sunflower |
| morning glory | zinnia |

mark out flowing sweeps on the prepared bed. Broadcast each sweep with a different kind of seed, rake lightly, and briefly sprinkle a fine spray of water over the bed to settle the soil. If the garden is large enough to allow it, repeat the same variety of annual in several sections. Remember to keep plant height in mind while broadcasting your seeds. Place taller varieties toward the rear of the bed and the lower ones at the front (or with a bed that can be viewed from all directions, sow the taller plant seeds in the center).

When the young seedlings sprout, they'll need to be thinned to prevent overcrowding. When thinning, adjust the space you leave between the plants according to their growth characteristics:

Tall, upright-growing plants such as feathered cockscomb, bachelor's buttons, and larkspur can be left much closer together than wide-spreading plants such as sweet alyssum, petunias, cosmos, and baby's breath. Surplus seedlings can be discarded, passed on to friends, or moved to grow in planters or other garden areas.

For a more formal garden design, make a precise plan on paper beforehand. Then carefully copy the layout onto the prepared seedbed. With this approach, each preselected variety is planted in rows or clumps in the appointed order—two or three seeds to a cluster, spaced 4 to 12 inches apart depending on their growth habits. When the plants are 1 to 2 inches tall, thin out all but the strongest one from each cluster. The resulting beds will have a neat, organized, well-planned look.

For large plants that need to be spaced a foot or more apart, it's easiest to lay mulch

*Plant a few seeds in each hole cut into a mulch sheet.*

over the bed prior to planting. Cut 3-inch holes at proper intervals in the mulch sheet. (If an organic mulch is used, push mulching aside for proper spacing.) Plant three seeds in a triangular pattern in each hole. Pat soil gently over each group. When seedlings grow their second set of true leaves, thin out the weaker plants, leaving just the strongest one to continue growing.

Another approach to flower bed layout is simply to mark off rows the length of the bed and plant each one with a different annual favorite. By planting the tallest kind in the back row and increasingly shorter ones in each row in front of it, it's possible to effectively display all varieties. Take into account the width to which each type grows when spacing the rows. You can mulch between the rows before or after sowing the seeds. Maintenance of this garden is easy because you always work along straight rows.

To decide which design style to use, consider what is best suited to your own tastes

*A simple solution: Sow each annual type in its own row.*

and talents, as well as to the style of the surrounding buildings and the already existing garden and lawn.

**PROPAGATING ANNUALS BY CUTTINGS** Most annuals are grown from seeds. However, you can start a number of annuals, including some impatiens, New Guinea impatiens, Swedish ivy, fibrous begonias, coleus, geraniums, bacopa, vining petunias, cobbity daisies, and fuchsia, by stem cuttings.

Select a mature plant that is in a stage of active midsummer growth. Prepare a container filled with rooting medium. It should be at least 3 to 4 inches deep, filled with 2½ inches or more of rooting medium. Clean, coarse builder's sand, a mixture of half perlite and half peat moss, or half perlite and half vermiculite are good choices. Fill the container with the moistened medium, then let it settle and drain for a half hour.

Take cuttings in the morning. Using a sharp knife, cut off growth tips just above the node, or the point where a leaf or side shoot attaches to the main stems. Each of the cut-

*You can propagate some annuals with cuttings.*

with rooting hormone powder. Just dip each stem in the rooting powder and shake off any excess. Poke a hole in the dampened rooting medium, insert the cutting in the hole to one-third of its length, and press the medium firmly around the stem with your fingers. When all of the cuttings are set in the medium, water the surface.

Place a plastic bag over the cuttings to form a tent, using bamboo stakes or wooden dowels as supports. This will serve as a mini-greenhouse, which should be kept out of direct sunlight. Leave the bottom edge of the plastic tent a bit loose to allow some fresh outside air to circulate up inside. This will help reduce the possibility of mildew and mold problems. Some growers prefer to hold

tings should be between 3 and 6 inches in length and have 4 to 6 nodes. The stem tissue should be easy to cut through.

Don't spend more than five minutes taking cuttings from the parent plants. To prepare a cutting for rooting, remove the leafless piece of stem at the bottom. Cut it off about ⅛ inch below the first node with a clean knife or razor, leaving no torn or dangling pieces of tissue hanging from the stem. Remove all of the leaves from the lower half of the cutting. These can be cut off with a knife or manually snapped off.

If there are any flower buds on the cutting, cut these off as well. Cut back the tips of any large leaves remaining on the cutting so that one-third to one-half of their surface remains. To help stimulate root formation, it's helpful to coat the lower one-third of each stem cutting

*Commercial hormones aid root development for cuttings.*

the plastic tightly against the container with an elastic band. In this case, it's necessary to remove the elastic and lift up the tent sides for a short period each day or else to poke holes in the plastic bag in order to supply the cutting with the necessary fresh air. With a plastic tent there will be little need for watering the cuttings.

Annual cuttings will root quickly. Check their progress in a week to ten days. Insert a narrow knife blade or a fork beneath one of the cuttings and gently lift it out. When the longest roots are ¼ inch long, remove cuttings from the rooting medium and transfer each to a 1- to 1½-inch pot filled with planting mix.

**SELECTING ANNUALS AT THE GARDEN CENTER** If you want to have an almost instant show of annual bloom, prestarted bedding plants are the answer. Every garden center and nursery, many roadside stands, and quite a few grocery and discount stores offer a selection of prestarted annuals. The main drawback to purchasing boxed bedding plants is the limited selection.

There can be a dramatic difference between the prices of annuals sold at discount centers and other retail outlets. While there are occasional bargains to be found at dis-count stores or other stores without knowledgeable horticulturists, annuals that have sat on the shelf for a few weeks may have been allowed to wilt or left out in blazing sun or unseasonable cold. Unfortunately, each time the plants wilt, some of their strength is lost. Plants that have suffered will be slow to recover when they're put in the garden.

*Check the quality of prestarted annuals closely.*

Wherever you shop, you can check annual quality in several ways.

🌡 Make sure plants are not wilted or limp and have a full set of leaves from the bottom to the top of the stem

🌡 The leaves should be a healthy shade of green, not yellow, brown, or bronze and shouldn't be riddled with holes or misshapen

🌿 The stems of upright annuals should be sturdy and compact, not floppy and leaning on their neighbors for support

🌿 You shouldn't find any insects hiding beneath the leaves, along the stems, or fluttering around when you brush the plants

🌿 Great masses of roots emerging from the drainage holes in the bottom of the pot indicate severely root-bound plants that may not transplant well

You also should check the number of plants in a box or cell pack. This may mean looking below the foliage and counting stems. One retailer may sell a "box" for $1.25 and another may sell the same "box" of the same variety for only $1.00. But if the first box contains eight plants and the second contains

*Dig a hole slightly larger than the annual to be planted.*

*Carefully remove the prestarted plant from the pot.*

only six, the higher-priced box is definately the better buy.

Even if the last frost date hasn't passed or your planting bed isn't fully prepared, it still makes sense to buy plants when they first arrive at the retailer's. Bring them home where you can care for them properly until you can plant them in your garden. (Keep most prestarted annuals moist, warm, and in the sun.)

**PLANTING ANNUALS** It's finally time to finish your annual garden by planting. Make planting holes with a hoe or trowel for your young plants. If you have seedlings in peat pots, score the sides and the bottom of the pot with a knife to ensure that the roots will escape even if the pot doesn't decompose, an

occasional occurrence. Drop the peat pots into the planting holes and firm the soil around the pot, making sure that the tops of the peat pots do not emerge from the soil.

Plants in multi-plant containers will need to be turned out of the container and separated before planting. Water the plants well before removing them. If the soil is moist, they'll slide out easily, subjecting the plants to less shock. Some roots are bound to be broken off in this process; pinching out the top growth on big plants will help keep the top and root areas in balance. Pinching also encourages side shoots to push out, helping to form a fuller flowering plant.

You can push the roots of annuals grown in cell packs out by pinching or pushing up

*Create a dam around new plants and keep them moist.*

on the flimsy plastic bottom of the cell. Often you'll find the plants are root bound, presenting a solid mass of roots entangled with each other. You need to loosen these roots up so they can begin to grow out into the soil instead of remaining tied in knots. Use your finger to gently tear free heavily clumped roots or to tease loose slightly tangled roots. Removing the dysfunctional root mats allows new roots to stretch freely into the soil.

After planting, mold an earth dam around the stem to form a water-holding area, and pour in a weak fertilizer solution. Keep newly planted annuals moist for several weeks or until they are growing strongly, a sign that they have begun to establish expanded roots.

*Gently firm the soil around the planted annual.*

# PLANT HARDINESS ZONE MAP

This map, based on the United States Department of Agriculture's official zone map, is designed to correlate average winter temperatures to selected areas of the country. Its purpose is to aid people in the choosing of plants for their particular area. It divides the United States into 11 zones based on average minimum winter temperatures, with Zone 1 being the coldest, and Zone 11 being the warmest.

This Zone Map should only be used as a general guideline, since the lines of separation between zones are not as clear-cut as they might appear. Plants recommended for one zone might do well in the southern part of the adjoining colder zone, as well as in the neighboring warmer zone. Factors such as altitude, exposure to wind, and amount of available sunlight also contribute to a plant's hardiness. Also note that the indicated temperatures are average minimums—some winters will be either colder or warmer than this figure.

Even though the Plant Hardiness Zone Map is not perfect, it is the most useful single guide for determining which plants are likely to survive in your garden and which ones are not.

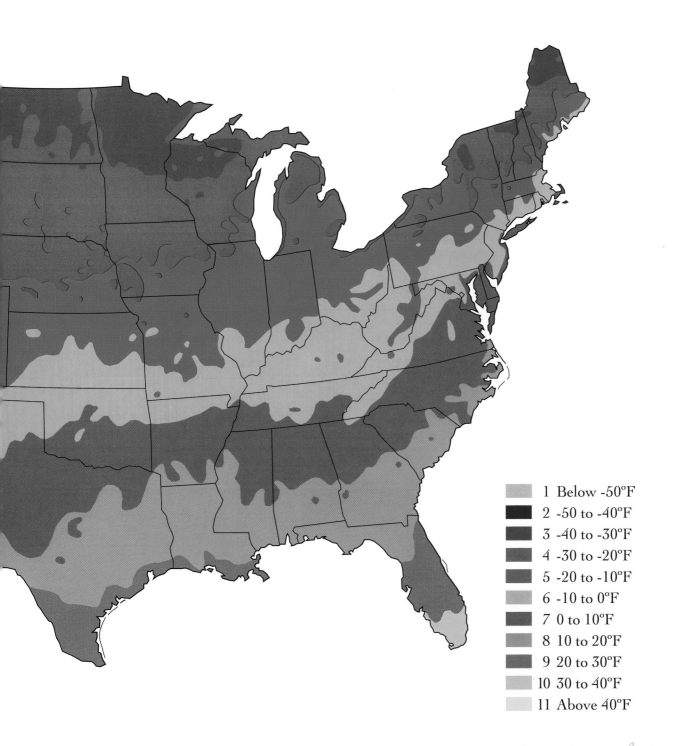

1 Below -50°F
2 -50 to -40°F
3 -40 to -30°F
4 -30 to -20°F
5 -20 to -10°F
6 -10 to 0°F
7 0 to 10°F
8 10 to 20°F
9 20 to 30°F
10 30 to 40°F
11 Above 40°F

# Chapter 5
# KEEPING THE GARDEN GROWING

**K**EEPING YOUR ANNUAL garden looking great is not difficult when you start with easy-care annuals and dedicate a healthy mix of business and pleasure. Ramble around your yard regularly, stopping to admire a healthy plant here, snapping off a few dead flower heads there, then pulling out some weeds in another area.

At the same time you're patting yourself on the back for a job well done, you also can be fine-tuning the garden. You'll notice clues that signal possible problems. If some of the plants have limp leaves, feel if the soil is dry and turn on the soaker hose if needed. If some leaves or flowers are peppered with

*'Purple Wave' petunias*

holes or totally eaten away, make a closer inspection to discover whether a caterpillar or other insect has invaded. Consult the illustrated troubleshooting guide on pages 76–79 to determine how best to deal with pests and other problems.

Making a hands-on inspection, you'll be glad to know, is best done on a sunny day or when the garden foliage is completely dry. Tiptoeing through the flowers when the foliage is wet can spread disease spores, something you can easily avoid with careful timing.

By selecting plants that are easy to grow and well-suited to your garden site, and then following gardening techniques that reduce the need for maintenance, your summer can be both carefree and color-filled.

**FINESSING FERTILIZER** Fertilizers, plant equivalents of people's vitamins, provide needed elements in minute quantities and shouldn't be confused with food (even though fertilizer may informally be called plant food). Provide enough fertilizer to correct any nutrient deficiencies discovered when you had your soil tested, to give annuals a subtle growth boost when they're newly planted, or when they need inspiration to bloom more profusely. However, be careful not to overdo it: Over-fertilizing can make annuals grow poorly or make them behave as if they are diseased.

**WHAT KIND OF FERTILIZER TO USE** As you study the NPK formula on each fertilizer product, you'll notice that different kinds of fertilizers contain varying

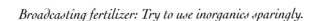

*Broadcasting fertilizer: Try to use inorganics sparingly.*

amounts of nitrogen, phosphorus, and potassium. When wanting to encourage rapid leafy growth, of a new seedling for instance, you can use a product with a higher nitrogen level. But for good flowering, look for either a balanced fertilizer with the same quantities of NPK or a product with more phosphorus and potassium than nitrogen.

Organic fertilizers contain lower percentages of nutrients per pound than do inorganic fertilizers. For the most part, this doesn't matter when fertilizing annuals. When trying to adjust a large garden bed's nutrient content at the beginning of the growing season, look for the more concentrated organic fertilizers. They can be found with nutrient ratios such as 8-8-8. In very poor soils that need even more fertilizer than this, it may be more practical to make major adjustments with inorganics, and then proceed with organics for minor adjustments in the future.

You can choose fertilizers in dry granular or powder form, or water soluble formulations for mixing with water for a liquid application. Broadcast the granular or powder fertilizers over the soil surface and dig them in. You also can side-dress existing plants, sprinkling the fertilizer in a broad circle around the plant and lightly scratching it into the soil surface. To apply liquid fertilizer, you can mix up small batches in your watering can or a hand sprayer, or blend a larger quantity in a special mixing nozzle that can be attached to your garden hose.

To supply fertilizer for immediate use by newly planted bedding annuals, pour a weak solution of water-soluble fertilizer—either fish emulsion or an inorganic type—from a watering can directly around each plant. If the soil is particularly rich in organic matter and naturally fertile, there probably isn't any need to add fertilizers. In more ordinary soils, you may want to add granular fertilizer periodically during the growing season. One of the best times to fertilize is after a large flush of flowers has begun to fade. Cut bushy annuals such as pansies and petunias back lightly and side-dress with granular fertilizer to stimulate resprouting and the creation of additional blooms.

For best absorption, fertilize when the soil is moist. Take care to apply it to the soil rather than the plant leaves. The plants, your hands, and the fertilizer should be dry when you fertilize. Caution: Always wash your hands after handling fertilizer.

**WATERING** If you live in a climate blessed with regular rainfall through much of the growing season, you may only need to water occasionally during times of drought. But in arid climates, honing your watering skills is a prerequisite for a beautiful annual garden. Growing drought-tolerant annuals such as

melampodium will help minimize water use, but even melampodium grows better when you keep the soil moist most of the time.

It's not easy, especially at first, to gauge exactly when plants require water—so much depends upon current weather and soil conditions. So how do you judge when to water and how much water to give? The one sure way to test moisture levels is by poking your finger 2 to 3 inches into the soil and feeling how moist or dry it is. Taking a pinch from the surface isn't good enough; you need to know the relative moisture in the root zone. Inexperienced gardeners should check soil moisture when there is little or no rainfall. Over time, you'll develop a feel for the overall conditions and check only when you suspect the soil may be turning dry. Remember, it's

*Using soaker hoses helps control fungal growth on foliage.*

*Sophisticated drip irrigation is the savvy way to water.*

always better to check too often rather than not often enough. Don't wait until drooping plants indicate that the soil is parched.

When you do water, water deeply. Many people briefly spray a thirsty flower bed with a hand-held hose. When they tire of holding it, become bored, or think they have watered enough because the water has stopped soaking into the soil as rapidly as it did at first, the watering session is ended. Unfortunately, only the surface of the soil will be moistened, just enough to help weeds sprout and not enough to nourish the roots.

A better approach is to use an automatic sprinkler, letting it gently "rain" for an extended period of time. Check at half-hour intervals to see how deeply the water has penetrated. Turn the water off when the soil is moistened to a 2-inch depth. Don't water again until your testing indicates the need.

However, one problem with sprinkler water is that it wets the foliage, creating an ideal environment for the spread of fungal diseases. In addition, flower clusters that become heavy with water are more likely to bend and break off or to become disfigured with disease.

Therefore, your best bet is to slake your plants' thirst with a soaker hose. The water slowly oozes from the hose's many tiny holes for several hours—even overnight. All of the water soaks directly on the soil and down to the plant roots without any waste or damage.

Drip irrigation is another excellent slow-soaking system. It is especially pertinent for gardeners in climates where irrigation is constantly needed in order for cultivated plants to survive. Once the network of tubes has been laid out, it can remain in place year

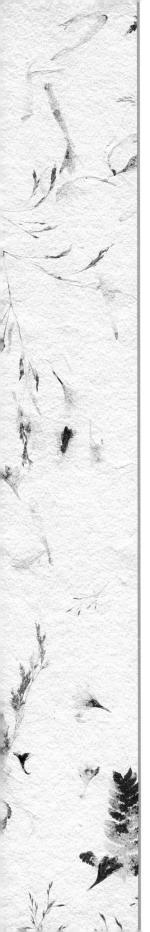

after year. In areas that freeze, however, it must be drained for the winter.

There are two additional factors that will help conserve moisture and thus reduce the need for watering. One is the incorporation of organic matter into the planting area, permitting light and sandy soils to soak up and hold water longer. (Conversely, when organic matter is added to heavy soils, it helps to lighten and aerate them.) Another excellent way to retain moisture is by covering the bed between plants with mulch, a task that will serve you well in several ways. Spread on the soil surface between the plants, a mulch protects the soil from the sometimes harsh effects of the sun and wind. It also discourages weeds. Organic mulch has the added advantage of bolstering the organic content of the soil as it decomposes. (See pages 73–74.)

By using mulch and soaker hoses or drip irrigation, you can cut down on the time needed to care for your garden and, even more important, help conserve water, one of nature's most precious resources.

*Pinching back* (above) *promotes side-branching* (left).

**PRUNING AND DEADHEADING** Even if you've chosen easy-care annuals that need little extra help to grow well, they can be made more beautiful with a touch of grooming. Every time you stroll around the garden, keep a pair of hand-held pruning shears in your pocket to take a little nip here and there to help make your plants look their best.

If you are growing annuals that are not self-branching (see pages 11–12), you may need to encourage them to fill out manually. This process is called "pinching back." Simply pinch or cut off the last inch or so of the main growing tip. This will redirect the plant's energy from this single shoot to the numerous latent side buds, located along the stem where each leaf is attached. Several days after pinching, you'll see several small shoots pushing from the remaining stem. These will grow into a cluster of stems to replace the original single stem. The plant will be shorter, stockier, and fuller than if you hadn't pinched it. It will also be neater-looking, more compact, and have many more branches on which to produce flowers. A second pinching can be done two weeks after the first one if you want an even fuller plant.

Pinching is best done when the plant is growing rapidly and before the first flower buds form. But since most bedding plants come already in flower, you can remove any

*Removing old flowers redirects energy to the plant and encourages new growth.*

faded flowers and the top buds on main stems and give them a little shot of fertilizer in order to encourage new growth when planting in the garden. When you grow annuals from seeds sown directly in the garden, pinch off the stem tips when they've grown to a height of 3 to 4 inches.

Deadheading bears no relation to the antiquated hippies of yore, but instead is one of the best ways to ensure that annual flowers will continue to look their best throughout the growing season. Deadheading works in several ways. It cleans away old, faded flower petals that detract from the good looks of the garden. Second, even though we say they're dead, old flowers are actually very much alive. They continue to produce seeds, a process that consumes more than its fair share of plant energy which would otherwise be available for new foliage and flower production. Third, when you remove old flowers, you are also pinching back the plant, redirecting energy to side shoots.

When deadheading, always cut back to just above the next plump flower bud on the stem. If there are no more flowers awaiting their turn to open, cut back to just above the first side bud that is already beginning to grow. If there is no active side bud below the bloom, cut back either to a side branch or immediately above a leaf node where a latent bud will be likely to push out new growth. Make a clean cut with a sharp knife or, better yet, with pruning shears, since ragged cuts take much longer to heal and are likely sites for the entry of rot and disease. Use the same techniques you learn here to removing cut flowers as well, and you will leave a better plant behind you.

If an annual grows too tall or sprawls over its neighbors, you can cut it back, a slightly more drastic operation than deadheading or pinching. Cutting back also works well when mid-season annuals don't want to bloom. You can remove old flowers and excess growth in one easy step, encouraging regrowth and new flowers to develop in the weeks to come. Cut these plants back by one-quarter or one-third

*Deadheading is necessary for some annuals.*

of their total length. As when deadheading, cut back to a side growth shoot or branch that is headed in the direction you want future growth to go. This way you can steer and control growth as you see fit.

**KEEPING WEEDS AT BAY** Weed seeds, opportunists of the plant world, are quick to germinate and grow rapidly. As soon as you turn the warm soil and bring them to within an inch of the soil surface, they'll begin to sprout. You can use this fast-rising weed habit to your advantage. After digging deeply in early spring to ready the bed for planting, wait a week or more before doing any planting or seed sowing. Let the weed seeds sprout, then strike them down by stirring up the top inch of soil with a hoe, leaving the lower soil, and the weed seeds it surely harbors, undisturbed. This will expose several cycles of young, sprouted weeds, letting them dry out and die in the sun and air.

It's particularly important to clean the soil surface of weed seeds when you're starting annuals from seeds so you'll know which new sprouts are annuals and which are weeds. But in places where only bedding plants will be used, you can discourage seed germination with a pre-emergent herbicide. Organic gardeners should try a revolutionary pre-emergent herbicide made out of benign corn gluten meal. Apply according to the package directions and avoid disturbing the soil thereafter to allow the herbicide to do its job.

Finally, the most popular way of dramatically reducing weed problems is by using some kind of mulch. Mulch is a layer of organic or inorganic material laid on the soil surface to shade out weeds, retain soil moisture, and moderate soil temperature.

You can use many materials for mulch, but some are more practical, less expensive, easier to handle, and more attractive than others. The list of organic mulches, which break down to improve the soil, includes: pine needles, leaves, straw, dried seaweed, tree bark strips, bark chunks, peat moss, old newspapers, sawdust, wood chips, compost, shredded leaves mixed with grass clippings, cocoa bean hulls, and cotton seed hulls. Inorganic mulches, usually covered with organic mulches for a more pleasing appearance,

## UNDERSTANDING ANNUAL LIFE CYCLES

How much you can manipulate the longevity and performance of annuals by fertilizing and pruning depends, in large part, on the nature of the annual itself. Deadheading, cutting back, and renewal fertilizing works well on tender perennials such as petunias, begonias, cockscomb, and impatiens. These plants could grow for years in frost-free climates and can be kept in prime condition with these techniques.

But annuals such as sweet alyssum and bachelor's button are short lived, genetically programmed to set seeds and fade away. Once that line has been crossed, the plants are

*Bachelor's button*

likely to die regardless of your manipulations. Similarly, some so-called annuals such as pansies, dianthus, and flowering cabbage have biennial roots. They are inspired to finish their life cycle after receiving a winter cold period. If they survive winter and come back to bloom in spring, they will likely disappear long before the growing season is through.

include "blankets" made from solid sheets of opaque plastic and landscape fabric mulches.

The least expensive way to mulch is with organic material such as old leaves and grass

*Organic mulches help keep weeds down.*

clippings found around your own yard. Or you can buy bags of shredded or chipped bark mulch. For a large garden, you can order mulch delivered by the cubic yard, but be sure that bulk mulch is sweet smelling before you lay it down. Stockpiled bark may get bad in the heart of the pile and burn annuals if it is layered too near. Another place to find reasonably priced mulch is from local industries such as mushroom farms, which regularly need to dispose of rich, leftover compost.

For all its benefits, mulch can have a few adverse effects in the garden. Woody mulches absorb nitrogen as they decay, so you may need to use additional fertilizer when you use them. Soggy soils, which aren't much good for growing annuals anyway, will stay even

soggier when mulched and are likely to become a breeding ground for plant-eating slugs and snails. You might try building a raised bed in this kind of wet area.

Despite these few adverse characteristics, mulches are a great time saver and should be a part of any easy annual garden, especially if you want to minimize the time and trouble of weeding and watering.

**TROUBLESHOOTING PESTS AND OTHER PROBLEMS** Fortunately, when growing easy annuals in ideal conditions, problems with pests and diseases are minimal. But it's an exceptionally lucky gardener who doesn't

*Mulches add a clean, rugged beauty to bedded annuals.*

encounter a few aphids or some powdery mildew sooner or later. Consult the following table (pages 76–79) to help you identify the most common garden pests and diseases. If you need more help, take a specimen to a horticulturist at your local garden shop or your county Cooperative Extension office to have it identified.

Once you know what is causing the problem, you'll need to decide how to control it. When an infestation is slight, you can simply remove the sick plants or individual insects. Sometimes a blast from the garden hose is all that's needed to dislodge intruders. For a heavy infestation, you'll probably need to turn to insecticides or fungicides, available in both organic and inorganic forms.

Using environmentally safe, organic products is an excellent way to encourage a healthy garden (and the overall environment). If you must apply pesticides, do so in the evening to avoid harming pollinating bees and butterflies. Use products like pyrethrin that kill quickly and then break down without leaving a harmful residue. Other products, such as Bacillus thuringiensis, a caterpillar disease, target the pest directly and ignore other beneficial insects such as ladybugs and spiders, which subsist on other insects. It is only when people spray and dust with the

## CULTIVATION OF NON-MULCHED AREAS

In beds where no mulch is used, frequent cultivation of the top 1 to 2 inches of soil is the best way to control weeds. Newly germinated weed seedlings die quickly when stirred up this way. Larger weeds should be hand-pulled and removed from the bed, since they can easily root again if left in the garden.

*Stir the soil to stop those weeds.*

attitude that "more is better"—whether the plants need it or not—that excessive poisons become a possibility.

One final note: New biological and chemical controls are continually being developed. Effective new products are being unveiled every year while some toxic inorganic products are taken off the market. Therefore, it is very important to correctly identify your pest or disease problem and to consult with your local nursery or garden shop. They can recommend the best available product for controlling your particular problem.

# INSECTS AND ANIMALS

| Symptom | Cause | Cure | Plants | |
|---|---|---|---|---|
| Cluster of small, soft-bodied insects on buds and growth tips (gray, black, pink, or green in color); sticky secretions may be evident | aphids | Spray with a blast of water, insecticidal soap, or pyrethrin in evening | dahlia<br>geranium<br>impatiens<br>pot marigold | nasturtium<br>primrose<br>salvia<br>sweet pea |
| Leaves chewed away; hard-shelled beetles on plant and burrowed into flowers | beetles of various kinds | Spray with rotenone or appropriate strains of Bacillus thuringiensis; attack grubs with parasitic nematodes; pick by hand and destroy | basil<br>American/French marigold<br>ornamental gourd<br>petunia<br>zinnia | |
| Growth tips wilted; small hole in plant stem at point where wilting begins | borers | Snap off at level of hole, dig out borer and destroy; spray with pyrethrin or rotenone | dahlia<br>American/French marigold<br>ornamental gourd<br>zinnia | |
| Leaves and flowers chewed away; caterpillars on plant | caterpillars of various kinds and sizes | Pick off by hand and destroy; spray with pyrethrum, neem, or Bacillus thuringiensis | ornamental or flowering cabbage<br>nasturtium<br>nicotiana<br>petunia | |
| Entire young plants wilted; partially or entirely chewed through at ground level | cutworms | Dig in soil around plant base; find rolled up caterpillars and destroy; circle plant with cardboard collar on edge (1″ below ground and 1″ above ground) | most seedlings<br>ornamental or flowering cabbage<br>nicotiana<br>petunia | |
| Leaves and stems chewed; insects seen hopping and flying | grasshoppers | Dust with sabadilla or Sevin[*1]; pick off by hand | ornamental grasses<br>petunia | |

[1] = inorganic treatment
[*] = copyrighted brand name

# Insects and Animals (continued)

| Symptom | Cause | Cure | Plants |
|---|---|---|---|
| Leaves peppered with small, round holes; small, triangular-shaped bugs seen when disturbed | leaf hoppers | Spray with pyrethrin or malathion[1]; cover plants with floating row covers; dust with diatomaceous earth | dahlia<br>pot marigold |
| Leaves "painted" with whitish, curling trails | leaf miners | Spray with neem or malathion[1]; remove and destroy badly infested leaves | China pink<br>ornamental pepper |
| White or pinkish fuzzy clumps on stems and at base of leaves; sticky to the touch | mealybugs | Spray with neem, insecticidal soap, light oils or pyrethrin; hand kill by painting each bug with an alcohol-soaked cotton swab | asparagus fern |
| Plants entirely gone or eaten down to small stubs; evidence of animal tracks or droppings | rabbits or deer | Spray with Hinder[*1] or other repellents; fence out rabbits with 3' high chicken wire or other close-woven fencing; surround garden with battery charged fencing for deer | impatiens<br>ornamental or flowering cabbage and kale<br>pansy<br>scarlet runner bean |
| Silvery slime trails on plants; soft sticky slugs on plants after dark (check with flashlight); holes eaten in leaves | slugs and snails | Set out shallow containers of beer; make barriers of diatomaceous earth; set out metaldehyde slug bait[1]; pick by hand after dark or on dark days | nicotiana<br>petunia<br>primrose |

[1] = inorganic treatment
[*] = copyrighted brand name

| SYMPTOM | CAUSE | CURE | PLANTS |
|---|---|---|---|
| Leaves yellowing with speckled look; fine spider webs on backs of leaves and at point where leaves attach to stem; very tiny bugs on backs of leaves | spider mites | Spray with pyrethrin, rotenone, or a miticide[1] from underneath to hit backs of leaves; wash or spray with soapy water | dahlia China pink impatiens marigold primrose salvia verbena |
| Small glob of white bubbles on plant stem or leaves; small insect hidden inside | spittlebugs | Ignore unless very pervasive; wash off repeatedly with water from hose | bachelor's button |
| Brown or white flecks on plant leaves | thrips | Spray with insecticidal soap, pyrethrins, or neem | tuberous begonia gladiolus |
| Cloud of tiny white flies fluttering around plant | white flies | Spray with neem or insecticidal soap; use yellow sticky traps | dahlia China pink impatiens marigold primrose salvia verbena |

[1] = inorganic treatment

# Diseases

| Symptom | Cause | Cure | Plants |
|---|---|---|---|
| Leaves become mottled, curl, and shrivel; plants become deformed | blights and viruses | Remove and destroy plants; buy blight-resistant strains; control disease-carrying aphids and leaf hoppers; wash hands before handling plants | aster<br>chrysanthemum<br>snapdragon |
| Newly sprouted seedlings fall over and die | damping off | Start seeds in sterile soil mix; thin out after emerging | all plants |
| Round, dusty brown or black spots on leaves; leaves drop from plant | leaf spot | Remove badly diseased leaves and destroy; spray with 0.5 percent baking soda solution | chrysanthemum<br>foxglove<br>annual phlox |
| Lower leaves and stems turn grayish and look slightly wilted | powdery mildew | Increase air circulation; spray with sulfur or antitranspirant | ageratum<br>bachelor's button<br>annual phlox<br>sweet pea<br>zinnia |
| Orange or reddish-brown raised dots form on backs of leaves; leaves look wilted | rust | Increase air circulation; keep foliage dry; buy rust-resistant varieties; spray flowers with sulfur | cleome<br>snapdragon |
| Leaves wilt and turn yellow; entire plant shuts down and dies | wilt | Remove infected plants and destroy; buy wilt-resistant varieties | dahlia<br>snapdragon |

# THREE GARDEN DESIGNS

Use these designs in your yard, or just take a look at them to get some ideas of your own. Each garden is designed for particular conditions. Remember to check the requirements for each plant that you decide to use.

The "Corner Garden with Trellis," from page 23, will work best when the trellis is partially shaded and the flower beds receive full sun. This is a garden of quiet contemplation and rest.

The "General Sunny Garden," from page 25, is an example of a formal, showy bed. This garden will become the centerpiece of your yard. It requires full sun.

The "Cottage Garden," from page 30, allows for individual flair. This is the "anything goes" garden that changes with the years as you do. Its conditions range from full sun to shade and it encompasses everything from fragrant flowers for cutting to edible herbs and vegetables. Cottage gardens usually include both annuals and perennials.

## CORNER GARDEN WITH TRELLIS

Trees: honey locust (*gleditsia triacanthos inermis*)

Shrubs: Japanese yew (*taxus baccata*)

On trellis: morning glory vine (*ipomoea nil*) and moonflower (*ipomoea alba*)

In planters: geraniums (*pelargonium*) and impatiens (*impatiens wallerana*)

In mulched area: impatiens (*impatiens wallerana*)

In curved bed: plumed cockscomb (*celosia cristata v. plumosa*); coleus (*coleus* x *hybrida*); creeping juniper (*juniperus horizontalis*); and French marigold (*tagetes patula*)

## GENERAL SUNNY GARDEN

Outer bed: gladiolus *(gladiolus hybridus)*; baby's breath *(gypsophila elegans)*; bridal wreath *(spiraea x vanhouttei)*; fountain grass *(pennisetum setaceum)*; black-eyed Susan *(rudbeckia hirta)*; sunflower *(helianthus annuus)*; and vining petunias, 'Purple Wave' *(petunia, spp.)*

Inner bed: black-eyed Susan *(rudbeckia hirta)*; snapdragon *(antirrhinum majus)*; vining petunias, 'Purple Wave' *(petunia, spp.)*; basil *(ocimum basilicum)*; parsley *(petroselenum crispum var. crispum)*; and dill *(anethum graveolens)*

Bush in yard: virburnum *(viburnum opulus sterile)*

## COTTAGE GARDEN

Tree: Japanese maple *(acer palmatum dissectum)*

Shrubs: Japanese yew *(taxus cuspidata)*

Bed along house: larkspur *(cosolida ambigua)*; signet marigolds *(tagetes tenuifloia)*; ferns (ostrich, and Boston); hostas *(hosta species)*

Beds along entry path: baby's breath *(gypsophila elegans)* and annual candytuft *(iberis hybridus)*

Smaller, sunny bed: black-eyed Susan *(rudbeckia hirta)* and blanket flower *(gaillardia pulchella and gaillardia x gradiflora)*

Larger, sunny and partially shaded bed: chives *(allium schoenoprasum)*; garlic *(alluim sativum)*; chamomile *(chamaemelum nobile)*; peppermint *(mentha piperita)*; onion, bulbing *(allium cepa)*; heliotrope *(heliotropium arborescens)*; blanket flower *(gaillardia pulchella and gaillardia x gradiflora)*; daylily

*(hemerocallis)*; ornamental grasses *(gramineae)*; rhubarb *(rheum rhabarbarum)*; periwinkle *(vinca minor)*; and pachysandra, *(pachysandra terminalis)*

In container in larger bed: asparagus fern *(asparagus densiflorus)*

Raised bed by tree: bleeding heart *(dicentra)* and ferns (ostrich and Boston)

Bushes in yard: bridal wreath *(spiraea x vanhouttei)* and lilac *(syringa vulgaris)*

# ENCYCLOPEDIA OF EASY ANNUALS

The plants selected for this directory cover a wide base—some are annuals, either easy-care species or more tolerant and durable cultivars of slightly temperamental species. Others are biennials. Still others are perennials in warm parts of the world that provide summer color until a killing frost. A few can even be recognized as houseplants. But you can use them all successfully to provide seasonal color outdoors as annuals.

You'll find annuals listed alphabetically by their most popular common name, with other common names and the reliable botanical name nearby for reference. Plant descriptions and photos will help you to discern what they can contribute to your garden design. Consult the tips for easy-care growing, identifying the right site, soil, and season so your garden will not just survive but thrive, trouble-free. Details on propagation, uses, and related species and varieties are also conveniently on hand.

Whether you live in a suburban home with a large yard or in a condominium 14 stories above the ground with only a windy balcony to plant in, you will find easy-growing annuals here that will work for you. Many of the plants listed in the directory are available in garden centers everywhere—a relatively reliable representation of their success rate. Some of the newer and more unusual varieties might be harder to find unless you start them yourself from seed, either from seed packets found on racks locally or from mail-order catalogs.

*American marigolds and salvia*

# AGERATUM, FLOSS FLOWER
### *Ageratum houstonianum*

Originally from Mexico and Central America, these fluffy, blue-lavender, white, and pink flowers are favorites for window boxes and edging in summer gardens. One interesting aspect of *ageratum* is that the eye sees the color of so-called blue varieties differently than film, which registers them as pink.

**DESCRIPTION:** Ageratum is covered with powder puff–shaped flowers about ½ inch in diameter on compact, mounding plants from 6 to 10 inches high. They will spread about 10 inches by season's end. Ageratum blooms continuously from planting out after all chance of frost has passed (it is very frost-sensitive) until fall.

**EASY-CARE GROWING:** Grow in any well-drained soil in full sun or partial shade. Space 6 to 10 inches apart for solid color. Occasional deadheading will improve their performance. Provide ample water to make sure that leaves never wilt.

**PROPAGATION:** By seed. Start seeds indoors 6 to 8 weeks before planting. Cover seeds very lightly, since they need some light to germinate well. Germination time will be 5 to 8 days at 70°F.

**USES:** Plant in the front of borders and beds. They also grow well in hanging baskets, window boxes, and other containers. Most of the newer varieties form compact mounds that provide the scarce blue color so seldom found in annuals. Taller, older varieties make good cut flowers.

**RELATED SPECIES:** Golden ageratum or *Lonas inodora* has the same flower effect in bright yellow.

**RELATED VARIETIES:** Several of the popular blue varieties are 'Adriatic' (mid-blue), 'Blue Danube' (lavender-blue), and 'Pacific' (violet-blue). 'Summer Snow' and 'Hawaii White' are white. 'Bavaria' has white-centered blue flowers. 'Pink Powderpuffs' and 'Swing Pink' cover the pink range. 'Blue Horizon' is a tall variety useful for cutting.

# SWEET ALYSSUM
### *Lobularia maritima*

Alyssum is covered with thimble-shaped clusters of small flowers for months on end, even through the winter in milder climates. Alyssum has a pervasive fragrance and is a member of the mustard family.

**DESCRIPTION:** Alyssum grows only a few inches high but spreads as much as a foot in diameter. The tiny, four-petalled flowers are closely packed around the small racemes that grow upward as the lower flowers fade. Although white is the most planted color, pink, lavender, and darker shades of violet are also available.

**EASY-CARE GROWING:** Alyssum grows best in full sun in cool weather, but it will tolerate partial shade. Plants will survive light frosts. Space 6 to 8 inches apart. Alyssum will reseed vigorously. If they begin to look shabby in summer, cut them back and fertilize to encourage fresh, new growth.

**PROPAGATION:** By seed. In the mildest climates it can be planted in the fall for cool season display. Otherwise, sow seeds outdoors as soon as the ground can be worked. For earliest bloom, sow seeds indoors 4 to 6 weeks earlier and transplant to the garden while plants are still small. Seeds germinate in 7 to 14 days at 65 to 70°F.

**USES:** Alyssum is traditionally used for edging beds and borders. However, it can also tumble over the rocks in a rock garden or be planted in niches between paving stones. Place it where the scent can perfume the air for passersby. It makes a good, sunny ground cover. It is also good in containers.

**RELATED VARIETIES:** 'Carpet of Snow' is the most planted, 'Snow Crystal' forms a mounded plant, while 'Snowcloth' is more spreading. The Basket Series includes 'Easter Basket Blend,' which combines the entire sweet alyssum color spectrum—rose, violet-blue, peach, and white flowers. 'Easter Bonnet' comes in rose, lavender, violet, and white.

# GLOBE AMARANTH
### *Gomphrena globosa*

Here's a weather- and soil-tolerant plant. This tropical native has small, cloverlike flowers that continue coming through the whole summer season.

**DESCRIPTION:** Globe amaranth can grow up to 2 feet tall, although newer, smaller varieties can stay as short as 6 inches. The flower heads are about 1 inch in diameter and are made up of many minute flowers held within showy, papery bracts, which are actually modified leaves. The basic color is violet, but varieties have red, orange, pink, and creamy white flowers.

**EASY-CARE GROWING:** The only demand for good performance is sun and well-drained soil. Plant in the garden after the last frost and, depending on variety, space from 10 to 15 inches apart.

**PROPAGATION:** By seed. Sow seeds in place in the garden after last frost. For earlier bloom, start transplants 6 to 8 weeks earlier. Seeds germinate in 14 to 21 days at 65 to 75°F.

**USES:** The tall varieties, especially good for cutting and drying, are ideal for mid-border. Use dwarf varieties for edging beds, borders, or for a colorful ground cover. Combine them with other plants for container plantings.

**RELATED SPECIES:** *Gomphrena haageana* has yellow to orange, pinecone-shaped flowers, each about 1 inch in diameter. It also dries well. 'Aurea' is orange-flowered, and 'Carmine' is magenta-pink.

**RELATED VARIETIES:** 'Buddy' is a compact, purple-flowered variety, growing only 6 to 8 inches tall. In the Gnome series, you can choose from similar-sized flowers with white, pink, and rose purple flowers. 'Strawberry Fields' is bright red and grows to 2½ feet with long stems. It is splendid for cutting. Several mixtures are offered including white, pink, rose, and reddish-purple flowers.

# ASPARAGUS FERN
## *Asparagus densiflorus*

Asparagus fern, of which there are many kinds, is related to the favorite springtime vegetable, and you'll notice that new shoots look like skinny asparagus spears. The most frequently used asparagus fern, loved for providing height and fullness in mixed planters and baskets, is *A. densiflorus* 'Sprengeri.'

**DESCRIPTION:** New asparagus growth expands to form feathery, branched shoots 1 to 2 feet long. From a small plant in spring with three to four stems, asparagus ferns can develop up to ten or more billowing stalks that emerge from pots or containers by summer's end.

**EASY-CARE GROWING:** Key factors to good growth include moderate water, a rich, well-drained soil, and full sunlight. Asparagus fern will tolerate low light (even existing satisfactorily as a houseplant), but growth will be diminished. Asparagus is a gross feeder; at planting use a slow-release fertilizer that will last all summer or feed weekly with a water-soluble fertilizer mixed at half the recommended strength.

**PROPAGATION:** By seed (must be fresh) or by division. It's most readily available as started plants.

**USES:** Asparagus fern excels as a filler plant in containers of mixed flowers growing during the summer. It works in wall boxes, hanging baskets, window boxes, and planters of all kinds. Asparagus fern also grows well in partially shaded ground beds, alone, or intermixed with larger, shade-tolerant flowers such as tuberous begonias. Because asparagus fern is a vigorous plant, combine with plants of some stature so they are not overpowered.

**RELATED VARIETIES:** Several other asparagus relatives are also used as ornamentals. *A. densiflorus* 'Myersii' is a selection with stiff, upright growth similar to foxtails. *A. asparagoides*, the florist's smilax, is sometimes planted in flowering containers. Leaves are coarser, and it is a definite trailer.

# Gypsy Baby's Breath
### *Gypsophila elegans* 'Gypsy'

Their light, airy texture and petite white or pink flowers make baby's breath a wonderful addition to the garden. This annual is native to the Caucasus and is related to carnations. Because ordinary baby's breath cultivars bloom for only 6 weeks and also usually need staking, you may want to try 'Gypsy,' a new award-winning cultivar.

**DESCRIPTION:** Annual baby's breath grows to 1½ feet tall, forming an airy bush with many forked branches covered with flowers. Although the flowers, up to ½ inch in diameter, are usually white, there are pink, rose, and carmine forms. In contrast, 'Gypsy' grows into a neat, self-branching and self-supporting mound to 12 or 14 inches high. Its semi-double, light pink flowers will bloom for an extended period.

**EASY-CARE GROWING:** Grow in full sun in well-drained, lime-rich garden soil. They grow rapidly and will come into bloom about 8 weeks after germination.

**PROPAGATION:** By seed. Sow seeds outdoors in place after the danger of frost has passed. For earlier bloom, sow indoors in peat pots 2 to 3 weeks before planting out, then plant—pot and all. (They grow so rapidly, it is difficult to separate the seedlings, so plant them in a clump.) Germination takes 10 to 15 days at 70°F.

**USES:** Baby's breath is effective in borders or cottage gardens, and 'Gypsy' works particularly well in the front of the garden or mixed flower pot. Taller forms of annual baby's breath also make superb cut flowers. It is used primarily as a filler to give unity to arrangements with strong vertical or horizontal lines.

**RELATED SPECIES:** *Gypsophila paniculata* is a perennial and widely planted. Rapidly gaining popularity is the creeping form of perennial baby's breath, *Gypsophylla repens*, which looks particularly handsome cascading over stone retaining walls.

# BACHELOR'S BUTTON, CORNFLOWER

### *Centaurea cyanus*

The boutonniere flower is reputedly where this favorite got its name. And "cornflower blue" has frequently been used in the fashion trade when displaying the intense blue of bachelor's button flowers. The flowers also come in soft shades of pink, lavender, maroon, red, and white.

**DESCRIPTION:** Bachelor's buttons grow 1 to 3 feet tall with innumerable round flowers held above the rather sparse, long and narrow gray-green leaves. The habit of growth is relatively loose.

**EASY-CARE GROWING:** Provide full sun in well-drained average soil. For earliest bloom, sow seeds outdoors in the fall so they will start to grow before the first frost and bloom the next spring. They may also be started indoors and transplanted. Otherwise, sow seeds outdoors as early in the spring as the soil can be worked. Thin to 8 to 12 inches apart. Early bloom is heavy and prolific; it tapers off later. Repeat sowings will maintain a lush bloom.

**PROPAGATION:** By seed. To grow seedlings indoors, germinate at 65°F four weeks before planting out. Germination time is 7 to 14 days.

**USES:** Bachelor's buttons lend themselves to informal planting, especially with other annuals and perennials in beds and borders. When planting in containers, the gardener should take into consideration their informal growth habit. The flowers dry well, but stems are weak and must be wired for arrangements.

**RELATED SPECIES:** *C. cineraria* 'Silver Dust' has lacy silver leaves and is sold as dusty miller. *C. moschata*, commonly called "sweet sultan," bears sweetly scented, fuzzy, 3- to 4-inch yellow, pink, lavender, or white blossoms. Growing to 2 feet, sweet sultans are good for cutting. Mountain blue *(Centaurea montana)* is a hardy, easy-spreading perennial with blue flowers.

**RELATED VARIETIES:** The Ball Series and the Boy Series, including 'Blue Boy,' grow to 2½ feet while 'Emperor William' reaches 3 feet. Award-winning 'Jubilee Gem' is shorter at 12 inches. 'Polka Dot Mixed' comes with flowers of blue, maroon, rose, lavender, red, and white, while 'Frosted Queen' has blue or crimson flowers with pale tips.

# SNOWSTORM BACOPA
### *Sutera cordata* 'Snowstorm'

This annual is new and taking America by storm. An Old World native, it was discovered filling out lush hanging baskets in an Australian nursery and brought to America as a Proven Winners introduction. Propagated by cuttings, and not by seed, it is a welcome newcomer for window boxes, planters, pots, and a garden ground cover.

**DESCRIPTION:** On creeping or cascading stems, hundreds of small, five-petaled, white flowers stand above rounded and toothed leaves. Stems can get to be a foot long, spreading across the soil surface or draping gracefully down the side of a pot.

**EASY-CARE GROWING:** Bacopa grows well from sun to shade, but requires abundant water in sunny areas. Provide well-drained but rich soil in a garden or planter. When grown in a basket or container, fertilize regularly with a high nitrogen fertilizer.

**PROPAGATION:** This is a patented plant and unauthorized propagation of it is illegal.

**USES:** Use alone or in combination with other annuals in pots, baskets, and other containers. Or let the stems creep around the base of taller annuals or perennials or along a retaining wall or front edging of a garden bed.

**RELATED VARIETIES:** 'Snowflake' is an older variety with smaller flowers, less vigor, and less tolerance to heat and diseases.

# ROSE BALSAM
## *Impatiens balsamina*

This old-fashioned flower is related to bedding impatiens and, like its close cousin, is widely adaptable, generously flowering, and ideal for shady gardens. The seed capsules on most plants in the genus *Impatiens* will explode if touched when ripe, catapulting their seeds across the garden.

**DESCRIPTION:** Narrow, elongated leaves emerge on plants that can reach from 1 to 2½ feet high, depending on the cultivar. Cup-shaped flowers, both singles and doubles that resemble camellias, emerge in open spikes usually punctuated with leaves. The flower clusters are particularly showy on compact varieties, which cluster their flowers high on the stem. The flowers are white, purple, pink, or red.

**EASY-CARE GROWING:** Provide rich and moist but well-drained soil in light shade or full sun in cool climates. Plant prestarted seedlings outdoors after the danger of spring frost has passed.

**PROPAGATION:** By seed. Plant seeds indoors 4 to 6 weeks before the last spring frost. Provide temperatures of 75°F. Expect germination to begin in 8 to 10 days.

**USES:** Use rose balsam in the middle of a mixed border or to fill an entire bed in shade.

**RELATED VARIETIES:** 'Carambole' reaches 14 inches high and gives a good color display. The 6- to 8-inch-high 'Topknot Mix' holds its double flowers above the foliage. 'Camellia Flowered' have huge double flowers in pink, rose, scarlet, and white. 'Extra Dwarf Tom Thumb Mixed' reach only 8 to 12 inches high and are able to tolerate some drought.

# BASIL
*Ocimum basilicum*

Basil is one of the world's favorite flavorings, used in all kinds of meat, fish, and vegetable dishes. The purple-leaved varieties can stand on their own in any ornamental garden, a feast for both a visual and culinary palate.

**DESCRIPTION:** Basil is an herb that grows rapidly to form a bright green (or purple) bush. Standard varieties will grow 12 to 18 inches high with a 12-inch spread. Dwarf varieties may only grow 6 inches high and as wide. The oval leaves are used for flavoring. The inconsequential flowers are best cut off when they appear, for they diminish foliage production. Plants can be sheared back hard to 6 inches to force young, new growth.

**EASY-CARE GROWING:** Full sun and hot weather suit basil perfectly. Avoiding extra-rich and fertile soil helps the flavoring oils intensify, making the leaves more pungent. For ornamental use, moderate water and fertility will increase basil's succulence and good looks.

**PROPAGATION:** Sow seeds indoors 4 weeks prior to the last frost date. They'll germinate in 5 to 7 days at 70°F. Or sow seeds outdoors when the soil is warm and danger of frost has passed. Depending on the variety, plant 8 to 12 inches apart for ornamental use.

**USES:** Compact, mounding varieties such as 'Spicy Globe' make ideal edging plants, while tall plants such as 'Green Ruffles' add a bright chartreuse note to borders. 'Purple Ruffles' and 'Osmin,' handsome, dark-leaved varieties, are an admirable contrast to whites, pinks, and shades of green. Any of these also grow well in containers on decks and patios. For crisp overtones of extra flavor, look for other basils reminiscent of cinnamon or lemon.

**RELATED VARIETIES:** 'Spicy Globe' and 'Minimum' (small, compact), 'Dark Opal' and 'Purple Ruffles' (purple), and 'Sweet Dani' and 'Citriodorum' (lemon-scented) are all available.

# Wax Begonia, Fibrous Begonia, Everblooming Begonia

### *Begonia semperflorens*

The brightly colored bedding begonias are equally at home in full sun (except where temperatures stay above 90°F for days on end) or dappled shade and will even bloom moderately well in full but bright shade (where trees are pruned high). From first setting them out until laid low by frost, they'll be packed with white, pink, rose, or red blossoms (some even have white petals edged in red), each flower centered by a cheery yellow eye. Virtually untouched by bugs or blight, their only shortcoming is a relatively narrow color range.

**DESCRIPTION:** Uniformity is the trademark of most tight mounds of closely packed leaves covered with blossoms. All four flower colors are available with your choice of leaf color: chocolate-red or shades of green. The deeper-colored or bronze-leaved varieties offer especially eye-catching contrast with flowers. Though not as well-known, there are also varieties with double flowers that resemble fat, little rosebuds and others with variegated foliage.

**EASY-CARE GROWING:** Begonias perform well in rich, well-drained soil but the soil must be allowed to dry between waterings. They'll form tight, compact plants in full sun, with increasingly looser form and fewer flowers as you move them deeper into the shade. Most hybrids will grow 6 to 9 inches high and spread as wide.

**PROPAGATION:** By seed or cuttings. Most hybrids are grown from seed, but great patience is required. Dustlike seeds (2 million per ounce) must be sown in December or January for large, husky plants by May. Seeds need light to germinate. The seeds should be covered with clear plastic in starting containers to maintain high humidity during germination. Germination temperature is 70 to 85°F and requires 14 to 21 days. Cuttings

also root readily. A good way to start plants is on a sunny windowsill or under fluorescent lights during winter.

**USES:** Wax begonias lend themselves to large, formal plantings because of their uniform size and shapeliness. They're also suitable in front of summer annual borders and combine well with other cool-colored (blue and green) flowers in mixed plantings and containers. (They tend to be overwhelmed by hot colors.) Even a small planting of begonias in a small pot by a window or door will bloom lustily all summer.

**RELATED VARIETIES:** The most popular, dark-leaved kinds are the Cocktail Series: 'Brandy,' 'Vodka,' 'Whiskey,' and 'Gin' and the Senator Series in pink, rose, salmon, scarlet, and white flowered forms. Good green-leaved varieties are found in the 'Olympia' and 'Prelude' series. 'Avalanche' begonias in pink or white are rangier, suited for containers and hanging baskets where their arching growth habit is handsome. 'Charm' begonias, grown only from cuttings, have green foliage marked with white. Calla lily begonias, which can be grown from seed, have green and white variegated foliage and pink flowers.

# TUBEROUS BEGONIA
*Begonia tuberhybrida*

A triumph of the breeder's art, tuberous begonias at their biggest have flowers of salad-plate size in fanciful forms and bright colors, even with petal edges tipped in a contrasting color (picotee). These beautiful flowers grow well in morning sun and light shade. They have been joined in recent years by new varieties with altogether more modest flowers but many more of them.

**DESCRIPTION:** The large-flowered tuberous begonias come with many flower types, both upright and pendulous, single or double-flowered, and with frilled or plain petals. Unlike their *semperflorens* cousins, tuberous begonias offer wide color choices: white, pink, rose, red, orange, and yellow. They grow upright with large, arrow-shaped leaves. Both the large- and small-flowered tuberous begonias alternately bear female (ravishingly beautiful) and male (single and smaller) flowers. The smaller-flowered tuberous begonias bear many flowers up to 3 inches in diameter.

**EASY-CARE GROWING:** Tuberous begonias grow best in midday and afternoon shade; otherwise the foliage will scorch. They need rich, well-drained soil with high organic matter. Allow soil to dry between waterings. The large-flowered varieties easily become top-heavy and require judicious staking, while the smaller-flowered ones can usually support their own growth. Powdery mildew is frequently a problem with tuberous begonias, especially if they are grown where the air around leaves and stems is stagnant. At the first signs of a white powder on leaves, spray with a fungicide.

**PROPAGATION:** By seed, tubers, or cuttings. Most of the big-flowered tuberous begonias are sold as named-variety tubers. When tiny, pink growth appears on the upper side (with a depression where last year's stem was attached), place the tuber with the hollow side up at soil level in a pot filled with packaged soil mix. Water well once to firm the tuber in the pot and provide a temperature of 65°F. As the top swells and grows, roots will be forming below the surface. Do not allow the soil to dry out, but avoid drenching until the leaves expand. Provide high light until time for planting outside (after all danger of frost has passed, the weather has settled, and the soil has warmed). Carefully plant at the same level as the begonia was growing in the pot.

**USES:** Grow the large-flowered kinds as specimen plants in semi-shady locations. Pendulous varieties, such as the heat-tolerant Illumination Series, make good container plants. The new, small-flowered kinds including 'Memory' and 'Non Stop' can be used in larger beds, containers, and hanging baskets. Watch container plantings to prevent from drying out.

**RELATED SPECIES:** The iron cross begonia *(Begonia masoniana)*, a widely grown indoor plant, makes a handsome foliage planting for shade in summer planted directly into the ground or plunged in its own pot. The chartreuse leaves strongly marked with a chocolate-brown cross make a bold statement. Be sure to take this plant inside before cool weather starts because it is very frost-sensitive. Rex begonias *(Begonia rex)* are foliage plants colored in every conceivable combination: steel-gray, red, pink, green, and with splashes of white. They do well outdoors in the summer in shady spots. Elatior begonia *(Begonia hiemalis)* are hybrid begonias produced by crossing several species. One series is upright, good for planters, while the other has a flowing character and is ideal for hanging baskets and other containers to be viewed at eye level or above. Because much of the early development work on this variety was done by the Rieger firm in Germany, they are frequently known by this name. Flowers are 1 to 1½ inches in diameter, single, semi-double, and double. Colors are red, orange, pink, and a luscious white that looks green when the light shines through it.

**RELATED VARIETIES:** Tubers of large-flowered varieties in separate colors and flower forms are usually available at garden centers and from specialists as named varieties. Smaller-flowered types are available as seed or started plants in garden centers.

# Bells of Ireland, Shell Flower, Molucca Balm

## *Molucella laevis*

**B**ells of Ireland form dramatic spires of green in the garden, the tiny white or pinkish flowers being almost hidden within the large, green bells (or calyxes). Native to western Asia, the name "Molucca balm" and "Molucella" were applied mistakenly, for at one time they were thought to be natives of the Molucca Islands.

**DESCRIPTION:** Bells of Ireland at their best grow in spires to 3 feet, surrounded by the netted, green, bell-like calyxes. The flowers are fragrant.

**EASY-CARE GROWING:** Grow bells of Ireland in full sun or partial shade in average garden loam with good drainage. Sow them outdoors in spring as soon as the soil is dry enough to be worked. Thin seedlings to space plants 12 inches apart. To prevent their toppling, plant them in areas protected from high wind or tie them to a bamboo stake. They mature fairly rapidly and do not rebloom. For a longer show, start plants at different intervals. They reseed themselves readily and may provide their own repeat performance. After maturity, plants grow ragged. You can pull them out or leave them behind other tall foliage to set seeds for another generation.

**PROPAGATION:** By seed. Sow in place. For earlier flowers, start 8 to 10 weeks prior to planting out. Seeds germinate in 23 to 35 days at 55°F. Don't cover seeds; they need light to germinate.

**USES:** Plant this stately annual at the rear of garden borders for a vertical thrust. The chartreuse color of the bells combines nicely with lemon-yellows, sky-blues, and pinks. Especially revered by flower arrangers, the light green flowers hold their color for a long time in arrangements. For drying, hang them upside down in a dark place. They'll mute to a warm tan when dry and will last well in winter arrangements. Bells of Ireland are especially attractive with other warm-toned components such as ornamental grasses and seed pods.

# BLACK-EYED SUSAN, GLORIOSA DAISY

*Rudbeckia hirta*

This widespread native of the prairie states has been turned into a horticultural delight. The name "gloriosa daisy" has been applied to the multitude of varieties that have grown out of this prairie wild flower. Although they're short-lived perennials, they'll bloom the first year and are often grown as annuals.

**DESCRIPTION:** Varieties of black-eyed Susan grow from 1 to 3 feet tall and are relatively erect. The flowers are available in many warm-toned colors: yellow, gold, orange, russet, and mahogany. Many of them have bands of color intermixed. The single varieties all have a large black or brown center, contrasting with the color surrounding it. Double flowers may reach 6 inches in diameter.

**EASY-CARE GROWING:** Bright sun is the gloriosa daisy's main requirement. It will tolerate poor soil and erratic watering, although it does flourish with better care. Transplant it into the garden in the spring after the last frost. Space plants 10 to 15 inches apart. The taller varieties may need protection from strong winds or staking to keep them from toppling. Avoid staking by planting more compact cultivars such as 'Rustic Dwarfs,' 'Sonora,' or 'Toto.' Cutting the flowers encourages increased blooming.

**PROPAGATION:** By seed. Treated as biennials or perennials, the seeds can be sown in the garden the preceding summer or fall. For bloom the same season, start seeds indoors 8 to 10 weeks prior to transplanting. Seeds germinate in 5 to 10 days at 70 to 75°F.

**USES:** Any sunny location is ideal. Beds, borders, and planting strips will benefit from them. Plant them with ornamental grasses. They'll do well in large containers and are good cut flowers.

**RELATED SPECIES:** 'Goldsturm,' a hardy perennial of *R. fulgida* var. *sullivantii*, has black-centered, single yellow flowers up to 5 inches in diameter.

**RELATED VARIETIES:** 'Rustic Colors' is composed of many gold, bronze, and mahogany shades. 'Irish Eyes' has golden flowers with green eyes.

# BLACK-EYED SUSAN VINE, CLOCK VINE
## *Thunbergia alata*

This quick-growing vine boasts many open-faced flowers, usually with dark centers (hence the name "black-eyed Susan"). In areas where this plant is not struck down by frost it is a perennial, but in most climates of the United States it grows as a beautiful annual. The name *Thunbergia* honors Swedish botanist Karl Pehr Thunberg.

**DESCRIPTION:** Black-eyed Susan vine can grow 6 to 8 feet tall in a season and has rough, hairy leaves. The blooms have five distinct petals and are symmetrical. Flower color can be white, yellow, orange, or cream-colored. Most of them have dark centers.

**EASY-CARE GROWING:** Generally, it grows best in full sun. It needs average, well-drained soil. Plant seedlings 3 inches away from supports. Space plants 5 to 8 inches apart. Pinch the tips to encourage branching. Since black-eyed Susan vines climb by twining, netting, or strings make good trellising materials. They will need a trellis to climb large posts or solid fencing.

**PROPAGATION:** By seed or by cuttings. Sow seeds outdoors after the last frost or start seedlings indoors 6 to 8 weeks before outdoor planting. Seeds germinate in 10 to 15 days at 70 to 75°F. Cuttings root easily in a commercial soil mix.

**USES:** Thunbergias can be used to cover posts, porches, arbors, pergolas, or fences. They also make good container plants. Plants in containers will also bloom over winter in sunny windows.

**RELATED SPECIES:** *Thunbergia gregorii* has somewhat larger flowers in a bright orange color.

**RELATED VARIETIES:** 'Susie Mix' is composed of orange, yellow, and white blooms, either with or without dark centers. 'Alba' has white flowers with dark centers.

# BLANKET FLOWER
### *Gaillardia pulchella*

The annual gaillardia is a native of the Plains states to the East Coast. The name "blanket flower" comes from its resemblance to Indian blankets, blooming in yellow, orange, red, and their combinations.

**DESCRIPTION:** The annual gaillardia grows erect, 1 to 2 feet tall, with narrow leaves 2 inches long and flowers on long stems. In addition to single-flowered varieties, there are doubles with numerous quilled petals. In these, the original orange, red, and yellow colors have been extended to bronze and cream colors.

**EASY-CARE GROWING:** The annual gaillardia will grow well in full sun in any well-drained soil. It does not like clay, excess water, or fertilizer. A fungicide may be needed in areas with high humidity. It continues to perform admirably under dry conditions. Space it from 9 to 15 inches apart.

**PROPAGATION:** By seed. Barely cover, since gaillardia needs light to germinate. Sow seeds outdoors after the danger of frost has passed. For earlier bloom, sow indoors 4 to 6 weeks prior to planting out. Seeds germinate in 4 to 10 days at 75 to 85°F.

**USES:** Plant gaillardia in groups. Grow it in meadows, in the cottage garden, at the edge of lawns, or near woodlands. The flowers are good for cutting.

**RELATED SPECIES:** Hybrids under the name *G. grandiflora* behave like perennials. Two dwarf forms are 'Goblin,' with flowers of deep red edged in yellow, and 'Yellow Goblin,' a pure yellow. 'Burgundy' has large, wine-colored flowers. 'Dazzler' and compact 'Baby Cole' have yellow-tipped red flowers.

**RELATED VARIETIES:** 'Double Mixed' flowers are 3 inches in diameter in cream, gold, crimson, and bicolors. 'Red Plume,' an award winner with chrysanthemum-like double flowers, tolerates heat and drought.

# BROWALLIA, SAPPHIRE FLOWER
### *Browallia speciosa*

Sapphire flowers bloom heavily from early spring to fall frost; year-round in sunny windows or greenhouses. They're at their best in cool or coastal gardens, but with partial shade or an eastern exposure they will consistently grow well.

**DESCRIPTION:** *B. speciosa* varieties grow in a loose mound to 18 inches high and as wide. Their lax growing habits allow them to trail. In the Troll Series they are more compact and bushy.

**EASY-CARE GROWING:** Plant in rich, well-drained soil but keep moist. Plant larger varieties 10 inches apart; dwarf varieties 6 inches apart. Browallia is a good shade plant, although with looser habit and sparser flowers. Feed lightly on a biweekly schedule or incorporate a summer-long, slow-release fertilizer in the soil at planting. Taller varieties can benefit from pinching for a fuller shape.

**PROPAGATION:** By seed or by cuttings. Start seeds indoors 6 to 8 weeks prior to planting out after the last frost. Seeds need light to germinate, so do not cover. At temperatures of 70 to 75°F, they'll take 14 to 21 days to germinate. Softwood cuttings taken in the spring or fall root promptly. For large plants in 10-inch hanging baskets, add 4 weeks to the growing time.

**USES:** Sapphire flowers are grown in beds, borders, or rock gardens. Compact plants make good edges for a tall border. They are also excellent container plants.

**RELATED SPECIES:** *B. americana* 'Sapphire' is an upright plant with deep blue flowers with a white eye. *B. viscosa* 'Amethyst' tolerates heat and full sun, has natural basal branching, and small dark purple flowers with white eyes.

**RELATED VARIETIES:** Most planted *speciosa* varieties are the cascading Bell Series including popular, mid-blue 'Blue Bells,' pure white 'Silver Bells,' deep indigo blue 'Marine Bells,' clear azure blue 'Sky Bells,' and pale blue 'Heavenly Bells.' Compact, self-branching browallias include 'Blue Troll,' a dwarf variety in mid-blue and its counterpart, 'White Troll,' as well as the entire Starlight Series.

# FLOWERING OR ORNAMENTAL CABBAGE (*B. O. CAPITATA*) AND KALE (*B. O. ACEPHALA*)

*Brassica oleracea*

These fancy-leaved cousins of our familiar vegetables make a bold statement in the cool season garden. In fact, the ornamental forms are edible too, but the taste is bitter, and when the white, pink, red, and purple leaves are cooked, they turn an unappetizing gray. Tolerant of mild frosts, they're colorful all winter in mild climates.

**DESCRIPTION:** Bold, round plants whose center leaves (not flowers) color up in cool or cold weather, ornamental cabbage and kale grow 18 to 24 inches in diameter and can grow 18 to 24 inches tall.

**EASY-CARE GROWING:** Their primary use is in the fall when they can linger in pots and beds long after autumn leaves have fallen. Grow in large pots in a rich soil mix and feed weekly with a water-soluble fertilizer as recommended on the package. Transplant to the garden or display container in September. Before transplanting, remove tatty bottom leaves. Plant into the ground so that the crown of leaves is flush with the soil surface (roots will grow along the buried stem). Cover plants with floating row covers if necessary to keep off leaf-eating caterpillars.

**PROPAGATION:** By seed. Sow 6 weeks in advance of outdoor planting at 65°F. Do not cover the cabbage seeds since light aids germination. Conversely, cover kale seeds with ¼ inch of soil.

**USES:** Kale or cabbage are best planted in areas where you can peer into the center—on slopes, doorsteps, decks, and patios. They're also successful in ground beds and in large plantings.

**RELATED VARIETIES:** Dynasty Series cabbage in pink, red, or white have semi-waved leaves. 'Color Up Improved' has a flashy open rosette and takes on its autumn colors early in the season. Ornamental kale in red or white include the Peacock Series, which are extra-compact with finely cut leaves.

# CALADIUM HORTULANUM
*Caladium hortulanum*

Tropical caladiums are grown entirely for their brightly colored and wildly patterned foliage. Gardeners can choose from many combinations of green, pink, red, white, and creamy yellow.

**DESCRIPTION:** Large, spear- or arrowhead-shaped leaves on long stems rise directly from the tuber buried in the ground below. Depending on weather and soil, each leaf on caladiums can grow up to 12 inches in length on l-foot stems.

**EASY-CARE GROWING:** In hot sections of Zones 9 and 10, caladium tubers are planted directly in the ground 1 inch deep, but in the rest of the country, it's customary to start them in pots indoors and plant them outside when the weather is warm. Plant tubers in pots 1 inch deep in soil high in organic matter. Kept moist and provide temperatures of 70 to 85°F. Caladiums thrive in high temperature and humidity. Outdoors, grow in moist, rich soil, and protect them from intense sun. High, overhead shade or eastern exposures will provide maximum growth and color development of the leaves. Feed weekly with a diluted water-soluble fertilizer to assure continued growth of new leaves. A slow-release fertilizer may also be mixed into the soil before planting. In the fall, dig tubers before frost, allowing them to dry gradually. Store in a frost-free location.

**PROPAGATION:** Cut tubers in pieces, similar to potatoes, being sure each piece retains growing "eyes."

**USES:** Caladiums are unexcelled for foliage color in bright, shady beds or borders, window boxes, or containers. Grow in moist areas to reduce water needs.

**RELATED VARIETIES:** 'Candidum' is primarily white with green ribs and leaves. 'Pink Beauty' has patterns of pink overlaid on a green background. 'Florida Sweetheart,' with brilliant pink-centered leaves, tolerates more sun than most of the others.

# CALENDULA, POT MARIGOLD
*Calendula officinalis*

These beauties bloom in all shades of white, gold, yellow, and orange. Some varieties have flower petals tipped in contrasting colors. They're known as stalwarts of the cool season garden, growing all winter in Zones 8 to 10.

**DESCRIPTION:** Cultivated calendulas grow 12 to 24 inches tall with rich green leaves. Plants will spread 12 to 18 inches. Flowers can be single daisies, semi-double, or fully double. Flower size ranges up to 4 inches in newer varieties.

**EASY-CARE GROWING:** Calendulas thrive in poor to medium soil with full sun and moderate moisture. They will survive several degrees of frost, and if properly hardened off, can be planted in the spring as soon as soil is workable. Plant 10 to 15 inches apart. Pick off the spent flowers for continued bloom. For fall bloom, sow seeds in July. Mildew is occasionally a problem in cool, damp weather.

**PROPAGATION:** By seed. For earliest bloom, sow seeds indoors 4 to 6 weeks early at a temperature of 65 to 70°F. Germination takes 10 to 14 days. After transplanting, the seedlings grow in cooler temperatures (50 to 55°F) until planting outside. Seeds can also be sown outdoors when the soil is workable, then thinned to a 10- to 15-inch spacing. For winter bloom in Zones 8 to 10, plant the seeds in late fall.

**USES:** Plant in beds, borders, planting pockets, and containers in full sun. Calendulas also make good long-lasting cut flowers.

**RELATED VARIETIES:** The Bon Bon Series has separate shades of yellow and orange, and a mixture that also includes apricot and soft yellow. The Fiesta Gitana Series bears semi-double flowers in yellow, orange, and a mixture, with most of the flowers having dark centers. Taller 'Pacific Beauty' and 'Prince Mix' have large flowers on strong stems and are good for cutting. 'Greenheart Orange' is a color breakthrough with orange florets around a green center.

# CALLIOPSIS, TICKSEED
## *Coreopsis tinctoria*

Native to many parts of the United States, calliopsis have bright, daisylike flowers. The name "tickseed" comes from the resemblance to an insect, as does the name *coreopsis*, which is derived from Greek (*koris*, meaning bedbug).

**DESCRIPTION:** Growing 1 to 3 feet tall, coreopsis plants are sparsely branched with bright, toothed, daisy flowers. Some have extra layers of petals and include double varieties. Colors range from yellow through orange and cinnamon-red to burnished mahogany. Many varieties are bicolored with sharply contrasting colors in the petals.

**EASY-CARE GROWING:** Any sunny site with good drainage will grow coreopsis. They will even tolerate poor or dry soils after seedlings are well established. They will reseed year after year if not deadheaded.

**PROPAGATION:** By seed. Seedlings grow quickly; sow them outdoors after final frost, covering them with ¼ inch of soil. Seeds may also be sown indoors 6 to 8 weeks prior to planting out. Germination takes 5 to 7 days at 70°F.

**USES:** The dwarf forms make good bed edgings, while the taller varieties are effective at mid-border. Coreopsis also makes good cut flowers and can be dried for arrangements.

**RELATED SPECIES:** Some perennial coreopsis can be grown as summer annuals. Medal-winning varieties of *Coreopsis grandiflora* are 'Sunray,' with bright, double-yellow flowers, and 'Early Sunrise,' with glowing, yellow, semi-double flowers.

**RELATED VARIETIES:** Most annual coreopsis is found in mixed colors, separated into dwarf and taller varieties. 'Tiger Flower Improved' is a dwarf mixture with bicolored flowers. In some seed catalogues, you can find individual colored cultivars such as 'Mahogany Midget,' with dark red flowers.

# ANNUAL CANDYTUFT
## *Iberis* hybrids

Candytufts have flowers in white, pink, lilac, red, and purple. Where *Iberis amara* "blood" predominates, they're called rocket candytufts, since their growth is upright. Globe candytufts, with a more mounding form, emphasize the *I. umbellata* parentage.

**DESCRIPTION:** Rocket candytufts have compact clusters of flowers on top of short, erect stems. In globe candytufts, the flower clusters are flat with a more bushlike appearance. Neither will grow more than 1 foot tall and they usually remain compact.

**EASY-CARE GROWING:** Candytuft needs full sun and good drainage. If your soil is acidic, add limestone to improve the growth of candytufts. Plant as soon as the danger of frost is over. Space 6 inches apart.

**PROPAGATION:** By seed. In mild climates, seeds can be sown in the ground in the fall for earlier bloom. Elsewhere, sow in the spring after the last frost. For earlier bloom, start candytuft indoors 6 to 8 weeks before planting out. Germination takes 15 to 20 days at 68 to 85°F.

**USES:** Candytuft naturally grows as an informal plant. However, with shearing, it can be tamed to a more formal appearance. Plant candytuft in the front of borders or as an edging for beds and borders. Grow it along sidewalks and pathways; tuck it into pockets in rock gardens; and display it in containers. The rocket kinds will have an erect growth habit, while the globe candytuft will drape over the edges. They combine effectively with other flowers in mixed plantings. Use the rocket candytuft for cut flowers and save the seed heads for everlasting arrangements.

**RELATED VARIETIES:** 'Dwarf Fairy Mixed' combines lilac, pink, maroon, red, and white. 'Flash' is a mixture that includes several shades of pink, bright red, maroon, purple, lilac, and white. 'Hyacinth Mixed,' 'Pinnacle,' and 'Mount Hood' are fragrant.

# CANNA
### *Canna* hybrids

The name *canna* comes from the Greek word for "reed," referring to the stems. The parentage of garden hybrids is very mixed, but breeders have provided many sturdy and colorful kinds.

**DESCRIPTION:** Cannas grow from fleshy roots with erect stalks from which broad, long leaves emerge. Flower stalks rising in the center bear large flowers. Foliage may be green, bronze, or purplish in hue.

**EASY-CARE GROWING:** Cannas need full sun and grow best in a deep, rich, moist, but well-drained soil. Incorporate extra organic matter and a slow-release fertilizer in the soil before planting. For earliest bloom, start in pots indoors. Otherwise plant roots directly into the ground after soil is warm and all danger of frost has passed. Use pieces of rootstock with two or three large eyes and plant 2 inches deep. Space 1½ to 2 feet apart. Remove spent flower heads for more prolific bloom. In fall after the first light frost, cut back stems to 6 inches, dig roots with soil attached, and store in a cool, frost-free place. While in storage, water sparingly.

**PROPAGATION:** By seed or by division of roots. Seed propagation is slow for most, with the exception of 'Tropical Rose,' an award-winning, fast-starting seed-strain. For other cultivars, cut roots into pieces, each with two to three eyes, in the spring just prior to planting.

**USES:** Use cannas in the center of island beds, at the sides or back of brightly colored borders, or near pools and ponds. They also dominate large containers.

**RELATED VARIETIES:** Tall ones that grow up to 4 feet include: 'Yellow King Humbert,' yellow with scarlet flecks; 'The President,' bright crimson; 'Pink Sunrise,' a blend of rose, yellow, and apricot; and 'City of Portland,' a deep pink. Dwarf kinds growing to 2½ feet tall include 'Pfitzers Primrose Yellow,' named for its German breeder, and 'Tropical Rose,' with rose-pink flowers. For theatrical, multicolored foliage, try 'Bengal Tiger' and 'Tropicanna.'

# CASTOR BEAN
*Ricinus communis*

This plant brings great distinction to the garden quickly, growing to a large shrub of treelike proportions in a single season. The seeds yield an oil that is used commercially. All parts of the plant are poisonous, especially the coats of the seeds which contain ricin, a deadly toxin. Avoid planting castor beans where a child or pet might have access to it. Castor bean is a native of Africa and is naturalized in tropical parts of the world.

**DESCRIPTION:** In the tropics, castor bean becomes a small tree. In areas with long growing seasons in the United States, it will reach 10 feet. The distinctive tropical character comes from the large, hand-shaped leaves that are up to 3 feet wide. Each one has from 5 to 12 deeply cut lobes.

**EASY-CARE GROWING:** Castor beans are indifferent to soil if they receive full sun, adequate heat, and plenty of moisture. In areas with long growing seasons, plant them directly in the ground after all danger of frost has passed and the ground is warm enough to germinate the seeds. In frost-free areas of Zones 9 and 10, they will live through the winter. Plant them at least 3 feet apart.

**PROPAGATION:** By seed. Before sowing the seeds, soak them for 24 hours in water or nick the seed coat with a file. Start seeds indoors 6 to 8 weeks prior to planting in the garden. Start them in individual pots for transplanting.

**USES:** Castor beans are one of the most useful plants for shielding eyesores or providing temporary screens in the garden. They need lots of room; this plant is not modest in size. Side branches with flowers are cut to make attractive floral arrangements; the spiny seed pods are used in dried arrangements. Some people have a skin reaction to the foliage and seed pods.

**RELATED VARIETIES:** 'Impala' has maroon-to-carmine young growth and sulphur-yellow blooms. 'Carmencita' has bronze-brown leaves. 'Zanzibarensis' has white veins on the green leaves.

# CHINA PINK
### *Dianthus chinensis*

These compact plants have clove-scented, colorful flowers. They produce blooms in pink, white, rose, scarlet, and crimson; many are bicolored. The original species comes from Eastern Asia.

**DESCRIPTION:** China pinks grow 6 to 12 inches high—clumps of blue-gray foliage topped continuously with the single, semi-double, or fringed flowers. In Zones 6 to 10, they will live in the garden for two or three years as biennials or short-lived perennials.

**EASY-CARE GROWING:** China pink grows and blooms best during the cool temperatures of spring and fall and in cool summer locations. In Zones 9 and 10, they're widely used as winter-flowering annuals. Plant them in full sun in well-drained soil on the alkaline side. (Amend acid soils by incorporating lime into the soil before planting.) Plant in the garden after danger of frost has passed. China pink should be spaced 6 to 10 inches apart.

**PROPAGATION:** By seed. Seeds germinate in 8 to 10 days at 70°F. You can sow seeds outdoors as soon as the soil is workable or in fall for spring bloom in mild winter areas. Or start them indoors 8 to 10 weeks ahead of planting out for an earlier display.

**USES:** Use China pinks in rock gardens, in rock walls, or plant in cracks in paving stones. Mass them in at the front of beds or borders. Grow them in containers, alone, or combined with other flowers. They're good cut flowers for small arrangements.

**RELATED SPECIES:** Biennial sweet William *(Dianthus barbarus)* has a cluster of often bicolored flowers in pink, white, and red that can reach 2 feet.

**RELATED VARIETIES:** The Carpet Series grows only 8 inches high and blooms particularly early. The Parfait Series present layers of color with dark crimson or scarlet eyes. The popular Floral Lace Series have finely fringed petal edges that give them a delicate, lacy look. Despite any appearance of fragility, these durable plants are very heat-tolerant.

# CHRYSANTHEMUM
*Leucanthemum* (syn. *Chrysanthemum*) hybrids

The huge number of species once all lumped under *Chrysanthemum* have been split by taxonomists into several different groups. Nevertheless, we still call these groups chrysanthemums and still use many types as annuals.

**DESCRIPTION:** Mound-shaped chrysanthemums range from 8 inches to 2–3 feet in height. You can choose from plants with yellow or white button-like flowers, open daisylike flowers, full doubles, and even exotics with spoon-shaped or spidery long-legged florets. Chrysanthemums flower in every color except blue.

**EASY-CARE GROWING:** Grow in rich, well-drained soil in full sun, keeping the roots cool and shaded by other plants or mulch. Select finished potted chrysanthemums that are in bud, but not yet blooming, to plant in late summer or early fall for an autumn display. You also can purchase young mums, sometimes sold in cell-packs or small pots, for spring planting during frost-free weather. These will need to be pinched several times although self-branching cultivars such as 'Judy' and 'Sunny Robin' fill out nicely with less manipulation. Space 8 to 12 inches apart for solid coverage.

**PROPAGATION:** By seed or by cuttings. Germination is 14 to 21 days at 60 to 65°F. Sow 6 to 8 weeks prior to transplanting to the garden. Plants will bloom approximately 10 weeks after sowing. Chrysanthemum cuttings root quickly and easily.

**USES:** Plant in rock gardens, on slopes, and in the front of beds or borders. Use at gates, along pathways, and at doorsteps where a colorful ground cover is desired. Trailing chrysanthemums add grace to hanging baskets, window boxes, and other containers. Use white chrysanthemums to cool down hot colors and intensify dark ones. Use gold, russet, orange, and red to complement autumn foliage.

**RELATED VARIETIES:** 'White Buttons' and 'Yellow Buttons' are commonly grown, long-blooming selections. White-flowered 'Allison' matures into a wide-spreading mound with some frost tolerance. 'Maggie' and 'Stacy' have daisylike flowers with yellow centers and flashy white and lavender florets.

# CLEOME, SPIDER FLOWER
## *Cleome hasslerana*

Cleome starts blooming early and flowers continue opening at the top of 3- to 5-foot stems. Exceedingly long stamens that extend well beyond the orchidlike flowers—somewhat like a daddy longlegs spider—are what give spider flower its name.

**DESCRIPTION:** Cleome flowers, with many openings at once, grow in airy racemes 6 to 8 inches in diameter. Flowers are white, pink, or lavender. When flowers fade, they are followed by long pods that extend outward from the stem below the terminal raceme. Leaves grow on long stalks from a single stem.

**EASY-CARE GROWING:** Cleome grows well in average soil in full sun or minimal shade. It is very drought-tolerant, although it will look and grow better if it is watered well. Space plants 1 to 3 feet apart.

**PROPAGATION:** By seed. Sow after the last frost when the ground is warm, later thinning to final spacing. Or start cleomes indoors 4 to 6 weeks earlier at a temperature of at least 70°F. Germination time is 10 to 14 days. In the garden, it reseeds prolifically.

**USES:** Plant cleome for its height, to back up borders, in the center of island beds, or for statuesque beauty where its dramatic quality stands out. It can also be used as a space-defining hedge, although other plants should hide its bare stems later in the season. Cleome can also be used for tall container plantings. It also makes a good cut flower for use in large bouquets.

**RELATED VARIETIES:** The Queen Series are the most popular selections to date and include 'Cherry Queen,' 'Pink Queen,' 'Violet Queen,' and 'White Queen' (which is also known as 'Helen Campbell').

# COBBITY DAISIES
*Agryanthemum frutescens*

These marvelous marguerite daisies hail from the University of Sydney and have been released in the United States as one of the vegetatively propagated Proven Winners varieties.

**DESCRIPTION:** Naturally compact, cobbity daisies grow between 10 and 18 inches high, varying according to the cultivar, and need no special pinching to take on a full, bushy shape. They have perky single to double daisylike flowers that open prolifically throughout the growing season.

**EASY-CARE GROWING:** Provide full sun to light shade, and well-drained, organic soil. Plant out after the danger of spring frost has passed and fertilize frequently to encourage steady growth and continued flowering.

**PROPAGATION:** This is a patented plant and unauthorized propagation of it is illegal.

**USES:** Cobbity daisies excel as container plantings, blended with lower growing and cascading annuals of a variety of colors and textures. They also can be used in clusters in the front or middle of a flower or mixed border.

**RELATED VARIETIES:** 'Summer Pink,' which grows 15 to 18 inches high, has single pink flowers that mature to darker mauve. 'Summer Angel,' which is of similar height, has fuller white flowers with a yellow center. More compact 'Sugar N' Ice' has small, fully double white flowers. 'Sugar Baby,' which grows 10 to 12 inches high, has white florets around a golden center.

# PLUMED COCKSCOMB
## *Celosia cristata* v. *plumosa*

The name *Celosia* comes from the Greek word for "burned." These airy, feather duster look-alikes bear the vibrant golds and reds of a candle flame but now come in a broader array of pinks and pastels. The exotic plumes make superb dried specimens, retaining their color long after harvest.

**DESCRIPTION:** Shades ranging from electric reds, yellows, pinks, and oranges, to more subtle sand tones are available. Height ranges from 8 to 30 inches. Bloom lasts from June to October.

**EASY-CARE GROWING:** Plant celosias in full sun and average soil when the weather becomes warm and frost-free. Once growing strongly, celosias are almost unstoppable.

**PROPAGATION:** By seed. Seeds may be sown in the garden after danger of frost has passed and soil has warmed. Initial flowers may last as long as 8 weeks after opening, but removing them will encourage development of side branches and new bloom. For earlier bloom, plant seeds indoors 4 to 5 weeks in advance of planting out. Germination is at 70 to 75°F and takes 10 to 15 days. Plants should not dry out.

**USES:** Tall varieties add complementary textures to the center and sides of beds and borders, while the short kinds are good edging plants. They're good container plants, too.

**RELATED SPECIES:** *Celosia cristata* bears the contorted flowers known as cockscomb. Varieties include: dwarf 'Jewel Box Mixture' and 20-inch-tall 'Prestige Scarlet,' a highly branched plant replete with small, red combs. *Celosia spicata*, including the Flamingo Series, have narrow, upright pink and purple flower plumes that resemble feathers or wheat spikes.

**RELATED VARIETIES:** 'New Look' is naturally self-branching with bronze foliage and scarlet plumes to 16-inches high. Award-winning 'Apricot Brandy' grows 16 to 18 inches high and has unique orange plumes. More compact plants in the 12- to 14-inch Castle Series include fluorescent 'Pink Castle' as well as scarlet, yellow, and orange. For amazing miniatures up to 6 inches tall with disproportionately large flower plumes, look for the Kimono Series in cherry red, cream, orange, red with bronze foliage, rose, salmon, salmon pink, scarlet, and yellow.

# COLEUS
### *Solenostemon scutellaroides* (formerly *Coleus blumei*)

Coleus, recently given the new botanical name above, is one of the few plants where late blooming is an asset, for the insignificant flowers detract from the beautiful foliage. Tender perennials, they're very frost-sensitive and are used as annuals except in frost-free areas.

**DESCRIPTION:** Coleus forms a well-branched, spreading plant up to 2 feet tall and as wide. The leaves vary tremendously, from intricately dissected and lobed forms to broad solids. Colors, too, are varied from solid colors of red, bronze, chartreuse, white, pink, yellow, or green, to variations that combine two or more colors.

**EASY-CARE GROWING:** Coleus is ideal in shade and will excel in northern exposures. It will grow in any well-drained, moist soil. Regarding light: The deeper the shade, the taller the plant. Leaves are less colorful in deep shade.

**PROPAGATION:** By seed or by cuttings. Sow seeds 6 to 8 weeks before setting outside. Wait until the ground is warm and all danger of frost has passed. Seeds need light to germinate, so do not cover. Seeds germinate in 10 to 15 days at temperatures above 75°F; lower temperatures inhibit germination. Cuttings root quickly and easily—even in water.

**USES:** Coleus are unparalleled shade plants. They are useful as ground covers, massed in the front of borders, or grouped in clusters. Coleus grow well in containers. Indoors, they make good foliage plants. Use mixed color blends of coleus with caution as they can be overwhelming.

**RELATED VARIETIES:** The Wizards Series have heart-shaped leaves with contrasting colors. 'Rose Wizard' has patches of rose in leaf centers and is edged with green and white to the margins. The Saber Series have narrow, tapered leaves in many colors. The Fiji Series features heavily fringed leaves with contrasting color combinations. For a real eye-opener, try 'Black Dragon' (also known as 'Molten Lava') with large, curling, red leaves with purple-black edges.

# COSMOS
*Cosmos bipinnatus*

osmos is one of the fastest-growing annuals. Some varieties reach up to 6 feet by summer's end. They're natives of Mexico.

**DESCRIPTION:** Cosmos forms a lacy, open plant with flowers 3 to 4 inches in diameter. These daisies are in pink, red, white, and lavender with a contrasting yellow center. Foliage is feathery.

**EASY-CARE GROWING:** Cosmos grows best in full sun, but it will bloom acceptably in partial shade. Grow in well-drained soil. It does not need fertilizing. Space at least 12 inches apart. Cosmos needs room to grow and is not easily staked. It reseeds vigorously.

**PROPAGATION:** By seed. Because it grows so fast, sow outdoors after frost danger has passed. Barely cover seeds, since they need light to germinate. For very early bloom, sow indoors 4 weeks prior to planting out. Germination takes 3 to 7 days at 70 to 75°F.

**USES:** Because of its height, plant cosmos at the back of borders and group it against fences or other places as a covering. Its informal habit works best in mixed plantings. Cosmos also can provide height for the center of an island bed. The flowers are good for cutting, especially for informal arrangements.

**RELATED SPECIES:** *Cosmos sulphureus* is the source of the hot red and yellow colors of cosmos. They're also more compact, growing up to 2 feet in the garden. Bloom is heavy from start until frost. A medal winner, 'Sunny Red,' has 2½-inch, semi-double flowers of vermilion red. Its companion is 'Sunny Gold.' 'Lemon Twist' is the first of this species to have a lemon-yellow flower.

**RELATED VARIETIES:** The 'Sensation Mix' grows to 4 feet and blends flowers of rose, crimson, white, and pink. For a more compact flower, look for the Sonata Series, which lingers at 24 inches and features purplish-red carmine, lavender-pink, pastel pink blush, and white. 'Sea Shells' has a unique form with rolled, quilled petals.

# DAHLIA
*Dahlia* hybrids

From huge, dinner plate–sized blooms down to midget pompons only 2 inches in diameter, dahlias show as much diversity as any summer flowering plant. Once they start blooming in the summer, there is a continuous flood of flowers until frost. They're tender perennials, forming tuberous roots that may be dug and stored in the fall and replanted the following spring. Where the ground does not freeze, they may be left in the ground over winter.

**DESCRIPTION:** Dahlias grow from 1 to 5 feet tall. Flowers come in every color except blue, and the form is varied: singles; anemone-flowered; peony-like; round, shaggy mops; formal, ball-shaped; and twisted, curled

petals. The flowers are carried on long stems above the erect plants. The American Dahlia Society has classified dahlias by both type and size. There are several different flower types: single, anemone-flowered, collarette, peony-flowered, waterlily, formal decorative, informal decorative, ball, pompom, incurved cactus, straight cactus, semi-cactus, orchid-flowered, fimbriated (fringed), and novelty. Flower size designations for dahlias are A (large, over 8 inches); B (medium, 6 to 8 inches); BB (4 to 6 inches); M (miniature, not over 4 inches in diameter); Ball (over 3 inches); Miniature Ball (2 to 3½ inches); and Pompom (not over 2 inches in diameter).

**EASY-CARE GROWING:** Dahlias are sun lovers and need free air circulation around them. Soil should be fertile, high in organic matter, and moist but well-drained. Incorporate a slow-release fertilizer into the soil before planting. Plant outdoors when the soil is warm and danger of frost has passed. To plant, dig a hole 10 inches deep and as wide. Place the tubers so that the eye is 2 to 3 inches below ground level. Plants growing in pots can be planted at the same level as they were growing in the pot. Space tall varieties 12 to 18 inches apart, reducing the spacing for dwarf plants to as little as 8 inches. Tall varieties, and particularly those with large flowers, must be staked to prevent toppling. Drive the stakes before planting to avoid damaging the plant underground.

**PROPAGATION:** By seed, division, or cuttings. Most of the large-flowered varieties are grown from tuberous roots available at garden centers or specialist growers. Each fleshy portion must have a piece of old stem with an eye attached in order to grow (unlike potatoes, which can be sliced into pieces so long as there is an eye in the cut piece). At the end of a summer's growing season, a roughly circular mass of tuberous roots will form a clump. You can dig up the clump and store it in a cool but frost-free location until spring. Where the ground does not freeze, you can leave the tubers in place. In the spring, divide these pieces (leaving an eye attached to a portion of the stem) just before planting. Sow dahlia seeds 4 to 6 weeks prior to planting out at 70°F. Germination will take 5 to 14 days. Cuttings root in 10 to 15 days.

**USES:** Plant taller varieties as a hedge with shorter flowers growing in front. Groups of three plants can be effective at the back of the border or in the center of large island beds. Use compact varieties in the front of beds and borders or planted in containers. For exhibition, disbud or remove the side buds to encourage the remaining flowers to be substantially larger. Dahlias, especially long stemmed types, make good cut flowers. Flowers with short stems or no stems at all may be floated in a bowl of water.

**RELATED VARIETIES:** There are hundreds of varieties; consult your garden center or a specialist grower. A few tuberous-rooted varieties are: 'Park Princess,' a cactus-flowered border dahlia about 2 feet tall with 4- to 5-inch-wide pink flowers; 'Lambda,' an anemone-flowered type, has lavender outer florets fading to a golden center; 'Barbarossa' has huge, 7- to 9-inch-wide red flowers on stems to 4 feet tall. Seed-grown varieties are available as started plants or can be grown from seeds at home. From seeds, tall varieties include "Cactus Flowered," growing to 4 feet with many different flower colors and curved petals. "Large Flowered, Double, Mixed" will grow to 5 feet and bears large, double, and semi-double flowers. Compact varieties include: 'Redskin,' growing up to 20 inches with bronze foliage—a remarkable contrast to the many different flower colors. 'Figaro Improved' grows 14 to 16 inches with semi-double and double flowers. 'Harlequin Mix' are semi-double flowered with an extra-early bloom and basal branching.

# DILL
*Anethum graveolens*

This beautiful annual is edible as well as ornamental. The foliage, flowers, and dill seeds have a marvelous flavor while the upright plants, feathery foliage, and yellow flowers look great in flower borders or mixed gardens.

**DESCRIPTION:** Dill has hollow, ridged, upright stems that reach to about 2 feet high and are topped with airy, umbrella-shaped clusters of tiny yellow flowers.

**EASY-CARE GROWING:** Plant seeds in full sun and well-drained, average to fertile soil, thinning seedlings to 8 to 12 inches apart. Dill grows quickly from a ferny sprout to a tall flowering specimen. Once it sets seed, the plant quickly deteriorates, a good reason for replanting every couple weeks through the early half of the growing season.

**PROPAGATION:** Plant dill seeds directly in the garden from late spring through the middle of summer. Self-sown seeds may emerge from around old plants if the soil is not disturbed.

**USES:** Dill makes a wonderful upright accent plant in large container gardens or mixed flower beds. Or use it for color and flavor in a decorative vegetable and herb garden.

**RELATED VARIETIES:** 'Bouquet' is a compact dwarf, less likely to tip over in the wind. Compact 'Fernleaf,' an award winner, is slower to flower and set seed and therefore provides a longer harvest of the aromatic leaves.

# DRACAENA, SPIKE PLANT
## *Dracaena* species

Dracaena was traditionally considered a houseplant for years. However, it is finding favor in annual container gardens where the spiky upright leaves provide height and textural contrast to bushy and cascading annual flowers.

**DESCRIPTION:** Dracaenas have lance-shaped, sharp tipped leaves, sometimes marked with colorful margins of white or pink.

**EASY-CARE GROWING:** Interplant dracaenas in containers of peat-based mix enriched with extra compost. They can tolerate full sun when the weather is cool and the soil is kept moist but do better in light shade during hot and dry weather. Keep the potting soil evenly moist and fertilize frequently with a water-soluble product to encourage healthy growth.

**PROPAGATION:** Propagation of colored leaf forms is by cuttings of stem sections, probably best left to professional growers. You can find a variety of suitable dracaenas in the houseplant section of garden centers and department stores.

**USES:** Place taller dracaenas in the back of a mixed container garden that will be viewed from the front or in the center of a garden that will be viewed from all sides. Use mound-shaped and cascading annuals to fill out the foreground.

**RELATED SPECIES:** *D. marginata* has narrow red-edged leaves to 24 inches long, handsome to highlight red or pink flower colors. *D. deremensis* 'Warneckei' has white stripes on narrow leaves produced in spiral whorls similar to a corn plant.

# DUSTY MILLER

*Senecio cineraria, Tanacetum ptarmiciflorum*
(originally *Chrysanthemum ptarmiciflorum*), *Cineraria maritima*

The term "dusty miller" originated from the effect of shimmering gray foliage rather than as a name for a particular plant. The name has been commonly applied to a variety of similar plants.

**DESCRIPTION:** *Tanacetum ptarmiciflorum* grows 1 to 2½ feet tall with finely divided leaflets. It has decorative white daisy flowers about 1½ inches in diameter. *Senecio cineraria* is a bushy subshrub that grows up to 2½ feet tall. The ornamental value is in the finely divided gray foliage.

**EASY-CARE GROWING:** Both plants do best in full sun and a rather ordinary, well-drained soil, although they will brighten lightly shaded areas, too. Plant in the garden when the soil has warmed and after danger of frost has passed. Space 8 to 10 inches apart. Pinch the tips of plants to induce shapely branching.

**PROPAGATION:** By seed or by cuttings. Germinate seeds of *Senecio cineraria* at 75 to 80°F and those of *Tanacetum ptarmiciflorum* at 72 to 75°F. Do not cover the seeds as they need light to germinate. Germination will take 10 to 15 days. Sow seeds 12 to 14 weeks before planting out.

**USES:** These are the classic plants to use in urns with bright summer flowers. They are effective in all kinds of planters. However, they also make great ribbons of light in flower beds and borders. They're especially good to use as a bridge between two clashing colors, to intensify cool colors like blue, or to tone down hot colors.

**RELATED VARIETIES:** 'Silver Lace' has very dissected, feathery leaves. It is not as vigorous a grower as *S. cineraria.* Of the latter, 'Silver Dust' reaches 12 inches high while 'Silver Queen' lingers at 8 inches.

# ENGLISH DAISY
## *Bellis perennis*

In nature, the English daisy, immortalized by poets, bears single flowers. However, breeding and selection have added semi-doubles and doubles to the array of varieties available to gardeners. Particularly in the Northeast, the English daisy has become naturalized. In order to enjoy the improved forms, the gardener must start with named-variety seeds.

**DESCRIPTION:** Flowers of white, pink, or red rise on 6-inch stems from a rosette of basal leaves. Single and semi-double flowers are centered in yellow, but in fully double varieties this distinguishing feature is covered. Normally, flowers are 1 to 2 inches in diameter; in newer varieties they are larger. Most flowers appear in spring and early summer, repeating again in the fall. In cool and coastal climates, they may bloom all year.

**EASY-CARE GROWING:** Grow in full sun or light shade in moist soil, well-enriched with organic matter. When used as an annual, set out large seedlings as early as the ground can be worked or plant in the fall for earliest bloom when weather warms (except in Zones 3 to 5 where they are not hardy except in well-protected cold frames). Plant 6 to 9 inches apart. You may want to replace them with warm season annuals in late June.

**PROPAGATION:** By seed or by division. Seeds germinate in 10 to 15 days at 70°F.

**USES:** English daisies will liven up small beds and are good for edgings and small containers during the cool spring period.

**RELATED SPECIES:** *B. rotundifolia* has white flowers; *B. r. caerulescens* bears blue flowers.

**RELATED VARIETIES:** The largest, flowered variety is the fully double 'Super Enorma Mix,' with flowers up to 3 inches. 'Pompanette Mixed' have 1½-inch flowers while 'Galaxy Mix' are particularly compact and uniform. More rare are golden leaved 'Aucubifolia' and 'Shrewly Gold.'

# FORGET-ME-NOT
### *Myosotis sylvatica*

A bed of spring bulbs—such as tulips or daffodils—underplanted with forget-me-nots is a sight to behold. Forget-me-nots are biennials that are native to the cool, moist areas of Europe and northern Asia. They are usually grown as annuals.

**DESCRIPTION:** Forget-me-nots are small plants seldom reaching more than 12 inches in height and equal in diameter. The tiny flowers are clustered together in racemes at the top of plants.

**EASY-CARE GROWING:** Forget-me-nots relish cool, moist weather with sun or partial shade. In Zones 8, 9, and 10, you can sow seeds in the fall where plants will bloom in the spring. When planting in the spring, plant as soon as the soil can be worked. When plants have finished blooming, replace them with summer annuals. Forget-me-nots will reseed, but seedlings in colder climates will not bloom until late spring or summer.

**PROPAGATION:** By seed. For early bloom in cold climates, plant seeds indoors in January, transplanting seedlings outdoors as soon as the soil can be worked. Seeds germinate in 8 to 14 days at 55 to 70°F. Be sure to cover seeds; they need darkness to germinate. When removing plants that have bloomed, shake the ripened seeds onto the ground where you want blooming plants the next spring.

**USES:** Plant forget-me-nots in masses for best results. They're suited for rock gardens, as an edging, or in the front of a border plant. Try them in window boxes and patio planters with spring bulbs. Grow forget-me-nots in meadows, along stream banks, or by ponds.

**RELATED VARIETIES:** 'Ultramarine' is a darker-colored selection that stays smaller than most varieties. 'Blue Ball' is a compact form with bright blue flowers. 'Snow Ball' is similar in form but has white blooms. 'Victoria Mixed' combines blue-, white-, rose-, and pink-flowered forms.

# FOUNTAIN GRASS
*Pennisetum setaceum*

This tender perennial, with beautiful, rosy flower spikes, comes in purple-leaved forms that are gaining popularity for use amid annuals, perennials, even in clumps around shrubs and trees.

**DESCRIPTION:** Slender, grasslike leaves, both ordinary green and purple, grow in a tufted mound. In late summer or early fall, graceful, bristling, pinkish flower spikes emerge over the leaves and rise from 3 to 5 feet high.

**EASY-CARE GROWING:** Provide well-drained and fertile soil in full sun or a peat-based growing mix in a large pot. Fountain grass, which is native to tropical Africa, the Arabian Peninsula, and other warm places in southwestern Asia, is only perennial in Zones 9 and 10. Space young plants 18 to 24 inches apart.

**PROPAGATION:** Fountain grass seeds, which must be started in late winter to be sizeable for spring planting, take 21 days to germinate when kept at 65 to 75°F. It is likely to be cost effective to purchase strapping seedlings from a reliable nursery.

**USES:** Interplant fountain grass among sun-loving and prairie perennials like coneflowers and coreopsis. Mingle it with tall and medium annuals in naturalistic gardens. Or blend it into large container plantings, using the tall plumes as a high point in the rear of the pot. Purple-leaved types make wonderful color combinations with pink, blue, or yellow flowers.

**RELATED SPECIES:** *P. alopecuroides* is a hardier perennial.

**RELATED VARIETIES:** 'Purpureum' has purple leaves and red flowers.

# FOXGLOVE
## *Digitalis purpurea*

A widely used heart medicine comes from this biennial plant, but its garden value is due to the spikes of bell-shaped flowers in late spring. It's a native of western Europe.

**DESCRIPTION:** Foxglove grows for months as a rosette of gray-green leaves; then a tall spike surrounded by buds quickly arises, growing from 3 to 7 feet tall. Most flowers, which are white, cream, pink, salmon, lavender, or red, are marked with blotches of contrasting color.

**EASY-CARE GROWING:** Foxglove thrives in light woodlands or at the fringes of tree or shrub plantings. It will grow in average soil if kept moist. When flower spikes appear, fertilize with a general fertilizer. The sturdy spikes normally do not need staking. The seeds are tiny and widely distributed by the wind. To prevent reseeding, cut flower spikes after bloom.

**PROPAGATION:** By seed. To grow as a biennial, sow seeds outdoors in June or July so husky plants will overwinter. For bloom the first year, sow indoors 8 to 10 weeks prior to planting outdoors. Except for selected varieties, these will bloom in late summer or fall. Seeds germinate at 70°F in 15 to 20 days.

**USES:** Foxglove deserves a place in the mixed cottage garden. Plant it in groups at the back of the border, against fences, near tall shrub hedges or woodlands. They're also useful in the perennial border, providing the height that early perennial gardens often lack. They make useful cut flowers. Because the plants are poisonous, keep them out of reach of young children and pets.

**RELATED SPECIES:** *Digitalis lutea* brings yellow flowers to the foxglove clan. It grows to 3 feet.

**RELATED VARIETIES:** 'Foxy' has a full range of colors and grows to 3 feet tall. 'Excelsior Mixture' contains many colors of tall-growing foxgloves. 'Apricot' is a buttery, copper color and 'Alba' is pure white.

# ANGEL'S EARRINGS FUCHSIA, LADY'S EAR DROPS

### *Fuchsia hybrida* Angel's Earrings Series

There are hundreds of named varieties of fuchsias, beautiful plants with pendulous blossoms that bloom heavily from spring to fall. Most of them have been developed from two species. The name "lady's ear drops" is self-evident, but the name *Fuchsia* is more commonly used. The name honors a German botanist by the name of Fuchs. Commonly grown as hanging basket plants, fuchsias tend to falter in heat with the exception of new, heat-tolerant Angel's Earrings Series derived from parents found in hot and humid parts of South America.

**DESCRIPTION:** 'Angel's Earrings' fuchsias produce compact upright or horizontal stems, bearing dangling flowers of red and blue. The flowers are composed of a calyx, a blue cylinder or tube that points downward, which is topped by flaring, red petal-like lobes called sepals.

**EASY-CARE GROWING:** Fuchsias bloom more freely when they get some shade. They're at their best in cool coastal or mountain regions with good humidity, but Angel's Earrings thrive in temperatures up to 90°F as long as they are kept moist. Fuchsias are heavy feeders. Apply a slow-release fertilizer at planting or feed

biweekly with a water-soluble fertilizer. For large-blooming plants by mid-May, plant 3 to 5 rooted cuttings in a 10- to 12-inch basket. To develop full and shapely plants, make sure to pinch out tips as soon as two sets of leaves have formed and continue this process until March 1.

**PROPAGATION:** By seed or cuttings. Seeds germinate in 21 to 28 days.

**USES:** Fuchsias are at their best in hanging baskets where the pendulous flowers can be viewed from below. Place them where they can be seen frequently—on decks, on porches, or beside walkways. Upright varieties of fuchsia are eye-catching in containers raised on railings or porch steps.

**RELATED VARIETIES:** 'Dainty Angel's Earrings' is a petite, upright form. 'Cascading Angel's Earrings' has horizontal stems and is larger than the former.

# IVY-LEAF GERANIUM
### *Pelargonium peltatum*

Ivy-leaf geraniums have an entirely different character than their zonal cousins. Long, trailing stems make them ideal for containers of all kinds. Their flowers are generally less strident and more toned to the pastel range of their hues. Older varieties are a bit intolerant of long periods of heat and humidity, but newer varieties are somewhat more heat-resistant. The common name springs from the shape of the leaves.

**DESCRIPTION:** Two distinct groups of ivy-leafed geraniums are available to home gardeners. All of them have the cascading form of ivy geraniums, but a group of varieties from Europe, such as the Matador Series, are proving more floriferous and heat-tolerant. Many varieties are available—from miniatures with a spread of only 12 inches through vigorous ones that can grow to 5 feet tall.

**EASY-CARE GROWING:** Ivy-leaf geraniums grow best in cool, coastal, or mountain climates with lots of sun. In other locations they may need partial shade. Ivy-leaf geraniums in containers relish full sun if temperatures are not above 85°F for long stretches. Where this occurs, give them northern or eastern exposure where they can be protected from hot midday and afternoon sun. Do not let them dry out. Plant ivy-leaf geraniums outside after danger of frost has passed and the soil is warm.

**PROPAGATION:** By cuttings or by seed (although only a few varieties are seed-grown). Take cuttings from stock plants 10 to 12 weeks prior to planting outside. Pinch tips once or twice to encourage branching.

**USES:** Ivy-leaf geraniums are excellent container plants. They develop into shapely hanging baskets clothed with foliage and flowers. As window box plants, they excel and are ideal in patio planters. You also can use them as ground covers or for cascading over retaining walls.

**RELATED VARIETIES:** Among the heavy flowering, European types, the new Matador Series, including 'Matador Burgundy' and 'Matador Light Pink,' have large single and slightly double flowers with extra-broad petals. They are naturally well-branched at the base and tolerate heat well. One traditional favorite is alpine 'King of Balcon' with light coral pink flowers used in European window boxes. Its kindred 'Princess Balcon' has orchid-colored flowers. Among the miniatures, 'Evka' has white-edged leaves and abundant scarlet flowers on a highly branched plant. Seed-grown varieties include 'Summer Showers' with red, white, pink, lavender, and plum-colored varieties and the Tornado Series, with citrus-scented leaves and extra-early flowers of lilac or white.

# SCENTED GERANIUM
## *Pelargonium* species

Perhaps you've noticed the carrot-like fragrance of bedding geranium leaves. A number of species pelargoniums have perfumed leaves—with fragrances of spice, citrus, fruit, and flowers—best enjoyed by rubbing the leaf surface or drying the leaves and using them in fragrant potpourri or sachets. Some have attractive foliage, but in most the bloom is modest.

**DESCRIPTION:** Scented geraniums are a diverse bunch with upright plants that can grow to 2 feet high, or more prostrate plants staying under about 1 foot high and spreading more horizontally. The leaves vary from finely cut, to broad and felted, to petite and rounded with a undulating leaf margin. Some are variegated with white. Open clusters of white, pink, or purple five-petaled flowers appear in summer.

**EASY-CARE GROWING:** Plant scented geraniums in well-drained but moist and moderately fertile soil, either in a garden bed or in a large pot during warm, frost-free weather. Provide full sun or light afternoon shade in hot climates.

**PROPAGATION:** By seed or cuttings. Sow indoors 10 to 12 weeks before the last spring frost date. Germination occurs in 7 to 14 days at 70 to 75°F. Take cuttings of vigorous, young side shoots in late summer to winter over indoors and move outside again next spring. You also can take cuttings in spring and summer, allowing 8 to 10 weeks to root. Cuttings root more reliably when treated with rooting hormone before they are placed in rooting medium.

**USES:** Scented geraniums make interesting potted plants, kept close to the house where you can partake of their fragrance frequently. They are a wonderful addition to the ornamental/edible garden, as lemon and rose forms can be called for in herbal recipes. They also can blend nicely into the annual border, adding subtle beauty and fragrance to more common plants.

**RELATED SPECIES:** *Pelargonium crispum* has lemon-scented leaves, and a wide number of varieties including 'Variegated Prince Rupert' have been selected from it. *P. odoratissimum* is apple-scented, while *P. grossulariodes* is coconut-scented. *P. fragrans* smells like nutmeg. One of the most popular is *P. tomentosum,* which has a strong peppermint scent. *P.* 'Rober's Lemon Rose' is a favorite for herb teas.

# ZONAL GERANIUM

## *Pelargonium* x *hortorum*

Many gardeners consider zonal geraniums the epitome of summer flowers. These stalwart garden beauties are tender perennials that must be replanted each year except in the most favored climates. Most pelargonium species (true geraniums are hardy perennials) come from South Africa, but through hundreds of years of breeding, the parentage of today's varieties is obscured.

**DESCRIPTION:** Zonal geraniums are upright bushes covered with red, pink, salmon, white, rose, cherry red, and bicolored flowers on long stems held above the plant. Flower clusters (or umbels) contain many individual flowers and give a burst of color. Plants from 4-inch pots transplanted to the garden in spring will reach up to 18 inches high and wide by the end of summer.

**EASY-CARE GROWING:** Zonal geraniums benefit from full sun and moderate-to-rich, well-drained, moist soil. Incorporate a slow-release fertilizer into the soil at planting time. Plant after all danger of frost has passed and the soil is warm. Space them 12 inches apart. The only other care requirement is deadheading spent blooms.

**PROPAGATION:** By seed or by cuttings. Most of the magnificent semi-double, flowered varieties are grown from cuttings. The cuttings root easily. Make cuttings 8 to 10 weeks prior to planting out for husky plants. Seed-grown varieties should be started 10 to 12 weeks prior to garden planting. Seeds germinate in 7 to 10 days at 70 to 75°F.

**USES:** Zonal geraniums are among the best plants for formal beds. They can provide pockets of color in any sunny spot. Group three or more together for color impact in flower borders or along walks and pathways. They're classics in containers, all by themselves, or mixed with other kinds of plants. You can also buy geraniums grown as standards—a single stem is trained to the desired height with a bushy canopy of flowers and leaves. Zonal geraniums will bloom through the winter in sunny windows.

**RELATED VARIETIES:** There are many varieties available at garden centers in the spring. For full and compact plants look for 'Bubble Gum,' 'Cotton Candy,' and 'Red Hots.' 'Starburst Red' has streaks of white through salmon-red flowers. Larger geraniums include 'Melody' and 'Melody Red' and the Patriot Series. 'Wilhelm Langguth' has white-edged leaves with scarlet flowers. Seed-grown singles come in many colors. Look for the Orbit Series, the Elite Series, and the Ringo 2000 Series. For unique colors, look for 'Raspberry Ripple,' with salmon-pink petals spotted with red and 'Orange Appeal,' the first true orange flower.

# GLADIOLUS, GLAD
## *Gladiolus hybridus*

The name *Gladiolus* means "little sword" in reference to the sword-shaped leaves of the plant. Every flower color but blue is represented in modern hybrids, and the flowers themselves vary immensely. They are members of the iris family.

**DESCRIPTION:** The erect spikes of flowers, from 1 to 4 feet tall, grow through the swordlike leaves from the corm, a modified stem planted underground. The individual flowers are classified by size by the North American Gladiolus Council, from miniatures with flowers under 2 inches in diameter to giants over 5½ inches in diameter.

**EASY-CARE GROWING:** Gladiolus grows best in well-drained soil high in organic matter, in full sun. Provide shelter from heavy winds. Where the ground does not freeze, you can leave the corms in the ground from year to year. Elsewhere, plant each spring in succession to assure continuous bloom. Plant the first about the time deciduous trees are sprouting new foliage, continuing about every 2 weeks until the first of July. Bloom occurs 60 to 70 days after planting. Fertilize a month after planting and again just before the first flowers open. Water regularly if dry.

**PROPAGATION:** By corms. When digging up corms in fall, save the tiny cormlets that form around each corm. Keep them separate and label by variety, then plant in the spring to increase their size.

**USES:** Gladiolus can be used to provide a stunning succession of color, especially in perennial borders when early blooming perennials have finished. Plant them in clusters or groups. They make superb cut flowers, and if wanted primarily for cutting, can be planted in rows in the cutting garden.

**RELATED VARIETIES:** There are named varieties by the hundreds.

# GOLDEN AGERATUM, AFRICAN DAISY

*Lonas inodora*

The name "African daisy" comes from a portion of this plant's native territory, areas surrounding the Mediterranean Sea including northern Africa. Because it somewhat resembles the more common ageratum *(Ageratum houstonianum)*—but with yellow flowers—the name "golden ageratum" is sometimes used. However, the flower clusters are a bit more formal-looking than ageratum.

**DESCRIPTION:** Although lonas is a member of the daisy family, it does not have the long-ray flowers that give the daisy look. Instead, the small flowers are grouped together in clusters up to 5 inches across. The branched plants grow up to 1 foot tall, and leaves are finely divided into long, narrow segments.

**EASY-CARE GROWING:** African daisy grows best in full sun. It's not particular regarding garden soil as long as it is well-drained. It should be planted outside after frost danger has passed. The plant grows best if spaced 6 inches apart; it does not need staking.

**PROPAGATION:** By seed. You can sow the seeds outdoors in early spring where plants are to grow, thinning to a 6-inch spacing. Or start them indoors 6 to 8 weeks prior to outdoor planting for earlier bloom. Germination will take 5 to 7 days at 60 to 70°F.

**USES:** Plant African daisy in flower borders, combined with other flowers in complementary shapes and colors. They blend beautifully in informal mixed plantings and add a bright, golden note to wildflower gardens. For best effect, plant them in groupings, rather than as single plants. They are effective if used to make a bright, golden ribbon through a border. They also can be planted in rows in the cutting garden and used in fresh or dried arrangements. The flowers last a long time on the plant.

# ORNAMENTAL GOURDS

## Yellow-flowered Gourd
*Cucumis pepo* v. *oviferis*

These are closely related to squash. Hard-shelled fruits of many shapes and colors (both solid and striped) grow on long-stemmed vines. The gourds are variously warty or smooth; golden, green, white, yellow, orange, or red; and round, pear, or even crown shapes.

## White-flowered Gourd
*Lagenaria siceraria*

This is a rapidly growing vine with large fruits of many sizes and shapes. Depending on the shape, they are often known as bottle gourd, calabash, dipper gourd, siphon gourd, snake gourd, and sugar-trough gourd. Besides being used as ornaments and containers, they can also be used as musical instruments.

## Dishrag Gourd, Vegetable Sponge
*Luffa aegyptiaca*

The long, gourdlike fruits have a fibrous skeleton, which, once the skin is removed, can be used for scrubbing purposes. They grow on a vigorous vine.

**EASY-CARE GROWING:** Full sun, a rich soil high in organic matter, and plentiful moisture are important for good growth. Sow seeds outdoors when the ground is well-warmed and all danger of frost has passed. Plant seeds in hills of six to eight seeds to a group. Thin seedlings to four per hill, selecting the strongest ones. Space hills 8 feet apart.

**PROPAGATION:** By seed. Roots of gourds resent disturbance, so sow seeds in place outdoors. If started earlier indoors, plant in peat pots that can be transplanted into the ground, pot and all. Seeds germinate in 4 to 8 days at 70°F.

**USES:** Let the vines of gourds ramble over arbors, trellises, pergolas, fences, and arches, or let them spread across the ground. Their rapid growth and size will allow them to reach 15 to 30 feet. After harvesting mature fruit, wash well, dry, then coat with floor wax or varnish before using in ornamental arrangements.

# HELIOTROPE, CHERRY PIE
## *Heliotropium arborescens*

Fragrance is one of the most alluring attributes of old-fashioned heliotrope, although it has been lost in some modern cultivars. Deep blue, violet, lavender, or white flowers appear in copious quantities during the summer. A perennial shrub in South America, it is used in the United States, except in frost-free areas, as an annual.

**DESCRIPTION:** Heliotrope is a branched shrub with long, gray-green leaves with deep veins. In nature it grows to 4 feet, but as a summer plant a height of 1 foot and equal spread is reasonable. Many tiny flowers are clustered in the large heads carried well above the foliage. The most commonly available varieties are deep blue and white.

**EASY-CARE GROWING:** Any good garden soil with medium fertility in full sun will grow good heliotropes. Normally, plants are started early indoors (from seed or cuttings) and transplanted outdoors when danger of frost has passed and the ground is warm. Depending on the size of transplants, space from 8 to 15 inches apart.

**PROPAGATION:** By seed or cuttings. Sow seeds 10 to 12 weeks before planting out. Seeds germinate in 7 to 21 days at 70 to 85°F. Root cuttings in 4-inch pots in February in order to have husky plants for planting outdoors in May. Pinch the tips of both seedlings and cutting varieties to create bushy plants.

**USES:** Tuck heliotropes into rock gardens, or grow them in the front of borders. Plant them by doorsteps where the fragrance will be appreciated. They are superb as container plants. Grow them indoors if you can provide enough sunlight. To use as cut flowers, plunge the stems and necks deep in water and keep in a cool, dark place for several hours before arranging.

**RELATED VARIETIES:** 'Marine,' grown from seed, has dark violet-blue flowers. For fragrance, try 'Regal Dwarf,' 'Princess Marina,' or white-flowered 'Alba.'

# CHINESE HIBISCUS, HAWAIIAN HIBISCUS, ROSE OF CHINA

### *Hibiscus rosa-sinensis*

Hardy only in frost-free parts of Zones 9 and 10, hibiscus is widely used as an annual elsewhere. It is a member of the mallow family and is found throughout the year in garden centers as a blooming pot plant for indoor enjoyment, but it can be used outdoors as well.

**DESCRIPTION:** In nature, Chinese hibiscus are shrubs up to 15 feet tall, but for summering outdoors they will probably reach a maximum of 3 to 5 feet tall and wide. The glossy, evergreen foliage is a handsome background for the large—up to 6-inch—flowers. These flaring bells with a distinctive column of yellow stamens in the center are red, yellow, pink, salmon, orange, or white.

**EASY-CARE GROWING:** Hibiscus needs full sun for best bloom production, but it can tolerate partial shade. Soil should be rich, high in organic matter, and well-moistened. Hibiscus also grows best in high humidity. When grown in a container, apply slow-release fertilizer to the soil before planting. Pinch out the tips of young growth to induce branching and make hibiscus more shapely.

**PROPAGATION:** By cuttings. Semi-hardwood cuttings root quickly in summer under mist.

**USES:** Hibiscus is best used in containers. You can cut it back severely in the spring to maintain its size.

**RELATED SPECIES:** *Hibiscus moscheutos,* or rose mallow, is a perennial with large flowers. 'Disco Belle Mixed,' grown from seed, has large flowers in red, pink, and white. *H. syriacus*, or rose of Sharon, is a hardy shrub.

**RELATED VARIETIES:** There are hundreds of named varieties of *Hibiscus rosa-sinensis.* 'Cooperi' is distinct for brightly variegated leaves in pink and white; blooms are red.

# IMPATIENS, PATIENCE
## *Impatiens walleriana*

Impatiens flower in almost every color (except true blue and yellow). Their tidy, mounding habit makes them ideal low-maintenance plants. Impatiens were stowaways on trading ships from Africa and naturalized in Central and South America.

**DESCRIPTION:** Breeders have developed compact, self-branching plants whose flowers are borne above the foliage. Flowers are white, pink, rose, orange, scarlet, burgundy, violet, and many variants. Other varieties have star-shaped patterns of white against colored backgrounds. Double varieties are also grown. Foliage is deep, glossy green or bronze in color. Most varieties grow 12 to 15 inches high in dappled shade. Heavy watering encourages vigorous growth; higher light dwarfs them.

**EASY-CARE GROWING:** Impatiens will grow in any average soil. Keep them well-watered. In deep shade, bloom diminishes.

**PROPAGATION:** By seed or by cuttings. Sow seeds 10 to 12 weeks before the last frost date. Impatiens need light to germinate; do not cover seeds, but keep moist. Germination takes 10 to 20 days at 75°F. Use a sterile soil mix, because young impatiens seedlings are especially subject to damping off. Cuttings root in 10 to 14 days.

**USES:** Impatiens can be used in beds, borders, planting strips, and containers. Their mounding habit is beautiful in hanging baskets and planters. They can be grown indoors in bright, filtered light.

**RELATED VARIETIES:** There are many varieties: the Dazzler Series, the self-branching Accent Series, the bold-colored Deco Series, and the huge-flowered, extra-compact Super Elfin Series. 'Mosaic Hybrid' has misty splashes of white on a rose or lilac background. 'Victorian Rose,' an award winner; 'Rosette Mix'; and the Confection Series all have double flowers that resemble rosebuds as they open.

# NEW GUINEA IMPATIENS
## *Impatiens* species

When a plant-hunting expedition went to Southeast Asia, they made significant discoveries. Species impatiens found there are now being developed into varieties that are quite different from traditional impatiens.

**DESCRIPTION:** New Guinea impatiens form compact, succulent subshrubs with branches growing 1 to 2 feet tall by summer's end. Leaves are long and narrow, green, bronze, or purple. Flowers, growing up to 2 inches in diameter, are white, pink, lavender, purple, orange, and red.

**EASY-CARE GROWING:** Fertile, moist soil that is high in organic matter is preferred by New Guinea impatiens. They are more sun-loving than the other impatiens, especially if their roots are kept moist. Incorporate a slow-release fertilizer into the soil before planting. Wait to plant until the danger of frost has passed and the ground has warmed. Space 9 to 15 inches apart.

**PROPAGATION:** By seed or by cuttings. While cuttings are the standard means of propagation, a number of New Guinea impatiens are available from seed, including the Spectra Series and 'Tango.' Sow 10 to 12 weeks before planting outside. Germinate at 75 to 80°F. Do not cover, since seeds need light to germinate, but mist to keep moist. Cuttings root quickly and easily in 2 to 3 weeks.

**USES:** Mass impatiens for sweeps of color in beds and borders. Cluster three or more in groups beside garden features. Plant them in containers and in hanging baskets.

**RELATED SPECIES:** 'African Queen' is the first yellow-flowered impatiens, in a group called African, and is joined by related and unique-looking Seashells Series flowering in yellow, papaya, apricot, and salmon rose. 'Blue Angel,' a Himalayan species, has lilac flowers and red-tinged foliage.

**RELATED VARIETIES:** 'Tango' has fluorescent-orange flowers. The Celebration Series have large flowers, branch naturally, and come in many shades of red, lavender, and pink, as well as white. The Carnation Series are extra compact growers, while the Socialite Series offer fragrance as well as color.

# LANTANA

*Lantana camara*

These shrubby plants are abundantly covered throughout the summer with brightly colored blossoms. The garden varieties bear white, yellow, gold, orange, and red flowers; usually the older flowers in each cluster are a different color than the younger ones.

**DESCRIPTION:** Lantanas are woody shrubs with large, rough leaves. They grow about 3 feet tall and as wide over a summer's growth. When protected against frost, they can grow to 15 feet or more in height over a period of years.

**EASY-CARE GROWING:** Lantana needs full sun and hot weather to perform best. It is actually best in poor soil. It is very frost-sensitive, so plant outdoors after spring frosts have passed and the ground has warmed

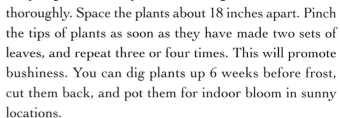

thoroughly. Space the plants about 18 inches apart. Pinch the tips of plants as soon as they have made two sets of leaves, and repeat three or four times. This will promote bushiness. You can dig plants up 6 weeks before frost, cut them back, and pot them for indoor bloom in sunny locations.

**PROPAGATION:** By cuttings. For May or June planting outdoors of 4-inch pots, take cuttings in February or early March. For larger hanging baskets, take cuttings in January. Dipping in a rooting hormone speeds rooting. Root under mist or keep from wilting during rooting.

**USES:** Lantanas are most often used in containers. They grow well in sunny window boxes, hanging baskets, or patio planters. You also can use them in ground beds if soil is not too rich.

**RELATED SPECIES:** *Lantana montevidensis* is a widely grown, pink-lavender flowering variety. Its growth is more trailing.

**RELATED VARIETIES:** 'Radiation' has tones of orange and red, while 'Festune Pink' combines pink and yellow in the same flower clusters. There are many other varieties.

# LARKSPUR, ANNUAL DELPHINIUM
## *Consolida ambigua*

Larkspur resembles the delphinium, with its stately spikes of flowers in cool pastel colors. Larkspur was formerly lumped with delphiniums until botanists split them off and named them *Consolida ambigua,* an old Latin term for "an undetermined plant."

**DESCRIPTION:** Larkspur grows up to 4 feet tall with delphinium-like flowers, single or double, evenly spaced around the long stem above lacy, gray-green foliage. Although blue is favored, larkspur also flowers in pink, salmon, rose, lavender, purple, and white.

**EASY-CARE GROWING:** Grow in moist, well-drained soil in full sun. If exposed to high winds, larkspur may need staking. It performs best in cool weather. In Zones 7 to 10, you can sow seeds early enough in the fall so that young plants will bloom early in the spring. In other zones, sow seeds late in the fall so that they will germinate in the spring. Remove spent blossoms to encourage new blooms.

**PROPAGATION:** By seed. Sow in place because larkspur does not transplant well. Sow in the fall or as soon as the ground can be worked in the spring. For summer and fall blooms in cool climates, successively sow 2 to 3 weeks apart until mid-May.

**USES:** Groups of delphinium backing informal annuals can give a cottage garden look. Cluster them at the side or at the back of the flower border or center them in island beds to lend height. They're good cut flowers and may be dried for winter bouquets.

**RELATED SPECIES:** Many of the true perennial delphiniums may be grown as summer annuals. Pacific hybrids are often used as larkspurs. Compact hybrids (2 to 3 feet high) grown from seed include 'Dwarf Blue Heaven.'

**RELATED VARIETIES:** A favorite is the Imperial Giant Series that branch freely from the base. For shorter plants less likely to need staking, look for the Dwarf Rocket Series or the Dwarf Hyacinth Series.

# LAVATERA, ROSE MALLOW
## *Lavatera trimestris*

Lavatera, also called rose mallow, is an annual originally from the countries around the Mediterranean Sea. It is related to both hibiscus and hollyhock.

**DESCRIPTION:** Rose mallow grows to 3 to 5 feet by the end of summer. It branches vigorously to form a sturdy bush. Lower leaves are rounded, but upper ones are lobed and toothed. The flowers, borne in leaf axils, are 3 to 4 inches in diameter.

**EASY-CARE GROWING:** Grow rose mallow in full sun in average soil. Make sure soil is well-drained. Soil that is too rich causes excess foliage and deters flowering. Plant outdoors as soon as the ground can be worked in the spring. Make sure to provide plenty of moisture. Space 1 to 1½ feet apart. Remove spent flowers to prevent seed formation.

**PROPAGATION:** By seed. Sow in the ground outdoors. Space the seeds thinly to 1- to 1½-foot spacing because thinned seedlings will probably die. For earlier bloom, sow indoors 6 to 8 weeks prior to outdoor planting. Sow in individual peat pots and transplant, pot and all, into the ground outdoors. Seeds germinate in 14 to 21 days at 70°F.

**USES:** Use lavatera along pathways or walks. Cluster groups of three or more at the end or sides of borders, or grow a row of them near the rear of the border, depending on border height. Rose mallows make good container plants. Individual specimens make a rounded bush in urns, tubs, and other planters. The pink and white colors also mix well with other flower colors. Lavatera makes good cut flowers.

**RELATED VARIETIES:** 'Mont Blanc' has pure-white flowers; 'Mont Rose' is rose-pink; and 'Silver Cup' has large, pink flowers.

# LICORICE PLANT
## *Helichrysum petiolare*

The desire for interesting foliage in mixed planters and even in annual beds has created intense demand for this intriguing plant, which is related to strawflowers and comes from arid lands in South Africa.

**DESCRIPTION:** Licorice plant is a mound-forming or trailing shrub which, when grown as an annual, bears stems that reach about 20 inches long. They are covered with furry, silver, heart-shaped leaves, also available with cream or yellow coloration. If allowed to flower late in the growing season, it produces cream-colored flower heads.

**EASY-CARE GROWING:** Grow in well-drained soil of moderate fertility or ordinary peat-based potting mix in full sun to light shade.

**PROPAGATION:** Root cuttings of firm shoots in summer to winter indoors and then replant in spring.

**USES:** Blend a single, silver-leaved plant in a pot with cool blue and purple or warm red and pink flowers. Try the golden-leaved form with warm orange and red flowers. You also can plant masses of either color in annual beds for the contrasting foliage and season-long color.

**RELATED VARIETIES:** 'Limelight' has yellow-green leaves and grows best in light shade. 'Variegatum' has cream-variegated silver leaves.

# LOBELIA

### *Lobelia erinus*

Few flowers have the intense blue provided by some varieties of lobelia. They are perennials, but are too tender to live over the winter in most parts of the country and are grown as annuals.

**DESCRIPTION:** Lobelias have small, round leaves and flowers up to ½ inch in diameter. Some varieties are compact and mounding; others are definite trailers. The most prominent flower color is blue, but there are also crimson, pink, and white varieties. The trailing varieties will reach 12 to 18 inches by summer's end; the mounding ones grow 6 to 8 inches high.

**EASY-CARE GROWING:** Lobelia grows best in cool areas or where cool nighttime temperatures moderate the weather. They will bloom well in partial shade and thrive if you mulch their roots and keep the area moist. Space seedlings 4 to 6 inches apart in the garden or in containers.

**PROPAGATION:** By seed. Seeds are tiny and need light to germinate, so they should not be covered. Start plants indoors 10 to 12 weeks before planting outdoors. Seeds germinate in 20 days at 70 to 80°F. Seedling growth is slow, and the early stages should be watched carefully to prevent damping off. Don't try to separate individual seedlings at transplanting; instead, plant clumps of several seedlings.

**USES:** Use the mounding forms for edgings, as pockets in rock gardens, between patio stones, or in the front of taller plantings beside walks and pathways. The trailing varieties can cascade over rock walls and are among the best for containers of all kinds.

**RELATED SPECIES:** Cardinal flower (*L. cardinalis*) and great blue lobelia (*L. siphilitica*) are popular hardy perennials.

**RELATED VARIETIES:** Mounding forms include: 'Crystal Palace,' with deep-blue flowers and bronze foliage; 'Cambridge Blue' with sky-blue flowers; 'Mrs. Clibran,' dark blue with white eyes; and 'Rosamund,' cherry-red. 'Riviera Blue Splash' has blue flowers with a white edge. Some trailers are: the Fountain Series in blue, rose, crimson, lilac, and white and 'Sapphire,' deep blue with white eyes. Trailing 'Regatta Blue Splash' has white flowers splashed with blue.

# LOVE-IN-A-MIST, DEVIL IN A BUSH

## *Nigella damascena*

These frothy, quick-to-bloom annuals add an airy note to garden plantings with their soft colors that combine well with other flowers. Love-in-a-mist is native to Mediterranean areas.

**DESCRIPTION:** Love-in-a-mist grows up to 2 feet tall and has many branches. The finely cut foliage is lacy, and the flowers float above the foliage, which is highlighted by large bracts on which the flowers sit. Flowers are most often powder-blue, but there are also pink, rose, and white varieties.

**EASY-CARE GROWING:** Nigella thrives in any sunny location in soil of average fertility or better. Sow the seeds outdoors in the spring as early as the ground can be worked. Thin to a spacing of 5 to 15 inches. For continuous bloom all summer, make successive sowings until early July. Protect them from high winds and stake the plants if necessary.

**PROPAGATION:** By seed. For earlier bloom, start love-in-a-mist indoors 4 to 6 weeks before outdoor planting. Because they are difficult to transplant, start them in peat pots that can be transplanted into the garden, pot and all. Seeds germinate in 10 to 15 days at 65 to 70°F.

**USES:** Nigella is a good see-through plant, allowing other plants behind it to peek through. Consider using it with other pastels and creamy whites. It's best in informal situations. The seed pods are widely used for winter arrangements. Cut them off after they have ripened and dry them upside down in a dark place.

**RELATED SPECIES:** *Nigella hispanica* has mid-blue flowers with black centers and red stamens.

**RELATED VARIETIES:** 'Persian Jewels' combines the popular blue with white, pink, rose, mauve, lavender, and purple. Miss Jekyll Series has white, rose, and light and dark blue flowers. 'Midget Blue' reaches only 10 inches high.

# Love Lies Bleeding, Joseph's Coat, Prince's Feather

*Amaranthus tricolor, A. caudatus*

**B**rightly colored foliage in yellow, red, and orange is the appeal of various ornamental varieties of *A. tricolor*, hence the common name of "Joseph's coat." *A. caudatus* is known as "love lies bleeding" for its brightly colored ropes of flowers in red, white, or bright green.

**DESCRIPTION:** These tropical foliage and flowering plants, with their bright plumage, vary in different, visually stimulating ways. Because they grow rapidly in hot weather, choose different amaranthus for specific needs of color and texture.

**EASY-CARE GROWING:** Plant in warm soil after all chance of frost has passed and in full sun to develop the most vibrant color. Amaranthus tolerate poor soil, heat, and drought. However, poor drainage or excessively wet soil may cause root rot.

**PROPAGATION:** By seed. Start indoors at 70°F 6 weeks prior to planting out or sow directly in place.

**USES:** Because of its height, *A. tricolor* makes a good background plant. The shorter *A. caudatus* is useful grouped in mid-border. Several plants together will effectively highlight their tassels. They make striking container plants. The flowers may also be cut and dried.

**RELATED SPECIES:** Prince's feather *(A. cruentus)* has purple or red spikes that will reach 5 feet by season's end.

**RELATED VARIETIES:** Plants of *A. tricolor* can grow to 4 feet high and spread 2 feet wide. Varieties include 'Flaming Fountains,' with long, willowy, crimson leaves; 'Joseph's Coat,' with yellow, scarlet, and green foliage; and 'Illumination,' which adds bronze to the previous colors. Varieties of *A. caudatus* are shorter, up to 2 or 3 feet high with a 2-foot spread, and include 'Green Thumb,' with upright, green spikes, and 'Love Lies Bleeding,' with blood-red flowers.

# AMERICAN MARIGOLD
*Tagetes erecta*

lthough these annuals are native to Mexico, *Tagetes erecta* are known as American or African marigolds. These flashy annuals are the biggest and boldest of marigolds.

**DESCRIPTION:** American marigolds can be tall plants, growing up to 36 inches high, although breeding has produced shorter heights. They have large, fully double flowers in yellow, gold, and orange.

**EASY-CARE GROWING:** American marigolds grow best in full sun with moist, well-drained soil, although they will tolerate drier conditions. Plant them outdoors as soon as all danger of frost has passed. Space seedlings 10 to 18 inches apart.

**PROPAGATION:** Seeds may be sown in place. For earlier bloom start indoors 4 to 6 weeks prior to outdoor planting. Seeds germinate in 5 to 7 days at 65 to 75°F.

**USES:** Grow taller tagetes toward the center or rear of beds and borders, or as planting pockets in full sun. Mass them in front of shrubs or trees for a big splash of color. You also can use them to make a small hedge around a vegetable or herb garden. American marigolds also work in containers if kept uniformly moist.

**RELATED VARIETIES:** The Antigua Series have large, 3-inch-wide flowers on compact plants only 12 to 16 inches high. 'Vanilla' produces off-white flowers—an unusual color for marigolds. The Jubilee Series, with primrose yellow, golden, and orange flowered varieties, are some of the taller American marigolds, reaching to 24 inches high. Even taller hedge types, which grow to 3 feet high, include members of the Gold Coin Series, 'Double Eagle,' 'Doubloon,' and 'Gold Coin Mix.'

# FRENCH MARIGOLD
### *Tagetes patula*

These all-American plants come in such an array of bright colors over a long season that they're a mainstay of gardeners everywhere.

**DESCRIPTION:** French marigolds are bushy and compact with small flowers and a neat overall appearance. Their flowers come in many colors and forms and often feature multiple colors in a single flower head, which is part of their charm. They usually grow no more than 12 inches.

**EASY-CARE GROWING:** French marigolds grow best in full sun with moist, well-drained soil, although they will tolerate drier conditions. Plant them outdoors as soon as all danger of frost has passed. Space French marigolds 6 to 10 inches apart. They get along with no deadheading but bloom more prolifically if you tackle this occasionally.

**PROPAGATION:** See American Marigold, page 143.

**USES:** Use French marigolds to line the edge of a sunny garden or to surround a vegetable garden as they are thought to repel some pests. They also grow nicely in containers.

**RELATED SPECIES:** Triploids, a cross between French and American marigolds, resemble French marigolds, but have larger flowers.

**RELATED VARIETIES:** One of America's most popular annual flowers is the French marigold 'Queen Sophia,' with gold-rimmed red flower heads. 'Janie' is an extra-early bloomer, only 8 inches high, and comes in yellow, orange, red and gold, gold, and mahogany with an orange center. Unique 'Mr. Majestic' has red stripes on yellow florets and golden centers.

# SIGNET MARIGOLD
*Tagetes tenuifolia*

Graceful, smaller-flowered marigolds—old-fashioned flowers with a delicate texture and more rounded habit—are coming back to popularity for informal or cottage gardens and edible ornamental gardens. Most have delightfully fragrant foliage.

**DESCRIPTION:** Tiny flowers average only a ½ inch in diameter but are borne in large quantities, forming a cloud of gold or orange over plants reaching about 1 foot high. The finely divided leaves often have citrus scents.

**EASY-CARE GROWING:** Provide well-drained, fertile soil in full sun. Plant seedlings during frost-free weather, spacing them 8 to 12 inches apart. Shear back faded flowers occasionally to deadhead and tidy plants.

**PROPAGATION:** See American Marigold, page 143.

**USES:** These make marvelous, perfumed edgings for a flower or vegetable garden and are delightful to brush by on a hot day. You also can use them in pots or interplant with vegetables for color and fragrance.

**RELATED VARIETIES:** 'Lemon Gem' and 'Tangerine Gem' have outstanding foliage fragrance. 'Paprika' has pimento red petals with golden edges. 'Starfire Mix' blends red-, gold-, and orange-flowered plants.

# MELAMPODIUM
*Melampodium paludosum*

**M**elampodium have large, bright green leaves and many perky, little yellow, daisylike flowers that peer forth all summer long. A member of the daisy family, it hails originally from Mexico and Central America—a legacy allowing it to flower profusely despite heat and humidity. *Melampodium paludosum* is one of 36 species in the genus. The name *melampodium* comes from the Greek and literally translated means "black foot," referring to the color of the stalks.

**DESCRIPTION:** Melampodium forms a vigorous, bushy plant 10 to 15 inches high in the garden. It will be 15 to 20 inches in diameter by the end of summer. The leaves are large and rough. They are paired, and each pair is at a right angle to the next. The flowers are small, up to 1 inch in diameter.

**EASY-CARE GROWING:** Melampodium needs full sun. An average-to-rich, moist but well-drained soil is satisfactory. Plants should not be allowed to dry out. Plant outdoors as soon as all danger of frost has passed and the ground is warm. Space melampodium 10 to 15 inches apart.

**PROPAGATION:** By seed. Sow seeds indoors 7 to 10 weeks prior to planting outdoors. Seeds germinate in 7 to 10 days at 65°F. For easier transplanting, grow in peat pots that can be transplanted into the garden, pot and all.

**USES:** Plant melampodium where you want some contrast between flowers and foliage. Use melampodium as a sunny ground cover or plant it in rock gardens in the front of flower borders. Grow in window boxes, patio or deck planters, and hanging baskets.

**RELATED VARIETIES:** 'Medaillon' is the most planted variety. It grows up to 20 inches tall and as wide and is covered all summer with small, golden-yellow flowers. 'Million Gold' and 'Derby' are dwarfs just 8 inches high.

# MOONFLOWER
## *Ipomoea alba*

While morning glories open early in the day, vining moonflowers open in the evening, reflecting the moonlight to make a lovely display for a twilight stroll. You can watch the flowers pop open as darkness descends.

**DESCRIPTION:** This quick-growing plant rapidly stretches vines up to 15 feet long. They bear oval or rounded leaves and large, white, trumpet-shaped flowers with a lovely fragrance.

**EASY-CARE GROWING:** Sow the seed directly outdoors in a sunny site with moderately fertile but well-drained soil.

**PROPAGATION:** By seed. Soak the seeds in water for 24 hours before planting to speed germination. In the North, get earlier bloom by starting seeds indoors in peat pots 4 to 6 weeks before planting out. Germination takes 5 to 7 days at 70 to 80°F. Transplant the peat pots to the garden—pot and all—without disturbing the roots.

**USES:** Like morning glories, let moon flowers climb fences and trellises, even mailboxes. You can cut the flowers in the evening for the dining room table.

# MORNING GLORY VINE

*Ipomoea nil, purpurea, tricolor*

This group of twining vines with bell-shaped flowers have become intertwined botanically under the name "morning glory." The name comes from the flowers, which open at dawn and usually stay open until midday. These rapidly growing vines are closely related to the sweet potato. Flowers are white, blue, pink, purple, red, and multicolored. There are even double forms. Because they're quick, easy, and dependably colorful, they're the most popular annual vine.

**DESCRIPTION:** The vines grow quickly to 10 feet or more only two months after seeds sprout. The leaves are heart-shaped, and the flowers are normally open from dawn to mid-morning, but new varieties will stay open longer, especially on overcast days.

**EASY-CARE GROWING:** Requirements are undemanding. Morning glories will thrive in full sun in any soil, especially if it is not too fertile or too moist. Sow the seeds outdoors when all danger of frost has passed. Provide support. Because they grow by twining, they need extra help if planted around large posts. Plant 8 to 12 inches apart.

**PROPAGATION:** See Moonflower, page 147.

**USES:** Morning glories are splendid for enhancing fences or for hiding eyesores. They will rapidly cover fences, arches, pergolas, and trellises, or can be made into their own garden feature with stakes and twine. They don't have to grow up. They're just as effective as trailers from hanging baskets and window boxes.

**RELATED SPECIES:** *Convovulus tricolor,* known as dwarf morning glory, forms bushy plants with pink, blue, purple, and rose flowers. 'Blue Ensign' is a selection with blue flowers and contrasting yellow and white centers. *Evolvulus glomeratus* is a prostrate plant, 10 to 15 inches in diameter, with many small, morning glory–like flowers in bright blue. 'Blue Daze,' with hairy white leaves and white-eyed blue flowers, is one selection.

**RELATED VARIETIES:** Most famous is 'Heavenly Blue' for refreshing azure color. 'Scarlet Star' has a strong pattern of red and white. 'Chocolate' has reddish-brown flowers. 'Platycodon Mixture' has white, red, and purple single and semi-double flowers.

# MUSK MALLOW, ABELMOSCHUS
### *Abelmoschus moschatus*

Newly introduced to ornamental gardens in the United States, this brightly colored flower is in the same genus as the vegetable okra. Hibiscus is also a close relative and their resemblance is striking. The 3- to 4-inch flowers appear in July from an early start indoors. Each flower lasts only a day, but the profusion of buds provides a continuous show of color.

**DESCRIPTION:** Plants grow 15 to 20 inches high and wide. Musk mallow flowers are pink or red with white centers and appear above the arrowhead-shaped leaves.

**EASY-CARE GROWING:** As with other members of the genus, it thrives in heat and full sun. Provide abundant water and a rich soil for best performance.

**PROPAGATION:** By seed. Seeds take at least 15 days to germinate at 70°F. For husky plants, start at least 8 weeks prior to planting in the garden. First bloom is approximately 100 days after sowing. Plant musk mallow 1 foot apart when the soil has warmed and nights remain above 50°F.

**USES:** This bright plant can be used for a sunny garden ground cover. Plant it mid-border or as an edging for borders in front of taller plants. Use it as a container plant where its mounding, flowing habit combines well with taller plants. Its tropical appearance looks attractive with cannas and other exotic-looking plants.

**RELATED VARIETIES:** Some varieties include 'Oriental Red,' which is cherry-red with white centers, and 'Pink,' white-centered with a pink blush. The Pacific Series include 'Pacific Pink,' 'Pacific Orange,' and 'Pacific Scarlet,' an orange-scarlet variety.

# NASTURTIUM
## *Tropaeolum majus*

Nearly every kid who's been near a garden has grown a nasturtium. And today's salad-conscious adult has certainly enjoyed the peppery tang of nasturtium leaves and flowers among the greens. Natives of Mexico, they're among our garden favorites.

**DESCRIPTION:** Nasturtiums started out as vigorous, vinelike plants, and many of them still are. Breeders have altered them so that some are now bushy, compact plants only 12 inches tall. The leaves are nearly round. The flowers have bright, open faces with long spurs behind them.

**EASY-CARE GROWING:** Don't overdo the care with nasturtiums. They need full sun in a dry, sandy, well-drained soil. They're at their best in regions with cool, dry summers—although they will grow elsewhere, too. Sow seeds outdoors after the last frost. Depending on the variety, space them 8 to 12 inches apart. The vigorous varieties can be trained upward only by tying them to supports; they have no means of attachment. Nasturtiums will reseed vigorously in warm climates but will not be the same colors you planted.

**PROPAGATION:** By seed. Seed germination takes 7 to 12 days at 65°F. Do not cover the seeds; they need light to germinate.

**USES:** Dwarf varieties are good for flower borders, beds, edging paths, and walks. Tie vining varieties to fences or posts or let them trail from window boxes, hanging baskets, or other containers or dangle over a retaining wall. Nasturtiums make good cut flowers, too.

**RELATED SPECIES:** *Tropaeolum peregrinum,* or canary creeper, is a vigorous vine with bright yellow flowers.

**RELATED VARIETIES:** 'Jewel of India' is a climber with variegated leaves and mixed-color flowers. The Alaska Series, available in yellow, orange, burgundy, and off-white, have similar white-marked leaves on dwarf plants less than 1 foot high. The Whirlybird Series, also compact, have spurless flowers held above the foliage. The Double Gleam Series, with fuller, semi-double flowers in light yellow, gold, orange, rose, crimson, and brownish-red flowers, are intermediate between a full-sized vine and a bushy dwarf. They grow to 3 feet.

# NICOTIANA, FLOWERING TOBACCO
### *Nicotiana alata* and *N.* x *sanderae*

Related to the tobacco plants of commerce, flowering tobacco has been bred for its ornamental value. The flowers exist in a variety of colors, including an intriguing lime-green. In addition, flowers have a rich, pervasive scent primarily in the evening, although it has been lost in some of the newer hybrids.

**DESCRIPTION:** A low rosette of large, flat leaves supports the tall, flowering stems covered with star-shaped flowers. Flower colors include white, pink, maroon, lavender, green, red, and yellow. The plants grow up to 3 feet tall. Botanists recently have split off similar looking flowering tobaccos of hybrid origin into their own species, *N.* x *sanderae*, which only reaches about 2 feet high.

**EASY-CARE GROWING:** Nicotiana grows best in fertile, humus-rich, moist, well-drained soil in partial shade or full sun in cooler areas. They are durable plants that will tolerate high temperatures as long as the soil is moist. Before planting out, incorporate extra fertilizer into the soil. Transplant to the garden when all danger of frost has passed, spacing 8 to 12 inches apart.

**PROPAGATION:** By seed. In areas with a long growing season, you can sow the seeds in place, thinning the seedlings to the correct spacing. Elsewhere, start the plants indoors 6 to 8 weeks prior to planting out. Seeds germinate in 10 to 20 days at 70°F. Don't cover seeds; they need light to germinate.

**USES:** Nicotiana can give much-needed height to beds and borders. Group them in clusters for more impact. They're also good when grown in containers.

**RELATED SPECIES:** *Nicotiana sylvestris* is a very fragrant species with white flowers. It grows up to 4 feet tall.

**RELATED VARIETIES:** The most popular *N. alata* series is Nicki Series, which reach only 18 inches high and come in red-, rose-, pink-, green-, and white-flowered forms. For a particularly exciting flower, look for pastel pink and white flowered 'Havana Appleblossom.' *N.* x *sanderae* varieties, often still listed under *N. alata*, include the extra dwarf, large flowered Starship Series only 10 to 12 inches high, and the Domino Series, with more upward-facing flowers, good basal branching, and a height of 12 to 14 inches.

# NIEREMBERGIA, CUP FLOWER
## *Nierembergia caerulea*

The name "cup flower," although not used much, refers to the shape of the flower, which is somewhat like an open-faced bowl. Native to Central and South America, it is a tender perennial grown like an annual in most of the country. In frost-free areas, it will winter over if given good drainage.

**DESCRIPTION:** Nierembergia has attractive thin, narrow leaves topped at the ends with bluish or purple flowers. A small yellow spot in the center of each flower highlights the display. The plants grow outward rather than up, up to 6 inches high, and will spread a foot.

**EASY-CARE GROWING:** Grow nierembergia in full sun in well-drained soil with adequate moisture and average fertility. Flowers hold their color without fading in full sun. Transplant to the garden when all danger of frost has passed. Pinch them to encourage more branching and a higher production of flowers. For full coverage, plant them 5 to 6 inches apart. Remove old flowers for increased floriferousness in weeks to come.

**PROPAGATION:** By seed. Sow seeds indoors 10 to 12 weeks prior to planting in the garden after the last frost. Seeds germinate in 14 to 21 days at 70 to 75°F. Plants will not grow rapidly until the soil is warm.

**USES:** Grow nierembergia as a flowering ground cover in full sun, massed in large patches or beds. It's an ideal edging plant for beds and borders, traveling along paths and walkways with ease. It's also a good plant for rock gardens. Use it in window boxes, hanging baskets, and patio planters—usually with other plants that will provide height and mass.

**RELATED SPECIES:** *Nierembergia repens* is a creeping species with creamy white flowers.

**RELATED VARIETIES:** 'Purple Robe' has glowing, violet-blue flowers. It makes a dramatic contrast with award-winning, white-flowered 'Mont Blanc.'

# PANSY
## *Viola* x *wittrockiana*

Pansies are the ultimate in cool season color, blooming until weather turns torrid and then thriving again when autumn chills return. Newer heat-tolerant cultivars bridge the summer gap, flowering nicely in northern climates throughout the growing season. They are related to violets.

**DESCRIPTION:** Pansies grow on sprawling plants that produce flowers continuously as they grow. Flowers range from 2 inches in diameter up to giants of 5 inches or more. Some have clear colors, but many have uniquely distributed colors. The color range is complete.

**EASY-CARE GROWING:** In mild winter areas, plant as soon as the weather cools in late summer. Even areas with short freezes can enjoy winter pansies; once the weather warms, they'll start opening blossoms. Elsewhere, plant in spring for a cool season display or allow heat-tolerant types to remain on the job all summer. Plant in the garden as soon as the ground can be worked. Space 6 to 9 inches apart. If plants become lank and leggy, shear back halfway to force new growth and bloom. Pansies prefer full sun and cool, moist soil. A bit of shade will help them extend the season in hot climates.

**PROPAGATION:** By seed. Start seeds 6 to 8 weeks prior to planting out. They will germinate in 10 to 15 days at 68°F. Do not cover seeds; they need light to germinate.

**USES:** Plant them anywhere you want a spot of color. They are suitable for the front of borders and beds, in small groups among other flowers, in cottage garden plantings, and in containers.

**RELATED VARIETIES:** Heat-tolerant hybrid Crystal Bowl Series flower early and have a contrasting throat color but lack the bicolor blotch. For blotched flowers with equal heat tolerance, look for the Maxim Series, available in blue, yellow, chiffon, black, purple, orange, red, rose, sherbet, sunset, and more. The largest flowers of all are in the Super Majestic Giant Series. The Bingo Series, with blue, purple, rose, red, yellow, white, and color blends, hold their flowers upright so they are prominent when viewed from above. 'Sprite Mix Hybrid,' a new ground covering type, grows in mats 5 inches high and 18 inches across.

# CURLY PARSLEY

*Petroselenum crispum* var. *crispum*

The curling, emerald leaves of parsley provide interesting texture and rich color for annual gardens and mixed borders. Grow plenty of it to make a big impact and have enough extra for kitchen use.

**DESCRIPTION:** Parsley has multiple sprigs of curling, divided leaves that grow into a handsome mound of greenery. The foliage reaches about 1 foot and remains fresh and appealing throughout the growing season. If allowed to remain in the garden during winter, parsley will go to seed the following year, sending up a flowering stalk several feet high topped with delicate, umbrella-shaped clusters of flowers.

**EASY-CARE GROWING:** Plant parsley seeds or seedlings in well-drained but rich and fertile soil, amended with extra compost and located in full sun or light shade. You can sow seeds directly in the garden when spring temperatures grow mild, but not necessarily frost-free. Wait to plant seedlings out, however, until frosts subside. Space seedlings 8 to 10 inches apart. Keep moist and fertilize with a high nitrogen product. In fall, mulch parsley with straw to keep the foliage green well into winter.

**PROPAGATION:** By seed. Sow directly in the garden or for a head start, indoors 6 to 8 weeks before the last frost date. To speed parsley seeds' sometimes slow germination, soak seeds in warm water for 8 hours before sowing. Place seeds ¼ inch deep in a peat-based seed sowing mix as they need darkness to sprout. They will germinate in 14 to 21 days (sometimes longer) at 70°F.

**USES:** Use clusters or masses of parsley between bedding annuals such as pansies and petunias or to make a transition between low plants such as sweet alyssum and moss verbena and medium-height plants such as nicotiana and American marigolds. Sweeps of parsley are particularly useful for separating conflicting colors. They also make a great edging for a flower or ornamental edible garden and blend beautifully into a mixed annual pot.

**RELATED VARIETIES:** Italian parsley, *P. crsipum* var. *neapolitanum* has flat leaves on taller plants. It is considered less decorative but has a more pungent flavor.

# ORNAMENTAL PEPPERS
## *Capsicum* species

Ornamental peppers are the only summer annuals grown primarily for the attractiveness of their fruit. That, combined with their contrast of foliage and form, is what makes them popular in the summer garden.

**DESCRIPTION:** Ornamental peppers grow into small bushes 12 to 18 inches high and as wide. Their dark green, purple, or variegated leaves are topped by bright-colored fruits that form in July and hold on the plant until frost. Depending on variety, fruits may be red, purple, yellow, or orange; the shapes range from conical to slim and tapered. There are even twisted forms. The small, white flowers that appear prior to the fruit are pretty but inconspicuous.

**EASY-CARE GROWING:** Ornamental peppers prefer full sun in rich, well-drained soil and perform best in hot weather. They're remarkably drought-tolerant, but will grow better if watered when soil becomes dry. Plant when the soil is warm and the weather has settled down.

**PROPAGATION:** By seed. Sow seeds 8 weeks prior to planting out after last frost date. The seeds germinate in approximately 12 days at temperatures above 70°F and should be covered.

**USES:** Bright-colored fruits on glossy, green plants decorate borders or bed edges. Mix them into an edible ornamental garden or a cottage garden. Peppers also make striking container plants.

**RELATED VARIETIES:** 'Pepper Fruit Basket' is a graceful, spreading plant with sweet, small orange fruit, the first of its kind suitable for hanging baskets. 'Sweet Pickle' is an upright pepper topped simultaneously with sweet red, orange, yellow, and purple peppers. 'Aurora' bears upright, hot peppers that change from green to lavender to orange, and finally to red. 'Pretty Hot Purple' has purple stems, flowers, and hot purple fruit. 'Bellingrath Gardens Purple' has purple-green leaves and stems with white variegation on the new foliage. The peppers are hot and change from purple-green to purple-orange to red.

# PERILLA, BEEFSTEAK PLANT
*Perilla frutescens*

Perilla is member of the mint family. Its foliage and stems have a pungent fragrance when they are crushed. It is widely used as a flavoring in Oriental cuisines and can be used to dye rice pink.

**DESCRIPTION:** Perilla has the square stems typical of mint family members. The oval leaves can be green, purple, or bronzy, although the most common are a deep purple. They also have a most attractive, metallic sheen. The leaves are deeply veined and crinkled, adding to the plant's attractiveness. Plants can grow as tall as 3 feet. Flowers are not noteworthy and appear at the end of summer.

**EASY-CARE GROWING:** Perilla will grow equally well in sun or in shade, but low light will create a lankier plant. You can plant it in average garden soil. Since perilla is a tender annual, you should plant it in the garden after all danger of frost has passed, spacing plants 12 to 15 inches apart. Pinch the tips once or twice to form a bushier plant.

**PROPAGATION:** By seed or cuttings. Sow seeds outdoors after the last frost date. Thin to the desired spacing when the seedlings are 3 or 4 inches tall. For larger plants earlier, sow seeds indoors 4 to 6 weeks prior to transplanting into the garden. Because perillas are difficult to transplant, grow them in peat pots to prevent root disturbance when transplanting. Seeds germinate in 15 to 20 days at 65 to 75°F. Cuttings root quickly and easily, even in water. Plants in the garden will self-sow readily.

**USES:** Plant perilla in beds or borders. Use it as a ribbon to contrast with other foliage and flower colors. Its bushy habit makes a good edging for pathways and along walks. Try it as a low hedge.

**RELATED VARIETIES:** 'Crispa' has attractively frilly-edged, purple or green leaves and grows 2 to 3 feet tall. 'Atropurpurea' has purple-red leaves.

# GRANDIFLORA PETUNIA
### *Petunia* x *hybrida* Grandiflora Group

Anyone who's been close to a garden is familiar with petunias, a longtime favorite for undiminished color through a long season. Actually tender perennials, they will flower through the winter in nearly frost-free climates. The name "petunia" comes from a South American word for "tobacco," to which they're related (along with tomatoes and potatoes). A plant that has long had the eye of breeders, petunias have flowers with charming variations—open bells, crisped, curled, waved, and doubled-up into fluffy balls. The enormous color range even includes a yellow.

**DESCRIPTION:** Grandiflora petunias, long the American favorite, have big and bold trumpet-shaped flowers 3 to 4 inches across and are available in single and double forms. Unfortunately, they are prone to damage and disease during wet weather and often grow lank and flowerless before the season has ended.

**EASY-CARE GROWING:** Well-drained but fertile soil in full sun suits petunias best. Grandifloras can excel in containers that can be moved under cover to avoid extended rain or overhead watering. Space petunias 12 inches apart. To promote more branching and increased bloom, shear plants back halfway in midsummer. Deadheading is extremely important for Grandiflora petunias—as the plants set seed, flowering is greatly reduced.

**PROPAGATION:** By seed. Start seeds indoors 10 to 12 weeks prior to planting outdoors. Seeds are very fine and can be more evenly sown by mixing thoroughly with a pinch of sand. Do not cover the seeds as they need light to germinate. Seeds germinate in 10 to 12 days at 70 to 75°F.

**USES:** Beds, borders, walkways, paths, containers—all will accommodate an abundance of petunias. Some varieties are especially recommended for containers, since they mound up and billow over the edges.

**RELATED SPECIES:** Milliflora petunias, a new species, make 8-inch-high mounds and bear dozens of inch-wide flowers. The Fantasy Series of millifloras includes cultivars with flowers of carmine, sky blue, blue, pink, red, or ivory.

**RELATED VARIETIES:** The Aladdin Series, with colors such as blue, burgundy, red, and peach, has a bushier habit than many grandifloras, and the plants are less likely to sprawl later in summer. 'Prism Sunshine Hybrid,' a multiple award winner, is a strong performer with a clear yellow throat fading to cream on the flower edges. Among double-flowered forms, 'Lavender Angel' is compact and uniquely colored. 'Purple Pirouette' and 'Rose Pirouette' are as full-flowered as a carnation with striking, white-edged petals.

# MULTIFLORA AND FLORIBUNDA PETUNIAS
### *Petunia* x *hybrida*

These two classes of petunias are more weather-resistant and durable than grandifloras, so are well-worth considering.

**DESCRIPTION:** The multiflora petunias have significantly smaller flowers than grandifloras, only an inch or two wide, but they are borne in abundance on graceful, bushy plants. Our fondness for big petunia flowers has been appeased recently with the development of floribundas, larger-flowered multifloras with blossoms reaching 2 to 3 inches wide. Floribunda petunias retain the neat, well-branched, and mounded habit of the multifloras.

**EASY-CARE GROWING:** Provide full sun and well-drained soil of average fertility. Deadhead or cut back plants if needed for rejuvenation.

**PROPAGATION:** See Grandiflora Petunia, page 157.

**USES:** Multifloras and floribundas are great for mass plantings because they provide a profusion of flowers and are nearly undaunted by drenching rains and high winds. The intricate, double varieties are probably best in containers for optimal enjoyment of their complex flowers. Petunias also make good, informal cut flowers.

**RELATED VARIETIES:** The Celebrity Series of Floribundas comes in pink, salmon, burgundy, blue, lilac, plum, red, and white. For a particularly pretty Celebrity, try 'Chiffon Morn' (an award-winning pink with a white throat). For eye-opening color, try Celebrities with contrasting colored veins including 'Raspberry Ice,' 'Strawberry Ice,' and 'Summer Ice.' Among the multifloras, the low-growing, spreading Carpet Series is widely available.

# VINING PETUNIAS
## *Petunia* spp.

While some old-fashioned petunias grew as ground-hugging semi-vines, interbreeding with wild South American petunias has created high-performance forms of vining petunias, a whole new look in annuals.

**DESCRIPTION:** Wave Series of petunias can spread to 3 or 4 feet wide while reaching only 6 inches tall. Their vining stems are covered with 2- to 3-inch flowers that emerge from top to bottom. Calibracoa petunias, developed using a close relative of the petunia, bear hundreds of small flowers on 2-foot-long stems. Surfinia hybrid petunias, popular in European window boxes, can grow to 4 feet long in containers or to 2 or 3 feet long and 12 to 15 inches high when grown as a garden ground cover.

**EASY-CARE GROWING:** Provide full sun and well-drained, average to fertile soil. Wave petunias are little troubled with diseases caused by wet weather and tolerate heat well. They do not need cutting back and actually perform better without it. Calibracoa and Surfinia petunias thrive if fertilized regularly with a nitrogen-rich product to encourage continued growth and flowering. The Million Bells Series of Calibracoa petunias are self-cleaning and do not need deadheading.

**PROPAGATION:** See Grandiflora Petunia, page 157. Calibracoa, Supertunia, and Surfinia petunias are patented plants and unauthorized propagation of them is illegal.

**USES:** Vining petunias are ideal for hanging baskets or window boxes, which can even be used to drape down and hide unsightly plumbing or other eyesores. They, along with the Wave Series, also are great ground covers, and can creep across the front of any sunny bed or around the bases of perennials, roses, and even taller annuals.

**RELATED VARIETIES:** The Supertunia Series, an introduction from Australia, includes nine different colors on plants that grow to 3 feet long in just 6 weeks. Popular Surfinias come in many variations of blue, purple, pink, and white. Million Bells Calibracoa come in 'Trailing Blue,' purple-blue with yellow center; 'Trailing Pink,' lavender-pink with a yellow center; and 'Cherry Pink,' hot-pink with a yellow center. The Wave Series includes 'Purple Wave,' 'Pink Wave,' 'Rose Wave,' and 'Misty Lilac Wave.'

# ANNUAL PHLOX, TEXAS PRIDE

*Phlox drummondii*

These bright-colored plants originally hail from Texas, but breeders have civilized them to be some of the most dependable garden performers. The name "phlox" comes from the Greek word meaning "flame," identifying its bright colors.

**DESCRIPTION:** Annual phloxes grow from 6 inches to 1½ feet tall. The flowers develop in large clusters of many colors and shapes. Colors include pink, red, rose, white, lavender, scarlet, crimson, and yellow.

**EASY-CARE GROWING:** Annual phloxes grow best in well-drained, sandy soil, high in organic matter. They require full sun and continuous moisture during the growing season. Place them where the air circulates

freely to prevent mildew. Plant seedlings in the garden as soon as the danger of frost has passed. Space 6 inches apart. Pinch the tips to encourage branching. At midsummer, shear the plants back halfway to reinvigorate flowering.

**PROPAGATION:** By seed. Sow plants outdoors where they are to grow after the last frost is due. Thin to the desired spacing. For earlier bloom, start plants indoors 4 to 6 weeks before setting out. Seeds germinate in 15 to 20 days at 55 to 65°F. Transplant in clumps of several plants to get a full color range.

**USES:** Grow annual phlox in beds or at the front of borders. Use them as edgings. Intermix them with other flowers in informal plantings and cottage gardens. Phlox are good container plants and hold well in water when cut.

**RELATED VARIETIES:** 'Promise Pink,' a double-flowered form, is naturally basal-branched and has coral-orange flowers on stems to 12 inches. 'Petticoat Mix' is a dwarf with a mix of all colors. Dwarf 'Cecily' is a bright mixture with a high number of bicolors with contrasting eyes. 'Twinkle' (syn. 'Sternenzauber'), an award winner, is a mix of ringed, pointed, starlike flowers.

# PINCUSHION FLOWER, SCABIOSA, MOURNING BRIDE

## *Scabiosa atropurpurea*

This native of southern Europe looks like a pincushion with flower heads up to 3 inches in size and scores of yellow or white stamens. The original flowers had a sweet scent.

**DESCRIPTION:** Scabiosa can grow up to 2½ feet tall. However, most modern varieties are shorter. The multi-branched plants are topped with flowers in white, pink, lavender, and deepest maroon (almost black), from which the name "mourning bride" comes. Both double and single forms are found.

**EASY-CARE GROWING:** Scabiosas grow well in any moderately fertile, well-drained soil. They need full sun. Plant outdoors after all danger of frost has passed, spacing them 8 to 15 inches apart, depending on variety. The taller varieties will need staking, but the shorter ones do not if protected from high winds. Scabiosas are sensitive to water. Apply water in the morning so that it can dry off before night.

**PROPAGATION:** By seed. Sow outdoors as soon as all danger of frost has passed, thinning seedlings to the proper spacing. For earlier bloom, sow seeds indoors 4 to 6 weeks prior to outdoor planting. Seeds germinate in 10 to 15 days at 70 to 75°F.

**USES:** Scabiosa is a delight in cottage gardens and mixed borders. It also makes good cut flowers.

**RELATED SPECIES:** *S. stellata* 'Ping Pong' develops globular seed heads suitable for dried flower arrangements.

**RELATED VARIETIES:** 'Ace of Spades' has reddish-black, lightly fragrant flower heads. 'Dwarf Double' is a mix of colors in white, lavender, lavender-blue, and rose, growing to 18 inches. 'Imperial Giants' features large flowers on long stems, ideal for cutting. They are a mix of lavender-blue, blue, white, rose, salmon, scarlet, and pink.

# CALIFORNIA POPPY
## *Escholtzia californica*

California hillsides are covered in spring with the golden-orange of California poppies. Gardeners now have a choice of color—white, rose, scarlet, crimson, or salmon.

**DESCRIPTION:** Perennials in mild winter areas, California poppies have finely cut, blue-green foliage in contrast to silky flower cups on slender, wiry stems 12 to 15 inches tall.

**EASY-CARE GROWING:** The best planting location for California poppies is sandy, slightly alkaline soil in full sun. They tolerate poor and dry soils as well. In all but Zones 8, 9, and 10, treat them as annuals that bloom best during cool weather. In cool seasons and maritime climates, they will continue blooming all summer if deadheaded.

**PROPAGATION:** California poppies have a taproot and don't transplant well, so they should be sown in place. In mild winter areas, this is best done in the fall, as small plants will winter over for earliest spring bloom. Elsewhere, sow as early in the spring as the ground can be worked. (If you want to start them indoors, transplant before the taproot is established.) Seeds will germinate in 4 to 10 days when the soil temperature is at 60°F. Water well.

**USES:** Grow them in rock walls or rock gardens or as a part of naturalized meadow plantings. Reseeding will occur and the offspring of hybrids will revert to the golden-orange colors of their ancestors.

**RELATED SPECIES:** *Papaver rhoeas,* the Shirley poppy, is the cultivated form of the Flanders poppy, a deep scarlet with black centers. There are many new forms including doubles in pink, white, rose, salmon, as well as red. 'Mother of Pearl' is a selection of pastel shades including gray, blue, lilac, dusty pink, and bicolors. 'Angels Choir' are double forms of 'Mother of Pearl' selections.

**RELATED VARIETIES:** The Thai Silk Series includes 10- to 12-inch-high 'Milkmaid' (butter yellow), 'Apricot Chiffon' (apricot highlighted with red), 'Rose Chiffon' (yellow-centered rose-red), and a mixture. 'Ballerina' is composed of semi-double and double flowers in yellow, rose, pink, scarlet, and orange. 'Milky-White' is a creamy white selection.

# ICELAND POPPY
### *Papaver croceum* (syn. *P. nudicaule*)

The glistening, translucent flowers of Iceland poppies are a glowing sight when backlit by the sun. The petals look like tissue paper or crinkled silk. Their spring and early summer splendor in warm parts of the country can be enjoyed throughout the summer in cooler climates. They're short-lived perennials that are best grown as biennials or annuals.

**DESCRIPTION:** A rosette of thin, narrow leaves forms the base. The tall, slender stems are topped by flowers in virtually all colors of the rainbow except blue, with many hues in between. The ring of prominent yellow stamens enhances the colorful blooms. Stem height varies widely from 1 to 2 feet. There are single and semi-double flowered forms.

**EASY-CARE GROWING:** Iceland poppies prefer full sun and a fertile, well-drained soil; otherwise their requirements are not demanding. Early flowers opening during cool weather will be the largest. To encourage continued flowering, remove seed heads when they form.

**PROPAGATION:** By seed. Seeds sown indoors in January will bloom the first season. You also can start plants the previous summer and overwinter them in the garden. In mild winter areas, they may begin blooming in winter. Seeds germinate in 10 to 15 days at 55°F. Poppies have taproots and do not transplant easily once the taproot is formed. Grow in peat pots and transplant into the garden, pot and all.

**USES:** A whole bed of poppies is spectacular. They can also be grown as clumps, groups, or as a ribbon in mid-border. They're especially beautiful when backed by the foliage of hedges or other green plants. They also make good cut flowers if you cut them in early morning just as the buds are showing color. Sear the cut ends with an open flame or plunge the stems in hot (not boiling) water for a few moments.

**RELATED VARIETIES:** 'Wonderland' series offers separate colors of white, orange, yellow, pink, and a mix. 'Garden Gnome Mix' are compact, sturdy stemmed, and blend scarlet, salmon, pink, yellow, white, and orange. 'Partyfun' mixes bicolor, pastel, and bold-colored flowers that reach 12 to 14 inches high.

# PORTULACA, MOSS ROSE
*Portulaca grandiflora*

**P**ortulaca's profusion of sunny flower colors combined with its toughness make it a natural for difficult garden sites. It will do even better under less difficult conditions. It is a native of Brazil.

**DESCRIPTION:** Moss roses grow nearly prostrate—a mat of fleshy leaves with stems topped by flowers. The flowers of newer varieties can reach 2 inches in diameter and are available in a myriad of jewel-like colors—lemon-yellow, gold, orange, crimson, pink, lavender, purple, and white. They're enhanced by the bright button of yellow stamens in the center. There are both single and double varieties. The latter is sparked by extra rows of petals.

**EASY-CARE GROWING:** Full sun with light, sandy soil and good drainage are musts for portulaca—although they respond to adequate moisture with lush growth and more flowers. Very frost-tender, wait to plant seedlings outdoors until the danger of frost has passed and the ground is warm. Space them 1 to 2 feet apart. The flowers of most varieties close at night and on cloudy days. Moss rose reseeds vigorously.

**PROPAGATION:** Sow in place as soon as danger of frost has passed and the soil is warm. For earlier bloom, start indoors 4 to 6 weeks ahead. Seeds germinate in 10 to 15 days at 70 to 80°F.

**USES:** Reserve your problem areas for portulaca. They're good container plants that do not languish if you forget to water them one day.

**RELATED VARIETIES:** 'Cloudbeater Mix' are unique, double-flowered types that don't close their blossoms during the day, even when the sun hides behind clouds. The Sundance Series are early blooming, double-flowered hybrids with a wide color range including cream, pink, gold, orange, scarlet, fuchsia, white, yellow, peppermint (pink flecked with red), and white flecked with lavender-blue.

# PRIMROSE
*Primula* species and hybrids

Primroses are favored in mild winter areas. They're also spectacular additions to other gardens for early spring color during cool weather. The two most popular varieties for gardens are P. Polyanthus Group, bred from a number of species with long stems topped by multiple flowers, and *P. vulgaris* (syn. *acaulis*), featuring many single-stemmed flowers clustered in the center of the plant.

**DESCRIPTION:** Primrose flowers grow from a rosette of long, narrow leaves. Acaulis types will grow up to 8 inches high, while Polyanthus primroses will grow to 1 foot high. The color range is immense—from sky to midnight blue, pinks, reds of all hues, yellow, orange, and lavender. Many of them are centered with a contrasting yellow eye; still others have narrow bands of color in the petals.

**EASY-CARE GROWING:** *P. vulgaris* is a hardy perennial but is often bedded out like an annual for early color. Blooms will start in midwinter through spring with a reprise of color in the fall when weather cools. Transplant well-hardened plants into the garden as soon as the ground can be worked. Space them 6 to 10 inches apart. Grow them in soil rich in organic matter and keep them moist. They're usually happiest with a canopy of high shade.

**PROPAGATION:** By seed or by division. To break seed dormancy, store in the refrigerator for 3 to 4 weeks before sowing. Sow seeds 8 to 10 weeks before planting in the garden. Seeds germinate in 10 to 20 days at 70°F.

**USES:** Primroses highlight woodland paths and walkways. Plant them in pockets by streams or ponds. They're also nice with pansies, forget-me-nots, and other spring flowers. In containers, they can be beautifully combined with all of the above and others.

**RELATED SPECIES:** There are between 400 and 500 species and much interest in growing them, including a Primrose Society for aficionados.

**RELATED VARIETIES:** The Crescendo Series are favorites among the Polyanthus primroses. Yellow-eyed flowers reach 8 inches high and bloom in violet, pink, red, purple, and white. For acaulis primoses, look for unusual 'Silver Lining Hybrid' with a white edge to the flowers. You can find multi-colored series such as the Bellissima Series and individual colors such as 'Cottage White' and 'Miss Indigo.'

# COMMON SAGE
*Salvia officinalis*

Sage is not just for Thanksgiving turkey stuffing. The lovely, leathery silver leaves, also available in golden and tricolor variegated forms, make handsome foliage plants for the mixed annual garden.

**DESCRIPTION:** Sage is a hardy shrub that reaches 2½ feet and bears elongated, oval, gray leaves that are lightly hairy and fragrant. It is easily grown as an annual, filling in fast to provide bright color. Open spikes of blue-purple flowers appear in summer. Its less hardy variegated cultivars are equally attractive with leaves of purple; yellow and green; or pink, white, and green.

**EASY-CARE GROWING:** Provide full sun and well-drained soil. Sages also grow easily in pots of ordinary peat-based mixes. You can set out well-hardened seedlings of common sage in spring before the last spring frost but wait until the weather warms to plant the less hardy, colorful-leaved cultivars. Space plants 12 to 18 inches apart.

**PROPAGATION:** By seed or cuttings. Sow seeds indoors 6 to 8 weeks before the last frost. They will germinate in 14 to 21 days at 70°F. Propagate colored leaf cultivars by softwood cuttings.

**USES:** Use sages for color in an ornamental edible garden or mixed pot of herbs and vegetables. The silver-leaved and purple forms blend nicely with annuals of cool colors such as blue and purple. Use sages with golden variegated leaves with gold and orange flowers. Sages with pink foliage highlights are best matched with similar pink flowers.

**RELATED VARIETIES:** 'Aurea' and 'Ictarina' have gold variegated leaves. 'Tricolor' has white variegation with pink on the new foliage. 'Purpurescens' has purple-toned leaves.

# SALVIA, SCARLET SAGE
## *Salvia splendens*

Salvias are best known for their spiky color that is dependable in any climate. Adaptable to full sun or partial shade with equal ease, these tender perennials are related to some of the best perennial plants for the garden as well as to common culinary sage. A native of Brazil, salvia comes in brilliant red, creamy white, rose-colored, and purplish variants.

**DESCRIPTION:** The native plants are reported to grow up to 8 feet high. In the garden, 3 feet is about as tall as the largest ones grow. There are dwarf variants that grow only 8 to 12 inches. The spikes of flowers are composed of bright bracts with flowers in the center of each. They are either the same color or contrasting.

**EASY-CARE GROWING:** Salvia is a good dual-purpose plant that will perform dutifully in full sun or partial shade. It needs average soil and continuous moisture to perform its best. Transplant plants to the garden after danger of frost has passed and the soil is warm. Depending on variety, space from 8 to 12 inches apart.

**PROPAGATION:** Although salvia seeds can be sown directly in the garden, earlier sowing indoors will bring earlier flowering. Be sure to use fresh seeds, since they lose their viability quickly. Sow the seeds 6 to 8 weeks before the final frost. The seeds germinate in 12 to 15 days at 70 to 75°F. Because salvia seeds need light to germinate, do not cover them. After germination, reduce the temperature to 55°F.

**USES:** Salvia provides some of the purest reds and scarlets in the garden world, and their vertical growth makes them superb accents in the garden. Plant them as spots of color against other colors. They're a classic combination with blue and white for patriotic plantings. Their ability to bloom well in light shade makes them especially useful with pastel colors that tend to fade in the sun. They also make good container plants.

**RELATED SPECIES:** *Salvia farinacea* is a perennial in milder climates that is now widely used as an annual throughout the country. Its common name is "mealycup sage" for the grayish bloom on its stems and foliage. It grows 18 to 24 inches tall and produces either blue or white flowers. 'Victoria' is the most popular blue; its counterpart is 'Victoria White.' 'Strata,' an award winner, has blue and white flowers. *S. patens*, gentian sage, is named for its rich indigo-blue flowers that have a long blooming season. *S. coccinea* 'Lady in Red' is a tender perennial with graceful, open spikes of hummingbird-attracting red flowers.

**RELATED VARIETIES:** The Carabiniere Series grows to 12 inches and, in addition to red, has separate colors of coral-shrimp pink, orange, blue-violet, and creamy white. The Sizzler Series, best used where summers don't get too hot and humid, include burgundy, lavender, pink, plum, purple, red, salmon, and white. Some showstoppers include 'Sizzler Burgundy' and 'Laser Purple.' Tallest reds are 'America' and 'Bonfire,' which will grow to just over 2 feet in the garden.

# SANVITALIA, CREEPING ZINNIA
### *Sanvitalia procumbens*

Although not a zinnia, sanvitalia has enough resemblance to it to fit its common name of "creeping zinnia." Bright, golden-yellow flowers bloom nonstop all summer until frost. A native of Mexico, it is a member of the daisy family.

**DESCRIPTION:** Sanvitalia is a creeping plant that will spread to 18 inches across and top out at 6 inches high. The flowers aren't large, but they're so abundant that they nearly obscure the foliage. The purple or brown centers are a pleasing foil to the yellow petals. Most sanvitalias are singles.

**EASY-CARE GROWING:** Sanvitalia prefers full sun but will adapt to partial shade. In the shade it will flower less. It thrives in well-drained, moderately fertile soil but is tolerant of most garden conditions. It is ideal for hanging baskets and planters. Plant outdoors when all danger of frost has passed and the soil is warm. Space plants 6 inches apart. Do not overwater or fertilize.

**PROPAGATION:** By seed. Sow seeds in place when ground has warmed. For earlier bloom, start indoors 4 to 6 weeks before outdoor planting. Seeds germinate in 10 to 15 days at 70°F. Do not cover the seeds; they need light to germinate. Because they do not transplant easily, grow sanvitalias in peat pots that can be planted in the garden, pot and all.

**USES:** Since sanvitalia is an annual that likes dry conditions, grow it in rock gardens or containers. Use it as an edging for the front of borders or along sidewalks and paths. It will even bloom near the sun-drenched or shade-dappled foundations of houses.

**RELATED VARIETIES:** 'Mandarin Orange' brings a new color to sanvitalia. 'Yellow Carpet' and 'Golden Carpet' are extra dwarf, growing to only 4 inches high.

# SCARLET FLAX

*Linum grandiflorum*

This showy annual provides bright red flowers with virtually no care. Each flower lasts a few hours and is followed daily by a procession of new ones. Originally from North Africa, it has become naturalized in parts of the United States.

**DESCRIPTION:** Scarlet flax grows to 2½ feet tall on slender, branched stems with narrow leaves. The round flowers, up to 1½ inches in diameter, have five broad petals. The primary color is red, which is featured in many shades.

**EASY-CARE GROWING:** Grow scarlet flax in full sun in any garden soil, preferably somewhat low in fertility. They perform best in cooler climates. Plants will tolerate mild frosts; in colder climates you can plant them in the fall for late spring bloom. Otherwise, sow in place as soon as the ground can be worked in the spring. Space 4 to 6 inches apart. Water during dry spells. Each plant blooms approximately 4 to 6 weeks. For all-season display, reseed at 4- to 6-week intervals.

**PROPAGATION:** By seed. For earliest bloom in most locations, start seeds indoors 6 weeks prior to outdoor planting. Grow in peat pots to aid in transplanting. Seed germination takes 5 to 12 days at 60 to 70°F.

**USES:** Scarlet flax is a good addition to wildflower or meadow gardens. Grow it in clumps in borders or beds and in mixed plantings such as cottage gardens. Plant it also in rock gardens.

**RELATED SPECIES:** *Linum perenne* is a hardy perennial with blue flowers.

**RELATED VARIETIES:** 'Rubrum' has deep-red flowers. 'Bright Eyes' is ivory white with chocolate-brown eyes. 'Caeruleum' has blue-purple flowers.

# SCARLET RUNNER BEAN
*Phaseolus coccineus*

In many parts of the world—especially in England and France—the scarlet runner bean is cultivated both as an ornamental and a vegetable. Until recently, the United States has embraced only its ornamental qualities. The lush, thick vines produce clusters of red flowers that are followed by the edible green beans. The Dutch runner bean, *P. c. alba,* has white flowers.

**DESCRIPTION:** Scarlet runner beans are quick-growing vines with typical, three-leaflet bean leaves. They grow 6 to 8 feet tall. The bean flowers are borne in clusters like sweet peas. The edible pods that follow are long, slender, green beans.

**EASY-CARE GROWING:** Scarlet runner beans need fertile soil and adequate moisture in full sun. Plant them where they can grow up some kind of support. The bean vines don't need to be tied—they twine around posts or poles. For covering fences, provide some kind of twine or netting for the beans to climb. If allowed to grow over the ground, they will form a tangled mass of leaves, and the flowers will be hidden.

**PROPAGATION:** By seed. Plant the large seeds directly in the ground after danger of frost has passed and the soil is warm. Plant seeds about 3 inches away from fences or posts, spacing them 2 to 3 inches apart. Thin the seedlings to a spacing of 6 to 8 inches. Seeds germinate in 5 to 10 days.

**USES:** These quick-growing vines are beautiful when trained up posts, arches, pergolas, or arbors. They make quick-growing screens to break up the garden.

**RELATED VARIETIES:** 'Lady Di' has tender, slim, 12-inch long pods. 'Musica' has wide, flat, stringless pods.

# SCAVEOLA, FAIRY FAN-FLOWER
## *Scaveola aemula*

Scaveola is a tender perennial from eastern Australia. Although it is a relative newcomer to American gardens, scaveola is rapidly gaining converts as a beautifully flowering cascader for hanging baskets and mixed containers.

**DESCRIPTION:** Scaveola has rounded basal leaves and narrower stem leaves on prostrate stems that reach only 6 to 8 inches high but grow 2 or more feet long. Blue or purple-blue flowers, shaped like folding, hand-held fans, emerge abundantly along the stems.

**EASY-CARE GROWING:** Provide full sun and rich, well-drained garden soil. For potted plants, use an enriched, peat-based potting mix. Plant 8 inches apart. Keep containers evenly moist but allow garden beds to dry out slightly before watering again. Use a fertilizer rich in nitrogen and lacking phosphate (which can damage this plant), every few weeks. Scaveola, particularly 'New Wonder,' can survive temperatures into the low 100s and down to freezing.

**PROPAGATION:** By cuttings. Take softwood cuttings in late spring.

**USES:** Let scaveola fill out an entire hanging basket with foliage and flowers or mingle it with other annuals in a mixed planter. You also can allow it to creep across the front of a garden like a ground cover or cascade over a retaining wall.

**RELATED VARIETIES:** 'New Wonder' is a popular, floriferous new variety. 'Blue Wonder,' an old standard, can produce stems 5 feet long.

# SNAPDRAGON
*Antirrhinum majus*

Children love snapdragons because they can snap open the flowers. Garden designers and flower arrangers cherish their columnar stateliness. Snapdragons endure cool weather and are widely planted for winter color in mild-winter areas.

**DESCRIPTION:** Snapdragons uniformly bear a whorl of flowers atop slender stalks. The best known are ones with snappable flowers, but new kinds have open-faced flowers including double forms. Colors include white, yellow, burgundy, red, pink, orange, and bronze.

**EASY-CARE GROWING:** Plant in rich, well-drained soil with a high level of organic matter. Grow in full sun, fertilize monthly, and water moderately. Space tall varieties 12 inches apart, small varieties 6 inches apart. Pinch tips of young plants to encourage branching. Tall varieties may need staking. After first bloom is finished, pinch off flower spikes to induce new growth and repeat flowering. For cool season bloom in Zones 9 and 10, plant in September.

**PROPAGATION:** By seed. Germination takes an average of 8 days at 70°F soil temperature. Keep seeds moist, but do not cover, since light is required for germination. For early bloom, sow seeds indoors 6 to 8 weeks before setting outdoors after last frost. You also can sow snapdragons directly in the garden 6 weeks prior to the last frost when soil is friable (workable).

**USES:** Use the tall varieties for the back of the floral border and for cut flowers. Short varieties are good in borders and as edgings for beds. All varieties can be used in containers.

**RELATED VARIETIES:** Tall snapdragons include the Rocket Series and open-faced 'Double Madam Butterfly,' which has improved basal branching. Medium varieties, up to 18 inches, include 'Princess White with a Purple Eye,' which will bloom all summer without special attention, and 'Black Prince' with bronze foliage and crimson flowers. Among dwarf snapdragons, the Bell Series have open flower forms and are particularly heat tolerant. The 8-inch-high Tahiti Series are rust-resistant and flower in rose, bronze, red, orange, and pink and white.

# SNOW-IN-SUMMER, GHOST WEED
### *Euphorbia marginata*

This annual is a native of the eastern United States. The names "snow-in-summer" and "ghost weed" come from the white, variegated margins on the edges of leaves. The sap can be irritating.

**DESCRIPTION:** Snow-in-summer grows rapidly from seedling stage, branching to a small bush 1 to 3 feet tall. The lower leaves are virtually all green, but progressively toward the top, more white appears on leaf edges. When flowering begins, the top leaves are mostly white. The real flowers are tiny, the color coming from the modified leaves called bracts.

**EASY-CARE GROWING:** Snow-in-summer grows well anywhere in full sun—from cool, moist locations to dry, rocky places. It reseeds vigorously. Space plants 12 inches apart.

**PROPAGATION:** By seed. Sow seeds outdoors after danger of frost has passed. Thin to desired spacing. Or start indoors 7 to 8 weeks prior to planting out. Seeds germinate in 10 to 15 days at 70 to 75°F.

**USES:** Plant large drifts anywhere you want the green-white combination to cool the landscape. Snow-in-summer also makes a nice border or temporary hedge for pathways and sidewalks.

**RELATED SPECIES:** *Euphorbia cyanthophora* (syn. *E. heterophylla*), "summer poinsettia," has bright red bracts about 4 inches in diameter on plants 2 feet tall. It is also called "Mexican fire plant," "painted leaf," and "fire-on-the-mountain." *Euphorbia lathyrus,* with the common name of "mole plant" or "gopher plant," is often planted because it is supposed to keep moles away, a hotly disputed claim. "Caper spurge" is a handsome perennial in areas with mild winters and grows up to 5 feet tall with long, narrow leaves.

**RELATED VARIETIES:** 'Summer Icicle' is a dwarf form growing to 2 feet tall.

# STATICE, SEA LAVENDER
## *Limonium sinuatum*

Many flowers that are good for cutting and drying end up with the common name of statice, which can get confusing when you are trying to order one particular type. Fortunately, you can rely on the botanical name to make some sense of this diversity.

**DESCRIPTION:** Statice *(L. sinuatum)* is a tender perennial with upright sprays of small flowers enclosed in papery calyces, which last for days as a freshly cut flower and for months when dried. They come in bright or pastel shades of yellow, pink, purple, blue, orange, red, and white. The plants have clusters of basal leaves and winged stems. They grow from 12 to 30 inches high.

**EASY-CARE GROWING:** Provide full sun and well-drained soil of moderate fertility. Set seedlings outdoors after the danger of frost passes and the soil is warm. Plant 12 to 15 inches apart. Once established, statice can withstand some drought. Cut the flowers when blooms are at least three-quarters open. Air dry them upside down in the dark.

**PROPAGATION:** By seed. Sow directly in place after the last spring frost in warm climates or, for earlier bloom, plant seeds 8 to 10 weeks before the last spring frost date. Seeds will germinate in 14 to 21 days at 65 to 75°F.

**USES:** Statice are naturals in a cut flower garden. You also can use them for upright accents in mixed flower gardens and for attracting butterflies.

**RELATED SPECIES:** *L. latifolium*, sea lavender, is a hardy perennial with airy plumes of everlasting, lavender-blue flowers. *Psylliostachys suworowii* (syn. *L. suworowii*) has long, branching spikes of small, everlasting flowers.

**RELATED VARIETIES:** 'Art Shades' has a handsome blend of orange, salmon-pink, yellow, red, rose-pink, carmine, white, lavender-blue, and blue flowers. 'Petite Bouquet Mix,' used for bedding, gets only 12 inches tall. The Soiree Series grow to 2 feet high. 'Sunset' focuses on warm shades of orange, apricot, peach, and rose and grows to 30 inches tall.

# STOCK
## *Matthiola incana*

Stock is appreciated for its cool, distinctive colors and exceptional fragrance in cool season gardens. In mild winter regions, it's grown as a winter or early spring annual for bloom before the weather gets torrid. In maritime or cool mountain climates, it's good for late spring or summer flowering.

**DESCRIPTION:** Most stock varieties have become well-bred doubles, an upgrade from their wild, single nature. Modern varieties vary in height from 12 to 30 inches and they all sport rather stiff columns surrounded by flowers. The flowers come in pink, white, red, rose, purple, and lavender.

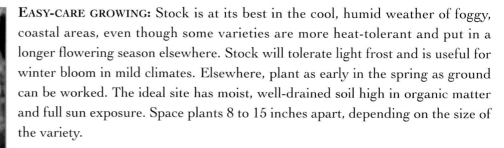

**EASY-CARE GROWING:** Stock is at its best in the cool, humid weather of foggy, coastal areas, even though some varieties are more heat-tolerant and put in a longer flowering season elsewhere. Stock will tolerate light frost and is useful for winter bloom in mild climates. Elsewhere, plant as early in the spring as ground can be worked. The ideal site has moist, well-drained soil high in organic matter and full sun exposure. Space plants 8 to 15 inches apart, depending on the size of the variety.

**PROPAGATION:** By seed. For winter use in mild climates, sow stock in the fall. In other locales, sow seeds indoors 6 to 8 weeks prior to when ground can first be worked in spring. Seeds germinate in 7 to 10 days at 70°F. Don't cover the seeds; they need light to germinate. A percentage of seedlings are singles. Doubles are usually the most vigorous seedlings and are lighter in color than the singles.

**USES:** Stock is best suited to formal beds. Plant where the fragrance reaches passersby—near walks and doorsteps. They're also adaptable to containers—combine them with informal flowers to break up the rigidity. They're also superb cut flowers, with the scent pervading an entire room.

**RELATED SPECIES:** *Matthiola longipetala* subsp. *bicornis* has a particularly strong scent at night; the daytime flowers are unexceptional, so plant them discreetly.

**RELATED VARIETIES:** The compact Cinderella Series flower in colors such as carmine, dark blue, lavender, pink, and white and grow to 10 inches high. These plants are graced with improved basal branching. Dwarf 'Trysomic Seven Week' stock is the earliest bloomer and is more tolerant of heat. 'Appleblossom' has double flowers blending pink and white and grows to 12 inches high.

# STRAWFLOWER
### *Helichrysum bracteatum*

The beauty of annual flowers can linger on in your house even when the garden is covered with snow. The trick is to grow everlastings that dry easily and look good in dried flower arrangements for months afterwards. Among the easiest everlastings to grow are strawflowers.

**DESCRIPTION:** These double, daisy-shaped flowers grow on compact plants 10 to 36 inches tall. The flowers come in a wide range of colors: white, yellow, orange, pink, crimson, bronze, purple, salmon, and pastel tones. They are composed of tiny florets and stiff bracts with the texture of straw, hence the name "strawflower."

**EASY-CARE GROWING:** Provide full sun and well-drained soil of moderate fertility. Plant seedlings out after the last spring frost passes, spacing them about 12 inches apart. Strawflowers can tolerate some drought once established. They must have a long season of growth to develop the flowers before fall. Cut for drying before the yellow centers are visible; use wire stems. Air dry upside down in the dark.

**PROPAGATION:** By seed and cuttings. Most varieties grow from seed, sown outdoors after the last frost or started indoors 4 to 6 weeks earlier. Leave seeds uncovered as they need light to germinate. At 70 to 75°F, they will germinate in 7 to 10 days.

**USES:** You can blend strawflowers into an annual bed, but may find that the mixed colors make a somewhat chaotic display. Pastels and flowers of a single color are more eye-appealing. Move the color mixes to the cut flower garden.

**RELATED SPECIES:** *Xeranthemum annuum*, also known as "immortelles," grow from 18 to 24 inches tall and have single or double flowers. Flowers are harmonious white, pink, rose, violet, and purple.

**RELATED VARIETIES:** 'Bright Bikini Mix,' with vivid, double flowers of red, yellow, hot pink, and white, grow to 12 inches high. The pastel-colored King Size Series includes 'Frosted Sulphur,' 'New Rose,' 'Silvery Rose,' and 'Silvery White.' 'Golden Beauty,' sold under the Proven Winner's brand, is propagated by cuttings instead of seeds. The Monstrosum Series grow to 30 inches tall and have large flowers to 2½ inches wide.

# SUNFLOWER
## *Helianthus annuus*

Whether giants of the garden at 15 feet tall or barely topping 1 foot, these natives of North America come in a variety of colors and forms. *Helios* is the Greek word for "sun."

**DESCRIPTION:** Typically growing from 10 to 15 feet tall, sunflowers have coarse leaves and flower heads up to 1 foot or more in diameter. Although they started out as yellow flowers with brown or purple centers, there are now variations with magenta, white, and orange flowers and still others that are fluffy doubles.

**EASY-CARE GROWING:** Sunflowers prefer full sun and will grow in any soil, except one that is light and well-drained. They're very tolerant of heat and drought. The tall varieties may need staking to prevent the wind from toppling them. Plant the tall varieties 12 to 18 inches apart; dwarf ones at 9- to 12-inch spacing.

**PROPAGATION:** By seed. Sow sunflower seeds outdoors after final frost. However, for earlier bloom, start indoors 4 to 8 weeks ahead. Seeds germinate in 10 to 20 days at 70 to 85°F.

**USES:** The dwarf kinds can be used in beds and borders, while the taller varieties are best at the back of the border. They can be used as a screen or as a clump at the end of driveways or along fences. The smaller-flowered varieties can also be used as cut flowers.

**RELATED SPECIES:** *Helianthus debilis*, which are particularly popular to grow for cut flowers, stretches 4 to 5 feet tall with long, branched stems of smaller yellow or creamy white flowers.

**RELATED VARIETIES:** 'Sunspot' has 8 to 12 inch blooms on plants only 18 to 24 inches high. 'Teddy Bear' has novel double, golden flowers 3 to 5 inches across on plants 2½ to 3½ feet high. 'Autumn Beauty' has 6-inch-wide flower heads of mahogany, yellow, golden, or red florets on 5-foot stems.

# SWEET PEA
*Lathyrus odoratus*

In cool, maritime or mountain climates, sweet peas will flower all summer. In Zones 9 and 10, they're best in cool seasons: winter and early spring. Natives of Italy, the original purple or white flowers now come in many hues.

**DESCRIPTION:** Sweet peas are vining plants that climb vigorously 6 to 8 feet over fences and other supports. Some cultivars are much more compact and need only branched twigs for support or can be pinched to remain bushy and self-supporting. The flowers are pink, white, red, lavender, purple, and almost (but not quite) blue.

**EASY-CARE GROWING:** In mild winter areas, sow seeds outdoors in the fall. Elsewhere, plant as soon as ground can be worked in spring. Sweet peas need full sun and a deep, rich soil. Dig a trench and fill with fertilizer and humus-rich soil. When seeds are up, mulch thoroughly to keep soil cool. When seedlings are 4 inches high, pinch the tips to develop strong side branches. Provide support for taller types to climb. Keep sweet pea blossoms picked in order to ensure continuous flowering.

**PROPAGATION:** By seed. Nick seed coats with a knife and soak seeds overnight in water. Before planting, treat with a culture of nitrogen-fixing bacteria available at garden stores. For earliest plants, start in peat pots 4 to 6 weeks before planting outside. Plant pot and all. Seeds germinate in 10 to 14 days at 55 to 65°F.

**USES:** Grow them against fences, over trellises, arches, and pergolas. Plant them on a tepee composed of stakes in the center or at the back of the bed. The dwarf varieties can be planted in the border. As cut flowers, sweet peas are superb.

**RELATED VARIETIES:** 'Giant Late Heat-Resistant Mix,' growing to 6 feet in height, flower after earlier types and withstand more heat. Tendril-free 'Explorer Mix,' an award winner, grows into bushes 2 feet high with blue, pink, red, purple, and white flowers. 'Winter Elegance Mix,' available in rose, salmon, white, lavender, pale pink, and scarlet, thrives during the short days of winter and early spring in warm climates.

# DECORATIVE SWEET POTATO

*Ipomoea batatas*

The sweet potato has broken free from the vegetable garden with colored leaf forms that are perfect for vining out of containers or stretching as ground covers across the front of a flower bed.

**DESCRIPTION:** Sweet potatoes grow into ground-hugging vines that can reach 5 feet long. The lobed leaves are at once graceful and dynamic, especially when you plant purple and golden-leaved forms.

**EASY-CARE GROWING:** Plant rooted cuttings in sun or light shade as soon as warm, frost-free, summer weather arrives. Provide rich, moist but well-drained soil—in a large pot or garden bed. Keep the soil moist and fertilize lightly. Plant sweet potatoes about 1 foot apart in garden beds or blend them with other plants in mixed containers.

**PROPAGATION:** By softwood cuttings or with small tubers.

**USES:** The dark purple foliage of 'Blackie' looks good with purple, pink, and blue flowers. Chartreuse forms are ideal for warm-colored annual flowers.

**RELATED VARIETIES:** 'Blackie' has purple leaves so dark that they appear black.

# TITHONIA, MEXICAN SUNFLOWER, GOLDEN FLOWER OF THE INCAS

## *Tithonia rotundifolia*

Tithonia, along with sunflowers, are the largest, most dramatic annuals for the garden. Some varieties can grow up to 8 feet tall. A native of Mexico and southward, its area of origin is the reason for the common names. A member of the daisy family, tithonia is also related to the sunflower.

**DESCRIPTION:** Tithonias have rough, hairy leaves on tall, vigorous plants. Shorter varieties are now available that will stay approximately 3 feet tall. The flowers are single and up to 3 inches in diameter. The color is usually a deep orange-red, even though there is a variety available now with chrome-yellow flowers.

**EASY-CARE GROWING:** Tithonia must have full sun, but it will grow in average soil with good drainage. It is one of the most heat- and drought-resistant plants, growing reasonably well in soils of low fertility. Plant in the garden after all danger of frost has passed. Space plants 2½ to 3 feet apart. Do not overwater. Protect the plants from high winds and stake them—this is particularly important in late summer and fall when they are tall and top-heavy. To avoid staking, choose naturally compact plants.

**PROPAGATION:** By seed. Seeds may be sown outdoors; for earlier flowering, start them indoors 6 to 8 weeks before the last frost. Seeds germinate in 7 to 21 days at 70°F.

**USES:** Its size and the coarseness of the foliage dictate planting it at the back of the border. The color is so intense that it only takes a few plants for impact. Tithonia is also useful for covering fences and shielding background eyesores in the garden. Tithonias attract butterflies and make good cut flowers as long as the hollow stems are seared after cutting by plunging them into 100°F water.

**RELATED VARIETIES:** 'Torch' is a medal winner that grows 4 to 6 feet tall, bearing the classic, deep orange-red flowers. 'Aztec Sun' has golden-yellow flowers and stays at 4 feet tall. Orange-flowered 'Goldfinger' can stay as low as 30 inches.

# TORENIA, WISHBONE FLOWER
*Torenia fournieri*

Torenia is a colorful, modest-sized plant that thrives in shade and hot, humid weather as a result of its original habitat in Vietnam. The common name comes from the two yellow stamens that arch over the center of the petals.

**DESCRIPTION:** Torenia forms a compact, well-branched mound about 1 foot high. Leaves are oval or heart-shaped. The flowers look a bit like open-faced snapdragons with prominent markings on the petals.

The most predominant color in the past was blue, but new varieties are pink, violet, rose, light blue, and white. Most have yellow throats and some may have deep blue or purple markings.

**EASY-CARE GROWING:** Torenias grow best in rich, moist, well-drained soil. They're widely used in frost-free areas for winter and spring display. Elsewhere, you can plant them in partial shade for summer bloom. They like high humidity and won't tolerate being dry. Plant outdoors after all danger of frost has passed. Space 6 to 8 inches apart.

**PROPAGATION:** By seed and cuttings. Sow torenia seeds 10 to 12 weeks prior to outdoor planting. The seeds are tiny; they are more easily sown evenly if mixed with a pinch of sand before sowing. Germination takes 7 to 15 days at 70°F. 'Summer Wave' is propagated by cuttings.

**USES:** Torenia is a good addition to a semi-shade garden, where it can bloom profusely. Plant torenia in groups of three or more in woodland bowers; grow clumps along paths or walkways. Because it grows evenly, it's a good candidate for formal beds in sun or partial shade. Torenia is well-adapted to containers.

**RELATED VARIETIES:** The Clown Series have flowers of blue, light blue, blush, rose-pink, burgundy, plum, rose, violet, and white on compact, self-branching plants 8 to 10 inches high. 'Summer Wave' is a trailing plant with bicolored light and dark blue flowers.

# MOSS VERBENA
## *Verbena tenuisecta*

Ground-covering annuals with bright flowers and handsome foliage make carpets of changeable color and are particularly in demand. Moss verbena, with its divided, lacy foliage and attractive clusters of small flowers, is one of the best. Native to South America, moss verbena grows vigorously in the southeastern United States.

**DESCRIPTION:** Moss verbena reaches about 1 foot high and often spreads wider. The leaves are divided into linear leaflets and the purple, white, or blue flowers cluster in headlike spikes.

**EASY-CARE GROWING:** Provide well-drained soil in sun, watering during dry weather until the plant is growing strongly. After this point, moss verbena can tolerate drought. Space plants 12 to 18 inches apart.

**PROPAGATION:** By seed or by cuttings. Verbenas are slow in the early stages. Sow seeds 12 to 14 weeks prior to planting in the garden. Cover the seeds; they need darkness to germinate. They are also sensitive to excessive dampness. Wet the seed flat 24 hours before sowing, sow the seeds without watering, and cover with black plastic until germination. Germination takes 10 to 20 days at 75 to 80°F.

**USES:** Moss verbena makes a handsome ground cover in dry, sunny areas, and even in tough areas such as a rocky bank. It excels in containers, window boxes, and hanging baskets, planted alone or mixed with more upright flowers.

**RELATED SPECIES:** *V. bonariensis*, a tender perennial, acts like an annual. It produces upright masses of lavender flowers, 3 to 4 feet high. *V. canadensis*, a hardy perennial, has rose-purple flowers, grows to 14 inches high, and is tolerant of mildew.

**RELATED VARIETIES:** 'Imagination,' an award winner sometimes listed as *V. hybrida* or *V. speciosa*, has violet-blue flowers and grows to 1 foot high and 2 feet wide. 'Sterling Star' is a slightly larger version of 'Imagination,' reaching to 16 inches high and to 2½ feet wide. 'Alba' is a white-flowered form that grows to 6 inches high. The patented Tapien hybrids, which are resistant to mildew, come in varying shades of pink, lavender, purple, and even pastel powder blue.

# Vinca, Madagascar Periwinkle
*Catharanthus roseus*

These tropical plants, native to Madagascar, stand up well to heat and humidity. Vinca was long used in folk medicine where it was found to contain cancer-fighting agents. Vinca has even been refined for use in modern medicine.

**DESCRIPTION:** Flowers are round, 1 to 2 inches in diameter, and borne at the tips of branches or shoots that bear glossy, green leaves. The flowers of many varieties are pink, white, or rose, often with a contrasting eye in the center of the bloom. You can grow two forms: somewhat erect types that develop into moundlike bushes and are the subject of much contemporary plant breeding, and also virtually recumbent trailers.

**EASY-CARE GROWING:** Vinca is at its best in hot conditions—full sun, heat, and high humidity. Grow in warm, rich, well-drained soil. Avoid overwatering to prevent soil-borne diseases. Plant bush types 8 to 12 inches apart; trailing types 12 to 15 inches apart. Avoid planting outdoors before soil is warm.

**PROPAGATION:** By seed. Sow seeds 12 weeks prior to setting out after last frost. Germination takes 14 to 21 days at a temperature above 70°F. Maintain warm temperatures after germination and be careful not to overwater.

**USES:** Trailing types make colorful ground covers, good container companions, and handsome edging plants. More upright plants can either back up trailers in the border or combine with other plants in pots or beds. Their heat tolerance makes them ideal for challenging locations.

**RELATED VARIETIES:** New colors are slowly arriving in the form of 'Apricot Delight,' a pastel apricot-pink flower with a raspberry eye growing on naturally basal branching upright plants. You can find extra large flowers, over 2 inches wide, on award winning 'Parasol,' which is white with a red eye, and 'Cooler Icy Pink.' The Pretty Series, in red, pink, and white, are particularly long blooming and grow 12 to 14 inches high.

# VIOLA, JOHNNY JUMP-UP, WILD PANSY
## *Viola tricolor* and *V. cornata*

These charming, petite bloomers for spring, fall, or even winter (in warm climates) resemble both violets and pansies, to which they are related. They are cute enough to mix in any spring pot but also bright enough for massing in spring bedding.

**DESCRIPTION:** Johnny jump-up, *Viola tricolor*, is an old-fashioned plant grown as a hardy annual, biennial, or briefly lived perennial. It blooms heavily in spring, producing purple, yellow, and white flowers. It often flowers again in summer or fall. The mound-shaped plants get to be 8 inches high. *V. cornata* is a tender perennial originally from Spain that grows to 6 inches high and over twice as wide and bears purple flowers, with an expanded color range of varieties available.

**EASY-CARE GROWING:** It is best to provide violas with well-drained but moist and fertile soil in either sun or shade. You can plant violas outdoors when spring weather becomes mild, spacing seedlings 6 to 12 inches apart.

**PROPAGATION:** By seed. These sprout in 7 to 14 days at 65 to 75°F. Johnny jump-ups freely self-seed, a clue to where it got its name. Sow seeds directly in early spring or fall. In cool climates, prestart seedlings indoors 10 to 12 weeks before the final frost.

**USES:** Let violas and small spring bulbs sweep across the front of a spring garden. Showcase them in pots or rock gardens or use them to edge an edible-ornamental garden.

**RELATED VARIETIES:** *Viola cornata* 'Arkwright Ruby' is a fragrant crimson and 'Chantryland' is apricot. The Princess Series comes in blue, cream, purple, lavender, and purple and yellow while the extra hardy Sorbet Series feature bicolors of purple and cream, light blue and cream, yellow and gold, dark and light purple, and blue and yellow. *V. tricolor* 'Bowles Black' have dark flowers with a yellow eye. 'Helen Mount' has extra large, yellow-and violet-faced flowers, 'Prince John' is a clear yellow, and 'Twilight' is dark blue and white.

# Hybrid Garden Zinnia
## *Zinnia elegans*

Zinnias are among the favorite American garden flowers, loved for their variety of colors, which ranges from bold and brassy to muted pastels. They often are troubled by mildew, however, which limits their life span in humid climates. The solution to this problem is as close as *Zinnia haageana* (see page 188) and its hybrids with *Z. elegans*.

**DESCRIPTION:** Zinnias are generally grouped into three classes: tall (up to 2½ feet), intermediate (up to 20 inches), and dwarf (up to 12 inches). Leaves and stems are coarse and rough like sandpaper, while the flowers bloom in almost every color except blue.

**EASY-CARE GROWING:** Zinnias need full sun and rich, fertile soil high in organic matter. They're best in hot, dry climates and are likely to suffer from powdery mildew when the humidity rises. To minimize problems, try to avoid watering from above and plant where there is good air movement. Plant zinnia seeds or seedlings after the final frost when the soil is warm. Space 6 to 12 inches apart, depending on the size of the variety.

**PROPAGATION:** By seed. Zinnias grow fast, and early bloom can be achieved in most climates by sowing seeds directly into the soil. For earlier bloom, sow seeds indoors 4 weeks prior to planting out. Seeds germinate in 5 to 7 days at 70 to 75°F. As zinnias can be reluctant transplanters, start seeds in peat pots to plant directly in the garden.

**USES:** Use dwarf and intermediate varieties in beds and borders or in container plantings. Move taller varieties to the back of the border or the cutting garden. Zinnias make good cut flowers.

**Related varieties:** Among tall zinnias, the double, early Ruffles Series have some disease resistance. 'Cherry Ruffles,' 'Yellow Ruffles,' and 'Pink Ruffles' are all award winners. Unique, tall varieties include 'Candy Stripe,' with 4-inch-wide white flowers splashed with pink and red. It grows to 2 feet and is self-branching. 'Big Red Hybrid,' which lives up to its name, bears flowers to 6 inches across on 3-foot-high plants. Among the medium varieties try the Border Beauty Series, which come in separate colors and a mix. Dwarf varieties include The Peter Pan Series, hybrids with large flowers in cream, gold, pink, scarlet, flame, orange, plum, and white on short, 10 to 12 inch stems. 'Thumbelina Mix' are tiny plants with miniature flowers while 'Lilliput Mix' have small flowers on taller plants to 18 inches high.

**Disease resistant zinnia hybrids:** New 'Profusion Cherry' and 'Profusion Orange,' hybrids between *Z. elegans* and *Z. haageana*, combine the disease resistance of the Mexican zinnia with the flashy, albeit single, flowers of garden zinnias. The older Pinwheel Series produces an abundance of single flowers in rose, salmon, and white. Both Series grow 12 inches tall.

# MEXICAN ZINNIA, SPREADING ZINNIA

## *Zinnia haageana* (syn. *Z. angustifolia*)

When you want the bright color of zinnias but don't want disappointing losses from powdery mildew that often strikes hybrid garden zinnias, this charmer is for you. It is native to the southeastern United States and, as you might guess, Mexico, and thrives in hot weather.

**DESCRIPTION:** Mexican zinnia can grow upright to 24 inches high and bears golden, orange, or red flowers that cover the plant all season and look a little like marigolds. Some varieties, such as 'Persian Carpet' and 'Orange Star,' grow more prostrate to about 8 inches high. All members of this species are untroubled by powdery mildew.

**EASY-CARE GROWING:** Plant in well-drained soil of moderate fertility in full sun. Mexican zinnias also thrive in containers filled with enriched, peat-based potting mix. Plant seedlings 8 to 12 inches apart after the final spring frost.

**PROPAGATION:** By seed. You can sow Mexican zinnia seeds directly into the soil. However, for earlier bloom, sow seeds in peat pots indoors 8 to 10 weeks prior to planting out. Seeds germinate in 5 to 7 days at 70 to 75°F.

**USES:** Use Mexican zinnias in sun-drenched pots or in the front of an annual or mixed flower garden. They are wonderful for cutting and drying and therefore deserve a place in the cut flower garden.

**RELATED VARIETIES:** 'Star Gold' has golden flowers. 'Crystal White,' an award winner, has white flowers. 'Golden Orange' has golden orange florets with a lighter lemon stripe. Dwarf 'Persian Carpet' has multicolored double flowers.

# INDEX

## A

Abelmoschus. *See* Musk mallow.
*Abelmoschus moschatus. See* Musk
　mallow.
*Acer palmatum dissectum. See* Maple,
　Japanese.
African daisy. *See* Golden ageratum.
Ageratum *(Ageratum houstonianum)*, 14,
　20, 24, 31, 39, 43, 52, 84
　'Blue Hawaii,' 14
　'Blue Horizon,' 13
*Ageratum houstonianum. See*
　Ageratum.
*Agryanthemum frutescens. See* Cobbity
　daisies.
*Allium cepa. See* Onion, bulbing.
*Allium schoenoprasum. See* Chives.
*Alluim sativum. See* Garlic.
Alyssum. *See* Sweet alyssum.
Amaranth. *See* Globe amaranth.
*Amaranthus caudatus. See* Love lies
　bleeding.
*Amaranthus cruentus. See* Prince's
　feather.
*Amaranthus tricolor. See* Love lies
　bleeding.
*Anethum graveolens. See* Dill.
Animals. *See* Insects and diseases.
Annual delphinium. *See* Larkspur.
Annuals
　cool season, 50–51
　defined, 8
　easy-care characteristics, 9–13
　growing conditions for, 14–15
　selecting, 17–19, 61–62
*Antirrhinum majus. See* Snapdragon.
*Asparagus densiflorus. See* Asparagus
　fern.
Asparagus fern *(Asparagus densiflorus)*,
　43, 52, 81, 87

## B

Baby's breath *(Gypsophila elegans)*, 20, 81
　'Gypsy,' 88
Bachelor's button *(Centaurea cyanus)*,
　20, 31, 39, 73, 89
Bacillus thuringiensis, 75, 76
Basal branching, 11–12
Basil *(Ocimum basilicum)*, 9, 19, 81, 92
　'Aussie Sweetie,' 19

Beans. *See* Castor bean; Scarlet runner
　bean.
Bedding masses, 24–26
Beefsteak plant. *See* Perilla.
Begonia, wax, fibrous, everblooming
　*(Begonia semperflorens)*, 14, 20, 39, 43,
　52, 59, 73, 93–94
Begonia, tuberous *(Begonia tuber-
　hybrida)*, 13, 20, 39, 43, 52, 73, 95–96
*Begonia semperflorens. See* Begonia, wax,
　fibrous, everblooming.
*Begonia tuberhybrida. See* Begonia,
　tuberous.
*Bellis perennis. See* Daisy, English.
Bells of Ireland *(Molucella laevis)*, 43, 97
Black-eyed Susan *(Rudbeckia hirta)*, 15,
　20, 39, 43, 81, 98
Black-eyed Susan vine *(Thunbergia
　alata)*, 99
Blanket flower *(Gaillardia pulchella)*, 20,
　39, 43, 58, 81, 100
　*(Galliarda* x *grandiflora)*, 81
Bleeding heart *(Dicentra)*, 81
*Brassica oleracea acephala. See* Kale,
　flowering or ornamental.
*Brassica oleracea capitata. See* Cabbage,
　flowering or ornamental.
Bridal wreath *(Spiraea* x *vanhouttei)*, 81
Browallia *(Browallia speciosa)*, 20, 39,
　43, 101
*Browallia speciosa. See* Browallia.
Burpee & Co., 52

## C

Cabbage, flowering or ornamental
　*(Brassica oleracea capitata)*, 39, 73,
　102
Caladium hortulanum *(Caladium
　hortulanum)*, 14, 20, 39, 43, 103
Calendula *(Calendula officinalis)*, 13, 20,
　31, 43, 51, 104
*Calendula officinalis. See* Calendula.
Calla lily, 14
Calliopsis *(Coreopsis tinctoria)*, 20, 29,
　43, 105
Candytuft *(Iberis* hybrids), 14, 20, 39,
　43, 52, 81, 106
Canna *(Canna* hybrids), 13, 20, 31, 39,
　43, 107
　'Brandywine,' 13

*Capsicum* species. *See* Peppers, orna-
　mental.
Castor bean *(Ricinus communis)*, 19, 20,
　39, 58, 108
*Catharanthus roseus. See* Vinca.
*Celosia cristata* v. *plumosa. See*
　Cockscomb, plumed.
*Centaurea cyanus. See* Bachelor's button.
*Chamaemelum nobile. See* Chamomile.
Chamomile *(Chamaemelum nobile)*, 81
Cherry pie. *See* Heliotrope.
China pink *(Dianthus chinensis)*, 20, 24,
　43, 73, 109
Chives *(Allium schoenoprasum)*, 81
Chrysanthemum *(Leucanthemum
　* hybrids), 11, 20, 31, 39, 43, 110
*Chrysanthemum ptarmiciflorum. See*
　Dusty miller.
*Cineraraia maritima. See* Dusty miller.
Cleome *(Cleome hasslerana)*, 20, 39, 43,
　52, 111
　'Royal Queen,' 22
*Cleome hasslerana. See* Cleome.
Clock vine. *See* Black-eyed Susan vine.
Cobbity daisies *(Agryanthemum
　frutescens)*, 20, 31, 59, 112
Cockscomb, plumed *(Celosia cristata* v.
　*plumosa)*, 20, 31, 33, 39, 43, 73, 80,
　113
　'Forest Fire,' 33
Cold tolerance, 11
Coleus *(Solenostemon scutellaroides)*,
　14–15, 19, 20, 24, 39, 43, 52, 59, 80,
　114
　'Burgundy Sun,' 25
*Coleus* x *hybrida. See* Coleus.
Color
　massing, 24–26
　planning with, 19–21
Compost. *See* Organic fertilizer.
Coneflower. *See* Black-eyed Susan.
*Consolida ambigua. See* Larkspur.
Container gardening, 26–28, 42
*Coreopsis tinctoria. See* Calliopsis.
Cornflower. *See* Bachelor's button.
*Cosmos bipinnatus. See* Cosmos.
Cosmos *(Cosmos bipinnatus)*, 14, 20, 39,
　43, 58, 115
Cottage gardens, 30–31, 80, 81
Creeping zinnia. *See* Sanvitalia.

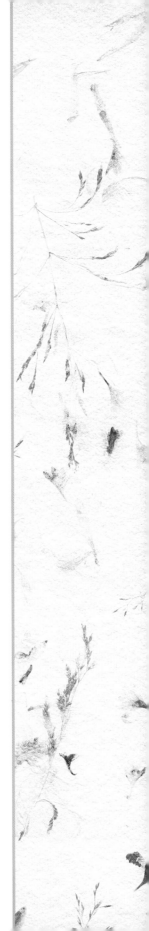

*Cucumis peop* v. *oviferis*. *See* Gourds, ornamental.
Cup flower. *See* Nierembergia.
Cut flowers, 31–33
Cutting back, 72
Cuttings, propogation from, 59–61

## D

Dahlia (*Dahlia* hybrids), 20, 39, 43, 52, 116–117
Daisy, English (*Bellis perennis*), 20, 39, 43, 121
Daylily (*Hemerocallis*), 81
Deadheading, 9, 13, 28, 71–72
Design, garden, 22–24, 80–81
Devil in a bush. *See* Love-in-a-mist.
Dianthus. *See* China pink.
*Dianthus chinensis*. *See* China pink.
Diatomaceous earth, 77
*Dicentra*. *See* Bleeding heart.
*Digitalis purpurea*. *See* Foxglove.
Dill (*Anethum graveolens*), 20, 43, 81, 118
Disease resistance, 10–11
Diseases. *See* Insects and diseases.
Dishrag gourd. *See* Gourds, ornamental.
Dolichos, 19
Dracaena (*Dracaena* species), 20, 39, 119
Drip irrigation, 69–70
Drying flowers, 33–36
Dusty miller (*Senecio cineraria, Tanacetum ptarmiciflorum, Cineraraia maritima*), 19, 43, 52, 120

## E

Eggplants, ornamental, 19
*Escholtzia californica*. *See* Poppy, California.
*Euphorbia marginata*. *See* Snow-in-summer.
Everlastings, 33

## F

Fairy fan-flower. *See* Scaveola.
Ferns, asparagus (*Asparagus densiflorus*), 43, 52, 81, 87
Ferns, Boston, 81
Ferns, ostrich, 81
Fertilizer (inorganic), 42–45, 56, 66–68. *See also* Organic fertilizer.
Floss Flower. *See* Ageratum.
Flower arrangements, 33
Flowering tobacco. *See* Nicotiana.

Forget-me-not (*Myosotis sylvatica*), 20, 24, 39, 43, 58, 122
Fountain grass (*Pennisetum setaceum*), 81, 123
Foxglove (*Digitalis purpurea*), 20, 39, 43, 124
Fuchsia (*Fuchsia hybrida*), 14, 20, 39, 43, 59
    'Angel's Earrings,' 18, 125
*Fuchsia hybrida*. *See* Fuchsia

## G

*Gaillardia pulchella*. *See* Blanket flower.
*Galliarda* x *grandiflora*. *See* Blanket flower.
Garlic (*Alluim sativum*), 81
Geranium, 16, 20, 39, 43, 52, 59, 80
Geranium, floribinda 'Maureen,' 12
Geranium, ivy-leaf (*Pelargonium peltatum*), 29, 39, 126
    'Matador Burgundy,' 11
    'Matador Light Pink,' 11
Geranium, scented (*Pelargonium* species), 127
Geranium, zonal (*Pelargonium* x *hortorum*), 128
    'First Kiss,' 12
    'Melody Red,' 12
    'Patriot Salmon Blush,' 12
Ghost weed. *See* Snow in summer.
Gladiolus (*Gladiolus hybridus*), 20, 39, 43, 81, 129
*Gladiolus hybridus*. *See* Gladiolus.
*Gleditsia triacanthos inermis*. *See* Locust, honey.
Globe amaranth (*Gomphrena globosa*), 14, 20, 31, 39, 43, 52, 86
Gloriosa daisy. *See* Black-eyed Susan.
Golden ageratum (*Lonas inodora*), 43, 130
Golden flower of the Incas. *See* Tithonia.
*Gomphrena globosa*. *See* Globe amaranth.
Gourds, ornamental, 43, 131
Grass, ornamental (*Graminae*), 31, 81
Growing conditions, 14–15
*Gypsophila elegans*. *See* Baby's breath.

## H

Hardening off, 57
Hawaiian hibiscus. *See* Hibiscus.
Heat tolerance, 11
*Helianthus annuus*. *See* Sunflower.
*Helichrysum bracteatum*. *See* Strawflower.
*Helichrysum petiolare*. *See* Licorice plant.

Heliotrope (*Heliotropium arborescens*), 20, 39, 43, 81, 132
*Heliotropium arborescens*. *See* Heliotrope.
Helipterum, 33
*Hemerocallis*. *See* Daylily.
Herbicide, pre-emergent, 73
Hibiscus (*Hibiscus rosa-sinensis*), 20, 133
*Hibiscus rosa-sinensis*. *See* Hibiscus.
Hinder, 77
Hosta (*Hosta* species), 81
*Hosta* species. *See* Hosta.

## I

*Iberis* hybrids. *See* Candytuft.
*Impatiens balsamina*. *See* Rose balsam.
Impatiens (*Impatiens walleriana*), 20, 24, 39, 43, 52, 59, 73, 80, 134
    'Busy Lizzie,' 9
    'Super Elfin,' 11
Impatiens, New Guinea (*Impatiens* species), 39, 59, 135
*Impatiens* species. *See* Impatiens, New Guinea.
*Impatiens walleriana*. *See* Impatiens.
Inorganic fertilizer. *See* Fertilizer.
Insecticidal soap, 76, 77, 78
Insects and diseases, 10–11, 55–56, 74–79
*Ipomoea alba*. *See* Moonflower.
*Ipomoea batatas*. *See* Sweet potato, decorative.
*Ipomoea nil, purpurea, tricolor*. *See* Morning glory vine.

## J

Johnny jump-up. *See* Viola.
Joseph's coat. *See* Love lies bleeding.
Juniper, creeping (*Juniperus horizontalis*), 80
*Juniperus horizontalis*. *See* Juniper, creeping.

## K

Kale, flowering or ornamental (*Brassica oleracea acephala*), 58, 102
Kitchen gardens, 29

## L

Labeling plants, 55
Lady's ear drops. *See* Fuchsia.
*Lagenaria sicenaria*. *See* Gourds, ornamental.
*Lantana camara*. *See* Lantana.
Lantana (*Lantana camara*), 14, 20, 39, 43, 136

Larkspur (Consolida ambigua), 20, 31, 39, 43, 81, 137
  'Imperial,' 12
Lathyrus odoratus. See Sweet pea.
Lavatera (Lavatera trimestris), 43, 138
Lavatera trimestris. See Lavatera.
Leucanthemum hybrids. See Chrysanthemum.
Licorice plant (Helichrysum petiolare), 20, 24, 139
Light, 38–40, 53
Lilac (Syringa vulgaris), 81
Limonium sinuatum. See Statice.
Linum gradiflorum. See Scarlet flax.
Lobelia erinus. See Lobelia.
Lobelia (Lobelia erinus), 20, 39, 43, 52, 140
Lobularia maritima. See Sweet alyssum.
Locust, honey (Gleditsia triacanthos inermis), 80
Lonas inodora. See Golden ageratum.
Love-in-a-mist (Nigella damascena), 20, 39, 43, 141
Love lies bleeding (Amaranthus caudatus), 142
Luffa aegyptiaca. See Gourds, ornamental.

M
Madagascar periwinkle. See Vinca.
Malathion, 77
Maple, Japanese (Acer palmatum dissectum), 81
Marigold, 13, 20, 39, 43, 58
Marigold, American (Tagetes erecta), 143
Marigold, French (Tagetes patula), 80, 144
  'Gold Lady,' 25
  'Queen Sophia,' 25
Marigold, signet (Tagetes tenuifolia), 81, 145
Matthiola incana. See Stock.
Melampodium (Melampodium paludosum), 11, 12, 20, 24, 68, 146
  'Medallion,' 12
Melampodium paludosum. See Melampodium.
Mentha piperita. See Peppermint.
Metaldehyde slug bait, 77
Mexican sunflower. See Tithonia.
Miticide, 78
Mixed gardens, 28–30
Molucca balm. See Bells of Ireland.
Molucella laevis. See Bells of Ireland.

Moonflower (Ipomoea alba), 20, 37, 80, 147
Morning glory vine (Ipomoea nil, purpurea, tricolor), 20, 37, 39, 43, 58, 80, 148
Moss rose. See Portulaca.
Mourning bride. See Pincushion flower.
Mowing strips, 46–47
Mulch, 70, 73–74
Musk mallow (Abelmoschus moschatus), 20, 43, 149
Myosotis sylvatica. See Forget-me-not.

N
Nasturtium (Tropaeolum majus), 20, 21, 43, 58, 150
Neem, 76, 77, 78
Nematodes, 76
Nicotiana alata. See Nicotiana.
Nicotiana (Nicotiana alata and N. x sanderae), 20, 31, 39, 43, 52, 151
Nicotiana x sanderae. See Nicotiana.
Nierembergia caerulea. See Nierembergia.
Nierembergia (Nierembergia caerulea), 20, 24, 29, 39, 152
Nigella damascena. See Love-in-a-mist.

O
Ocimum basilicum. See Basil.
Onion, bulbing (Allium cepa), 81
Organic fertilizer, 47–48, 67–68, 70
Organic matter. See Organic fertilizer.

P
Pachysandra (Pachysandra terminalis), 81
Pachysandra terminalis. See Pachysandra.
Pansy (Viola x wittrockiana), 20, 24, 31, 39, 43, 52, 73, 153
  'Majestic Giants,' 50
  'Maxim Marina,' 11
Papaver croceum. See Poppy, Iceland.
Papaver nudicaule. See Poppy, Iceland.
Park Seed Co., Inc., 52
Parsley, curly (Petroselenum crispum var. crispum), 39, 81, 154
Patience. See Impatiens.
Pelargonium peltatum. See Geranium, ivy-leaf.
Pelargonium species. See Geranium, scented.
Pelargonium x hortorum. See Geranium, zonal.
Pennisetum setaceum. See Fountain grass.
Peppermint (Mentha piperita), 81

Peppers, ornamental (Capsicum species), 19, 39, 52, 155
Perilla frutescens. See Perilla.
Perilla (Perilla frutescens), 19, 20, 39, 156
Periwinkle (Vinca minor), 81
Pests. See Insects and diseases.
Petroselenum crispum var. crispum. See Parsley, curly.
Petunia, 10–11, 20, 24, 39, 43, 52, 73
Petunia, grandiflora (Petunia x hybrida Grandiflora Group), 157
Petunia, multiflora and floribunda (Petunia x hybrida), 158
  'Summer Madness,' 10
Petunias, vining (Petunia spp.), 59, 159
  'Purple Wave,' 12, 15, 81
  Surfinia, 12
Petunia spp. See Petunias, vining.
Petunia x hybrida. See Petunia, multiflora and floribunda.
Petunia x hybrida Grandiflora Group. See Petunia, grandiflora.
Phaseolus coccineus. See Scarlet runner bean.
pH levels, 41
Phlox drummondii. See Phlox, annual.
Phlox, annual (Phlox drummondii), 20, 24, 39, 43, 160
Pinching back, 70–71
Pincushion flower (Scabiosa atropurpurea), 20, 31, 58, 161
Planning, garden, 17–24, 49
Plant hardiness zone map, 64–65
Planting techniques, 62–63
Plants, selecting, 17–19, 61–62
Poppy, 39
Poppy, California (Escholtzia californica), 13, 20, 58, 162
Poppy, Iceland (Papaver croceum), 163
Poppy, Shirley, 13, 57
Portulaca grandiflora. See Portulaca.
Portulaca (Portulaca grandiflora), 20, 24, 39, 43, 58, 164
Pot marigold. See Calendula.
Pressing flowers, 34–36
Pricking off, 56–57
Primrose (Primula species and hybrids), 20, 39, 43, 165
Primula species and hybrids. See Primrose.
Prince's feather. See Love lies bleeding.
Propogation
  from cuttings, 59–61
  from seed, 49, 51–57

Pruning, 72
Pyrethrin, 75, 76, 77, 78

**R**

Raised beds, 42, 44
*Rheum rhabarbarum. See* Rhubarb.
Rhubarb *(Rheum rhabarbarum)*, 81
*Ricinus communis. See* Castor bean.
Rose balsam *(Impatiens balsamina)*, 43,
   91
Rose mallow. *See* Lavatera.
Rose of china. *See* Hibiscus.
Rotenone, 76, 78
*Rudbeckia hirta. See* Black-eyed Susan.

**S**

Sabadilla, 76
Sage, common *(Salvia officinalis)*, 166
*Salvia officinalis. See* Sage, common.
Salvia *(Salvia splendens)*, 20, 31, 43, 52,
   167–168
   'Strata,' 15
*Salvia splendens. See* Salvia.
*Sanvitalia procumbens. See* Sanvitalia.
Sanvitalia *(Sanvitalia procumbens)*, 169
Sapphire flower. *See* Browlla.
*Scabiosa atropurpurea. See* Pincushion
   flower.
Scabiosa. *See* Pincushion flower.
Scarlet flax *(Linum gradiflorum)*, 170
Scarlet runner bean *(Phaseolus coc-
   cineus)*, 20, 39, 171
Scarlet sage. *See* Salvia.
*Scaveola aemula. See* Scaveola.
Scaveola *(Scaveola aemula)*, 172
Sea lavender. *See* Statice.
Seeds
   sowing directly, 57–59
   starting plants from, 49, 51–57
   suppliers, 52–53
   weed, 72–74
Seed Saver's Exchange, 52
Self-branching, 11–12
*Senecio cineraria. See* Dusty miller.
Sevin, 76
Shade, plants for, 39
Shell flower. *See* Bells of Ireland.
Shepherd's Garden Seeds, 53
Snapdragon *(Antirrhinum majus)*, 20,
   31, 39, 43, 52, 81, 173
Snow-in-summer *(Euphorbia mar-
   ginata)*, 20, 24, 43, 174
Snowstorm bacopa, 'Snowstorm'
   *(Sutera cordata)*, 43, 59, 90
Soaker hoses, 68, 69

Soil
   condition of, 38
   preparing, 42–46
   for seedlings, 53, 54
   testing, 40–41
   types and plant suitability, 43
*Solenostemon scutellaroioes. See* Coleus.
Spider flower. *See* Cleome.
Spike plant. *See* Dracaena.
*Spiraea x vanhouttei. See* Bridal
   wreath.
Sprinklers, 69
Statice *(Limonium sinuatum)*, 20, 33,
   175
Stock *(Matthiola incana)*, 20, 31, 39, 52,
   176
Stokes Seeds Inc., 53
Strawflower *(Helichrysum bracteatum)*,
   20, 33, 39, 177
Sulfur, 79
Sun, plants for, 39
Sunflower *(Helianthus annuus)*, 20, 39,
   58, 178
   'Sun Spot,' 12
*Sutera cordata. See* Snowstorm bacopa,
   'Snowstorm.'
Swedish ivy, 59
Sweet alyssum *(Lobularia maritima)*,
   8–9, 20, 24, 29, 39, 43, 58, 73, 85
   'Carpet of Snow,' 8
Sweet pea *(Lathyrus odoratus)*, 20, 31,
   39, 43, 179
Sweet potato, decorative *(Ipomoea
   batatas)*, 180
*Syringa vulgaris. See* Lilac.

**T**

*Tagetes erecta. See* Marigold, American.
*Tagetes patula. See* Marigold, French.
*Tagetes tenuifolia. See* Marigold, signet.
*Tanacetum ptarmiciflorum. See* Dusty
   miller.
*Taxus baccata. See* Yew, Japanese.
Texas pride. *See* Phlox, annual.
Thompson and Morgan, Inc., 53
*Thunbergia alata. See* Black-eyed Susan
   vine.
Tickseed. *See* Calliopsis.
*Tithonia rotundifolia. See* Tithonia.
Tithonia *(Tithonia rotundifolia)*, 20, 39,
   181
*Torenia fournieri. See* Torenia.
Torenia *(Torenia fournieri)*, 182
Transplanting, 56–57
*Tropaeolum majus. See* Nasturtium.

**V**

Vegetable gardens, 29–30, 31
Vegetable sponge. *See* Gourds, orna-
   mental.
Verbena, 39, 43, 52
   'Imagination,' 12
Verbena, moss *(verbena tenuisecta)*, 183
*Verbena tenuisecta. See* Verbena, moss.
Vinca *(Catharanthus roseus)*, 20, 31, 39,
   43, 52, 184
*Vinca minor. See* Periwinkle.
Vines, 36–37, 57. *See also specific vines.*
*Viola cornuta. See* Viola.
*Viola tricolor. See* Viola.
Viola *(Viola tricolor* and *Viola cornuta)*,
   20, 39, 185
*Viola x wittrockiana. See* Pansy.

**W**

Watering, 53–54, 68–70
Weed control, 72–74, 75
White-flowered gourd. *See* Gourds,
   ornamental.
Wild pansy. *See* Viola.
Wishbone flower. *See* Torenia.

**Y**

Yellow-flowered gourd. *See* Gourds,
   ornamental.
Yew, Japanese *(Taxus baccata)*, 80, 81

**Z**

Zinnia, 20, 31, 39, 43, 57, 58
Zinnia, hybrid garden *(zinnia elegans)*,
   10, 186–187
   'Profusion Cherry,' 10, 15
   'Profusion Orange,' 10, 15
Zinnia, Mexican or spreading *(Zinnia
   haageana)*, 10, 188
*Zinnia angustifolia. See* Zinnia, Mexican
   or spreading.
*Zinnia haageana. See* Zinnia, Mexican or
   spreading.
*Zinnia elegans. See* Zinnia, hybrid
   garden.

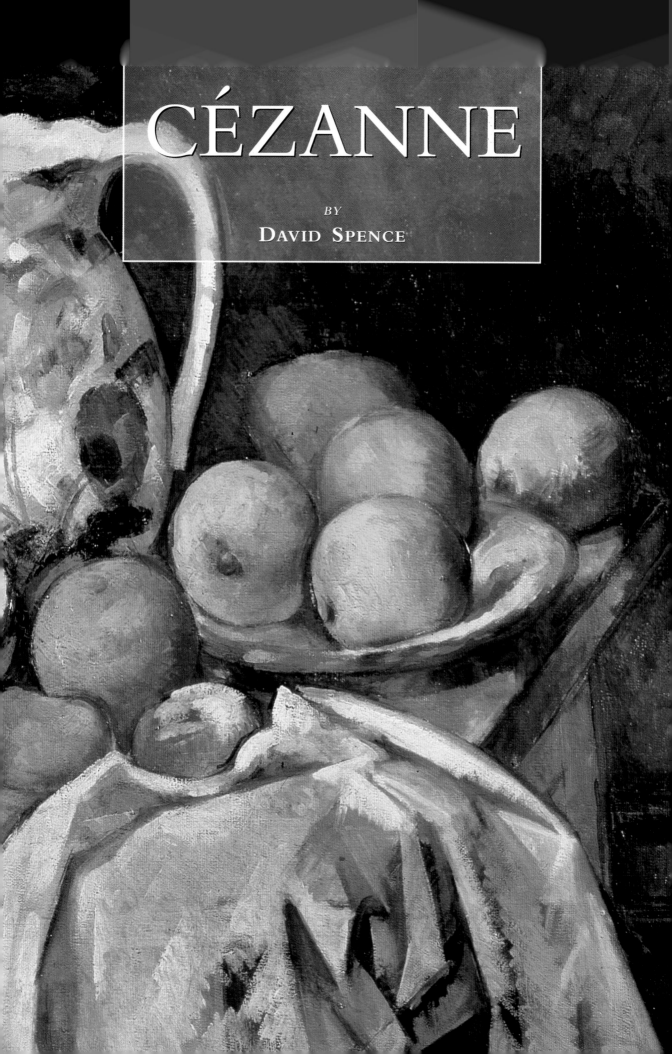

# CÉZANNE

BY

DAVID SPENCE

# THE WORLD OF CÉZANN

Approximately 20 miles (32 km) north of the Mediterranean port of Marseilles and 400 miles (650 km) south of Paris, Aix-en-Provence was a provincial town which proved idyllic for the growing child, but a conservative backwater for the young intellectual. Émile Zola left for Paris as soon as he had finished at the Collège Bourbon in 1858, while Cézanne stayed on to enroll at the university and attend life-drawing classes at the local free drawing school. Cézanne's father had decided that legal training was the best course for his son and of most help to the prosperous Cézanne Bank. It was obvious to the young Cézanne, however, that a career as a lawyer was not what he wanted, and he dreamed of joining his friend Zola in Paris and becoming an artist.

*P*aul Cézanne was born on the January 19, 1839, in Aix-en-Provence in the south of France. Paul was the eldest of three children born to Louis-Auguste Cézanne and Anne-Élisabeth Aubert. Paul's father made enough money as a felt-hat trader to become a banker, founding the Cézanne and Cabassol Bank in Aix in 1848. Paul grew up in a secur well-to-do family home with his two sisters enjoying the pleasant climate and attractive countryside surrounding Aix. When he was 13 years old he attended the Collège Bourbo in Aix as a boarder, and it was here he met Émile Zola who was to become a lifelong friend. Cézanne and Zola, together with a third friend Jean Baptiste Baille, became known to their school friends as the "Inseparables" who enjoyed nothing more than long walks in the countryside, fishing, and swimming in the nearby river Arc. Cézanne, encouraged by his father to study Law, eventually enrolled at the university of Aix.

## PAUL CÉZANNE

It was quite clear that Cézanne was not going to settle down at university in Aix to study Law, nor was he going to follow his father's footsteps into the family bank. Encouraged by Émile Zola, Cézanne decided to head for Paris and try his hand as an artist. Eventually Cézanne's father gave him his blessing and Cézanne traveled to Paris in 1861 to spend the summer with Zola. This was an unhappy time. Cézanne felt an outsider and did not feel comfortable with the sophisticated ways of the city dwellers. He missed the countryside of Provence and after his application to join the École des Beaux-Arts in Paris was turned down he returned, dejected, to Aix. It would not be long however before the urge returned and he made plans to return to Paris with the financial support of his father.

## ONE OF FOUR MURALS FROM THE SALON OF THE JAS DE BOUFFAN, 1859

The Jas de Bouffan was generally in a poor state of repair when the Cézanne family moved there, and Paul was given permission to paint on the walls of one of the rooms. In 1859, Cézanne painted a series of murals of the four seasons. These paintings are the earliest known works of Cézanne. The elongated female figures depicted in the murals show Cézanne's knowledge of art of previous generations. They show the distinct influence of artists such as the 16th-century Italian, Sandro Botticelli, and Cézanne himself recognizes his debt by signing the paintings, not in his own name, but that of Ingres, who was famed for his academic style.

## HOUSE AND FARM AT THE JAS DE BOUFFAN (detail), 1885/7

In 1859, Louis-Auguste Cézanne purchased a fine 18th-century house with surrounding grounds situated close to the center of Aix. The house had formerly belonged to the Governor of Provence and was called the *Jas de Bouffan* (House of the Wind).

**THE STRANGLED WOMAN**
*(detail)*, *c*.1870/2

In his early works painted during the 1860s, Cézanne's rapid fusion of brushstrokes and color borrow from the work of Delacroix, but also appear similar to the pictures of Honoré Daumier, an artist whose cartoons were full of biting political satire. The dark earthy realism of his solid figures could equally owe a debt to Gustave Courbet, whose work would have been known to the young Cézanne. Cézanne experimented with different painterly styles during this period just as he chose to depict a wide range of subject matter, from imaginary scenes of violence to still life.

# INFLUENCES & EARLY WORKS

*I*n 1862 Cézanne settled in Paris. Like all aspiring artists he was a frequent visitor to the Louvre, where he spent hours sitting in front of paintings meticulously copying the great masters. This was the established way of learning how to paint and Cézanne was no exception. Gradually he discovered the works of living artists such as Eugène Delacroix, who was a great source of inspiration for artists of Cézanne's generation. Delacroix symbolized rebellion against the Classical art, which dominated the art schools at the time, led by the great French artist and master draughtsman, Jean Auguste Dominique Ingres. The Romantic artists, led by Delacroix, considered color to be more important than draughtsmanship and favored exotic subject matter over the traditional subjects depicted by the followers of Ingres. The École des Beaux-Arts, taught in the Classical tradition, was still favored by the critics and by the public, but it was increasingly out of touch with the new generation of artists. The up-and-coming painters no longer sought the advice and approval of the established system of teaching and they were becoming dissatisfied with the official annual exhibition of paintings at the Salon.

APOTHEOSIS OF DELACROIX, *c*.1870/2

Cézanne made his palette of colors deliberately bright in emulation of Delacroix. Of color he said; *"Pure drawing is an abstraction. Line and modeling do not count; drawing and outline are not distinct, since everything in nature has color... by the very fact of painting one draws. The accuracy of tone gives simultaneously the light and shape of the object, and the more harmonious the color, the more the drawing becomes precise."*

## THE DEATH OF SARDANAPALUS *Eugène Delacroix*

When Delacroix painted this picture in 1829, he was angrily attacked by the art establishment for his use of brilliant color, exotic, and dramatic subject matter, and free handling of the paint, which was seen to be "anti-French" in its rejection of French Classicism. In 1832, he visited north Africa and this opened up a whole new field of subject matter as well as heightening his appreciation of color. He also used literary sources of inspiration including Byron, Scott, and Shakespeare, and his way of painting broke new ground enabling the Realist artists to follow.

Cézanne made a number of copies of Delacroix's paintings as well as making his own pictures which also contained images of violence, such as *The Abduction, The Murder, The Woman Strangled,* and *The Autopsy.*

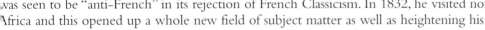

## THE HOUSE OF
## DR GACHET AT AUVERS, *c.*1873

Cézanne was encouraged by Pissarro to move to a small village near Pontoise called Auvers-sur-Oise. Cézanne stayed with the eccentric art enthusiast Dr Gachet who was a great supporter of the young artists. Pissarro and Cézanne painted landscapes in the pretty countryside.

# INFLUENCES & EARLY WORKS

*I*n Paris, Cézanne mixed with the most modern, adventurous painters and intellectuals who discussed their ideas about art and literature in the Paris cafés, particularly the Café Guerbois in the Batignolles district of Paris. The painter Camille Pissarro became a good friend and introduced Cézanne to artists such as Manet, Monet, and Renoir. Cézanne however did not feel at ease in this company, and complained in a letter *"I am just wasting my time in every respect… just don't go imagining that I shall become a Parisian…"* In 1863 the "Salon des Refusés" was set up to give the public the opportunity to see the works of artists rejected from the official Salon. The picture that caused the greatest sensation at the Salon des Refusé was, *Le Déjeuner sur l'Herbe* by Édouard Manet. The works of Manet and Courbet attempted to be true to life, depicting ordinary scenes of everyday life, *"bringing art into contact with the common people."* Cézanne submitted a number of paintings to the Salon, all of which were rejected.

## THE CUTTING, 1870

Cézanne traveled between Paris and his family home in Aix. In 1869 he met his future wife, Hortense Fiquet, who modeled for him when he was working in Paris, and they began living together. In 1870 they moved to the fishing village of L'Estaque, near Marseilles, to avoid the Franco-Prussian war. Cézanne became obsessed with painting the rocky Mediterranean landscape. Around this time he painted the landscape of a railway cutting near Aix. In the distance, behind the cutting, towers the Mont Sainte-Victoire—this feature of the Aix countryside was to dominate Cézanne's painting for the rest of his life.

## THE HOUSE OF THE HANGED MAN

This painting was made in 1873, when Cézanne was heavily influenced by the Impressionist style. The painting reveals Cézanne's continuing obsession with representing solidity of form. Heavy brushstrokes give it a physicality anchoring the imagery in the landscape, rather than relying on color to depict light, as in the works of the Impressionist painters. *The House of the Hanged Man* was exhibited at the first Impressionist exhibition where it was purchased by Count Armand Doria for the sum of 300 francs.

## PHOTO OF PISSARRO & CÉZANNE

Camille Pissarro (left) had been friends with Cézanne since they first met in Paris at the Académie Suisse in 1861. Pissarro, who was 10 years older than Cézanne, persuaded him to try painting outdoors. This *en plein air* way of painting was favored by Pissarro and became the hallmark of the Impressionist painters. They believed it was essential to get close to their subjects, to capture what they saw with immediacy. They concerned themselves with the fleeting effects of light on the subject, and rejected the studio-bound method of painting. Pissarro had a profound influence on Cézanne's painting in the early 1870s and was equally influential on other painters of the day. Pissarro was the only artist to exhibit in all eight Impressionist exhibitions.

## THE LIFE OF CÉZANNE

~1839~

Paul Cézanne born on
January 19 in Aix-en-
Provence, eldest of
three children

~1844~

Paul's parents, Louis-Auguste
Cézanne and Anne-Élisabeth
Aubert are married

~1852~

Attends the Collège
Bourbon where he
meets Émile Zola and Jean
Baptiste Baille. The three
become best friends

~1857~

Attends the drawing
school in Aix

~1859~

Attends the University
of Aix to study law

~1861~

Spends the summer in
Paris studying art at the
Académie Suisse where
he meets Pissarro

Reluctantly returns to Aix to
work in the family bank

~1862~

Cézanne gives up work
and his legal studies to
return to Paris with
a modest allowance
from his father

~1863~

Attends the Académie
Suisse once more and
meets Impressionist
painters Sisley, Monet,
and Renoir

~1866~

Submits work to the Paris
Salon but is rejected

**THE FLOOR STRIPPERS** *Gustave Caillebotte*

*La Deuxième Exposition* (The Second Exhibition) of Impressionism,
was held at the art dealer Durand-Ruel's gallery at 11 rue le Peletier
in Paris from April 11 to May 9, 1876. One of the paintings
that caused a great sensation was *The Floor Strippers* by Gustave
Caillebotte. Caillebotte was an extremely talented and wealthy artist.
He extended his interest in painting not only by buying artwork, but
by exhibiting it alongside his own. This painting depicts workmen
stripping the floor of his new Paris apartment.

## FOUR GIRLS ON A BRIDGE

*Edvard Munch*

Artists from all over the world flocked to Paris in the 1870s and
1880s, as its reputation as a vibrant exciting city with the most
modern trends in art spread. Wealthy Americans traveled to Paris,
some to collect this new art, some to become artists themselves.
A young Norwegian painter named Edvard Munch traveled to
Paris and much of his formative youth was spent in the city.
By 1892 Munch had attracted enough interest to be able to hold a
large exhibition of his work in Berlin. His art was very influential
and he soon became a powerful factor in the growth of the
Expressionist movement. Munch had himself been influenced in
Paris by the deeply personal vision expressed in the works of
Gauguin and van Gogh.

# THE ART OF HIS DAY

*E*arly in his career Cézanne exhibited alongside artists such as Manet, Whistler, and Pissarro. In 1877, Cézanne showed 16 paintings at the third Impressionist exhibition which was received with a torrent of criticism. Unlike many of his contemporaries Cézanne spent a great deal of time away from Paris, often in his home town of Aix and the nearby Mediterranean village of L'Estaque. Meanwhile fellow Paris-based artists such as Monet, Degas, and Manet continued to defy the critics with their determination to pursue the new style of painting and sweep away the traditional values of art. Manet's paintings of naked women depicted in recognizable settings shocked a public who were used to art which placed them in the socially acceptable realm of classical mythology. Degas' abrupt framing of everyday scenes copied the photographic "snapshot" which was challenging art as a visual record. Monet's "Impression" of a sunrise over water with bold daubs of orange paint was ridiculed by critics whose description of the painting christened the Impressionist movement. Cézanne became increasingly influential himself as he developed his own style alongside the Post-Impressionist artists such as van Gogh, Gauguin, and Seurat.

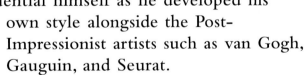

## LITTLE DANCER OF FOURTEEN YEARS

*Edgar Degas*

This sculpture, originally modeled in wax, incorporates real artifacts such as hair, dancing shoes, gauze tutu, and silk bodice. It was modeled on Marie van Goethem, a dancer at the Paris Opera, who was known to spend much of her time at the local Brasserie de Martyrs, also favored by artists. The incorporation of real materials in the sculpture was considered very shocking at the time. It was finally exhibited, in a glass case, at the sixth Impressionist exhibition.

On January 4, 1872 in Paris, Hortense Fiquet gave birth to a boy who was registered as Paul Cézanne. The artist was an indulgent father who was very attached to his young son. As Paul grew up, Cézanne began to depend upon him to help organize his affairs. He was later to become Cézanne's advisor, taking care of money matters and the sale of his pictures.

## THE ARTIST'S FATHER
*(detail)*, 1866

## THE LIFE OF CÉZANNE

~1869~

Meets Hortense Fiquet, who models for him, and becomes his mistress

Hortense moves in with Cézanne

~1872~

Son Paul is born

Cézanne, Hortense and Paul move to the village of Auvers-sur-Oise where Cézanne works with Pissarro

~1874~

Exhibits with the first group exhibition of Impressionist painters

~1877~

Exhibits 16 paintings at the third Impressionist exhibition

~1878~

Cézanne's father threatens to cut off the artist's allowance after hearing of his son's mistress and child who Cézanne had kept a secret

In 1874, already two years after the birth of his son, Cézanne wrote to his parents: *"You ask me why I am not yet returning to Aix. I have already told you in that respect that it is more agreeable for me than you can possibly think to be with you, but that once at Aix I am no longer free and when I want to return to Paris this always means a struggle for me; and although your opposition to my return is not absolute, I am very much troubled by the resistance I feel on your part. I greatly desire that my liberty of action should not be impeded and I shall then have all the more pleasure in hastening my return. I ask Papa to give me 200 francs a month; that will permit me to make a long stay in Aix... believe me, I really do beg Papa to grant me this request and then I shall, I think, be able to continue the studies I wish to make."*

# FAMILY, FRIENDS & OTHERS
## THE SECRET FAMILY

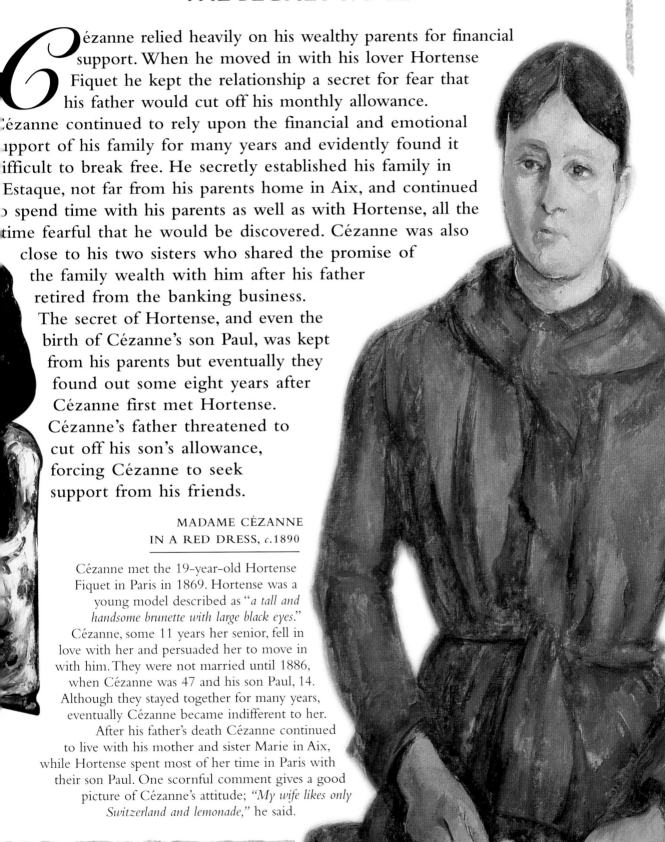

Cézanne relied heavily on his wealthy parents for financial support. When he moved in with his lover Hortense Fiquet he kept the relationship a secret for fear that his father would cut off his monthly allowance. Cézanne continued to rely upon the financial and emotional support of his family for many years and evidently found it difficult to break free. He secretly established his family in Estaque, not far from his parents home in Aix, and continued to spend time with his parents as well as with Hortense, all the time fearful that he would be discovered. Cézanne was also close to his two sisters who shared the promise of the family wealth with him after his father retired from the banking business.

The secret of Hortense, and even the birth of Cézanne's son Paul, was kept from his parents but eventually they found out some eight years after Cézanne first met Hortense. Cézanne's father threatened to cut off his son's allowance, forcing Cézanne to seek support from his friends.

MADAME CÉZANNE
IN A RED DRESS, *c.*1890

Cézanne met the 19-year-old Hortense Fiquet in Paris in 1869. Hortense was a young model described as "*a tall and handsome brunette with large black eyes.*" Cézanne, some 11 years her senior, fell in love with her and persuaded her to move in with him. They were not married until 1886, when Cézanne was 47 and his son Paul, 14. Although they stayed together for many years, eventually Cézanne became indifferent to her.

After his father's death Cézanne continued to live with his mother and sister Marie in Aix, while Hortense spent most of her time in Paris with their son Paul. One scornful comment gives a good picture of Cézanne's attitude; "*My wife likes only Switzerland and lemonade,*" he said.

## THE LIFE OF CÉZANNE

~1895~
First one-man exhibition at the gallery of Ambroise Vollard

~1886~
Publication of Zola's novel about a failed artist which was thought to be based on Cézanne. Their friendship breaks down

Cézanne marries Hortense

Cézanne inherits the family wealth after the death of his father, and moves to Jas de Bouffan, although Hortense and Paul spend most of their time in Paris

~1897~
Cézanne's mother dies

~1899~
Sells Jas de Bouffan and moves into an apartment in Aix

~1902~
Moves into a studio he has built in Chemin des Lauves, in the hills outside Aix with a view of Mont Sainte-Victoire

Zola dies

~1904~
Works exhibited in Paris and Berlin

~1905~
Exhibits in London with Durand-Ruel

~1906~
Cézanne dies of pneumonia on October 22, a week after getting soaked in a thunderstorm while out painting

~1907~
A retrospective exhibition of Cézanne's paintings is held at the Autumn Salon in Paris.

## THE ARTIST'S LIFE
# FAMILY, FRIENDS & OTHERS
## FRIENDS FROM AIX

Throughout his life Cézanne maintained friends from his home town of Aix. The "inseparables," the childhood friends Baille, Zola, and Cézanne, kept their friendship going into adulthood. Émile Zola remained very close to Cézanne until a book published by Zola in 1886 offended Cézanne to such an extent that he ceased to communicate with the writer. The acquaintances Cézanne made at the drawing school in Aix, where he studied from 1856 to 1859, lasted many years. When Cézanne left for Paris in pursuit of Zola, who had already decided to make a home there, he found familiar faces from Aix such as Solari and Valabrègue. These young hopefuls rubbed shoulders with the exciting avant-garde in the Parisian cafés where artists and intellectuals debated the latest artistic fashions long into the night.

### ACHILLE EMPERAIRE, c.1868

Emperaire was an artist from Aix who studied with Cézanne at the Académie Suisse in Paris. Cézanne was very attached to Emperaire who suffered from dwarfism. His painting portrays Emperaire's condition ruthlessly—the young man's feet are propped on a box because they would not reach the ground. However there is a sensitive handling of the face, which shows Emperaire gazing thoughtfully into the distance. Emperaire stayed with Cézanne in Paris in 1872, but only for a short time. When he left he wrote; *"I have left Cézanne—it was unavoidable, otherwise I would not have escaped the fate of the others. I found him deserted by everybody. He hasn't got a single intelligent or close friend left."* Later in life Cézanne is reported to have wanted to destroy the picture.

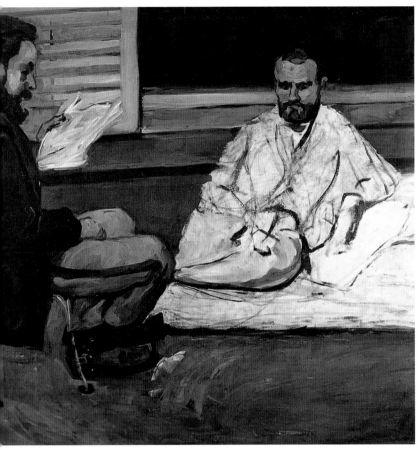

Zola and Cézanne had been intimate friends since childhood. Zola, a highly talented writer, became notorious for his Realist novels such as *Nana,* and *Germinal,* which although causing a scandal when they were published, today are considered to be among the greatest French novels of the 19th century. This painting, found in Zola's attic after his death, is clearly unfinished, showing Zola's body as a few bold brushstrokes against the cream canvas. In 1886, Zola published a novel called *L'Oeuvre* about a failed painter named Claude Lantier. The character was said to be based on Cézanne. This caused a permanent break between the two and their friendship never recovered.

On April 4, 1886, Cézanne wrote:

> *My dear Émile*
>
> *I have just received* L'Oeuvre, *which you were good enough to send me. I thank the author of* Les Rougon-Macquart *for this kind token of remembrance and ask him to permit me to clasp his hand while thinking of bygone years. Ever yours under the impulse of past times.*
>
> *Paul Cézanne*

The letter undoubtedly refers to the relationship in the past tense and is far more formal than his normal letters to the writer. Some years later Zola said; *"Ah yes, Cézanne. How I regret not having been able to push him. In my Claude Lantier I have drawn a likeness of him that is actually too mild, for if I had wanted to tell all…!"*

## JOACHIM GASQUET, 1896/7

Gasquet was a young poet from Aix and the son of one of Cézanne's childhood friends. Gasquet was very taken with Cézanne's work and set about publishing transcriptions of lengthy conversations he had with the artist. After a time their relationship became strained, as was the case with many of Cézanne's friendships.

## THE ARTIST'S VISION

# WHAT DO THE PAINTINGS SAY?

udden outbursts of wild painting characterized Cézanne's work in the 1860s and early 70s. It is difficult to understand how this fits with the rest of his work but when Cézanne's friend Zola wrote the controversial book *L'Oeuvre*, which was thought to be based on Cézanne, he said of Claude Lantier (the main character of the novel): *"It was a chaste man's passion for the flesh of women, a mad love of nudity desired and never possessed...Those girls whom he chased out of his studio he adored in his paintings; he caressed or attacked them, in tears of despair at not being able to make them sufficiently beautiful, sufficiently alive."*

The black maid in attendance in Manet's painting has a far more active role in Cézanne's picture, as she unveils the female figure to the man seated in the foreground.

Manet's *Olympia* includes a black cat representing promiscuity. The cat replaces the dog painted in Titian's version of Venus, which represented faithfulness. Cézanne includes a lapdog complete with red ribbon which suggests decadence.

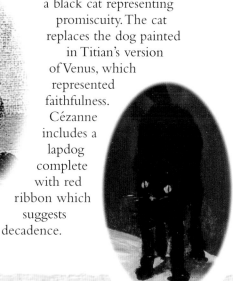

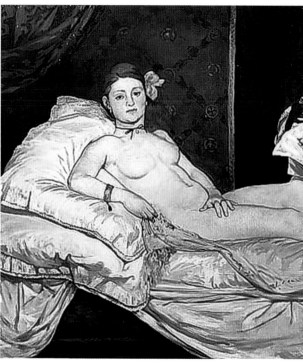

14

## A MODERN OLYMPIA, 1873

In 1867 Cézanne made a painting which he called *A Modern Olympia*. This painting was a homage to Manet's famous painting *Olympia* which was the sensation of the 1865 Salon. Apparently the subject came up in conversation some years later when Cézanne was staying with Dr Gachet in Auvers. The story states that Cézanne immediately took up his brushes and with uncharacteristic speed painted another canvas also called *A Modern Olympia*. This version of 1873 was exhibited at the first Impressionist exhibition in 1874. Criticism was heaped upon the exhibition. A female critic who wrote in the paper *L'Artiste* under the name Marc de Montifaud commented of *A Modern Olympia*; *"On Sunday the public saw fit to sneer at a fantastic figure that is revealed under an opium sky to a drug addict. This apparition of pink and nude flesh… has left even the most courageous gasping for breath. Mr Cézanne merely gives the impression of being a sort of madman who paints in delirium tremens."*

This man is undoubtedly a self-portrait with Cézanne's own distinct features.

## OLYMPIA

### *Édouard Manet*

Manet painted *Olympia* in 1863 but did not submit it for exhibition until 1865. Manet referred back to a well-known painting called *Venus of Urbino* painted by Titian in 1538. Manet's Olympia is a modern courtesan who is self-possessed and confident, unashamed of her nakedness. She looks directly at the viewer, thereby involving the spectator in the scene. This confrontation was shocking for the public, who were used to gazing on images of naked women safely portrayed as mythical goddesses.

# WHAT DO THE PAINTINGS SAY?

## MONT SAINTE-VICTOIRE

The mountain of Sainte-Victoire dominates the landscape around Aix. Mont Sainte-Victoire became Cézanne's *motif*, his subject to which he continually returned, painting the landscape again and again. It is perhaps for his views of Sainte-Victoire that Cézanne is best known. In 1881, Cézanne's brother-in-law, Maxime Conil, purchased a house called Bellevue which stood to the southwest of the town of Aix. The house was situated on a hill overlooking the Arc valley with the mountain of Saint-Victoire in the distance. Cézanne visited Bellevue on many occasions, setting up his canvas to paint the rural landscape, especially the view along the valley towards the flat-topped mountain. A viaduct in the middle distance formed a bold horizontal line running towards the foot of the mountain. Cézanne loved this countryside which he had known so well since childhood. He said that

*Mont Sainte-Victoire 1880*

conditions of light, exploring the form which appeared ever-changing under the harsh Provençal sun. However Cézanne's obsession was about making something with a strong underlying structure. He grew further and further away from the Impressionist painters whose fixation with the transient effects of light on color was for Cézanne "not permanent." In conversation Cézanne said to Joachim Gasquet; *"Impressionism, what does it mean? It is the optical mixing of colors, do you understand? The colors are broken down on the canvas and reassembled by the eye. We had to go through that… but now we need to give a firmness, a framework to the evanescence of all things."*

Mont Sainte-Victoire was the subject Cézanne chose to create this firmness, this permanence that he felt had eluded fellow painters such as Monet. It was more than just a mountain, itself the very essence of permanence. Sainte-Victoire was the foundation of Cézanne's beloved Provence countryside, the security of his family home, the solidity of his youthful friendships.

## MONT SAINTE-VICTOIRE SEEN FROM LES LAUVES

When his last link with his parents was cut after his mother's death in 1897, Cézanne was drawn nearer to the mountain, taking a studio in the hills at Chemin des Lauves overlooking Aix. This painting made between 1904 and 1906, is a view of Sainte-Victoire from Les Lauves. The same motif Cézanne was painting almost 30 years earlier became increasingly abstract, with sky and ground merging together as Cézanne searched for the underlying framework in his painting.

*Mont Sainte-Victoire 1885*

*Mont Sainte-Victoire 1890*

MOUNTAINS IN PROVENCE,
1878/80

Cézanne described how
he tried to paint from nature.
This description is a telling insight
into the way the artist works, his
thought process as he struggles to
create a work of art. *"If I reach too
high or too low, everything is a mess.*

*There must not be a single loose
strand, a single gap through which the
tension, the light, the truth can escape.
I have all the parts of my canvas under
control simultaneously. If things are
tending to diverge, I use my instincts
and my beliefs to bring them back
together again…I take the tones of
color I see to my right and my left,
here, there, everywhere, and I fix these
gradations, I bring them together…
They form lines, and become objects,
rocks, trees, without my thinking
about it. They acquire volume, they
have an effect. When these masses and
weights on my canvas correspond to the
planes, and spots which I see in my
mind and which we see with our eyes,
then my canvas closes its fingers."*

# HOW WERE THEY MADE?
## THE STRUCTURE OF THINGS

*C*ézanne was reaching for a way
of painting what was beneath
the surface, the basic form of his
subject expressed and modeled in
color. His fellow Impressionist painters worked
very quickly in order to capture the fleeting
impression of light on the surface, where
Cézanne worked slowly, laboriously, using
color to build solid shapes. He is famous
for his statement that he *"wanted to make of
Impressionism something solid and durable, like
the art of the Museums."*

He sought to create
images which represented
the subject as color and
tone together, that is to
identify a color which
could represent the tone
of an object and in this
way build something
solid out of color alone,
without the need for line
or shade. He expressed

BEND IN THE ROAD,
*c.*1900/6

Cézanne increasingly
analyzed his landscapes
as ordered brushstrokes
and parallel color blocks
which are described today
as *"constructive strokes."*
Through these building
blocks of color he
attempted to represent
sunlight on the landscape
rather than provide an
impression of its effects.
Although he rejected the
Impressionist style, he
still adopted the use of
complementary colors
famously used by the
Impressionists, such as
setting muted blues against
oranges to create depth
in the picture plane. It is
in canvases such as *Bend
in the Road* and the 1904
painting of *Sainte-Victoire*
(see page 17) that historians
have seen the beginnings
of Cubist and eventually
Abstract art.

this method of working when he said: *"I try to render
perspective through color alone… I proceed very slowly, for
nature reveals herself to me in a very complex form, and
constant progress must be made. One must see one's model
correctly and experience it in the right way, and furthermore,
express oneself with distinction and strength."*

PAUL CÉZANNE
SITTING IN
THE COUNTRY

This photograph,
taken by Cézanne's
friend Émile Bernard,
shows Cézanne as an
old man in his beloved
Provençale countryside.

FLOWERS AND FRUITS, *c.*1880

Cézanne derived enormous pleasure from creating fruits which were painted with such delicacy of color and yet were given real volume and weight.
It is almost as if the viewer can feel their roundness in the palm of the hand.

# HOW WERE THEY MADE?
## STILL LIFE

Cézanne said he wanted to conquer Paris with an apple—in other words to become famous for his modest still-life paintings. He applied the same methodical analysis to his still-life pictures as he did to his landscapes, which often resulted in the fruit rotting in the bowl before he could finish the painting, so eventually he used artificial fruit. The simple shapes of the fruit and bowls appealed to him; they were, after all, the basic spheres, cubes, and cylinders out of which all things can be said to be made. Another indication of the time he devoted to the paintings is the fact that sometimes contradicting shadows can be seen. Each time he returned to the subject he would paint exactly what he saw, even if the shadow had moved. He would spend weeks, sometimes months or longer on a painting, and if he was not happy with the result would abandon the picture or sometimes destroy it.

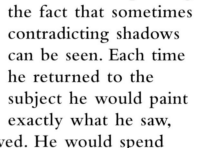

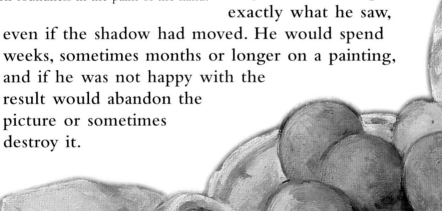

## VESSELS, BASKET AND FRUIT, 1888/90

The still life pictures appear at first glance to be simple representations of everyday objects, and yet these paintings are some of the most sophisticated images to have been created at the end of the 19th century. The artist's viewpoint has been very carefully selected and is in fact not one but several shifting viewpoints. The objects are seen from a number of different angles at the same time, so the jug appears to be tipping forward

but the plane of the table top contradicts it. The distortions of perspective are deliberate so that important shapes and colors balance each other pictorially rather than present a true representation of the still life. This playfulness broke with the rules of art which had been established for generations and stretched back to the Renaissance. Cézanne flattens the perspective where it pleases him to do so, pursuing harmony of shape and color to create a painting which cares more for the "abstract" elements of composition than for a perfect illusion of objects on a table.

## STILL LIFE WITH CURTAIN, c.1898/9

This still life was carefully arranged in order to present exactly the combination of shapes and juxtaposition of colors that Cézanne wanted.

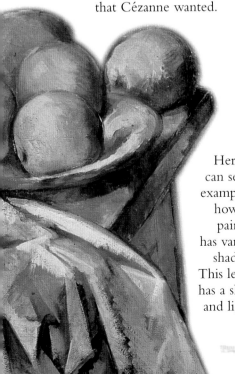

Here we can see an example of how this painting has varying shadows. This lemon has a shadow on the top, and light at the bottom.

The shadow and light are reversed here.

## THE CARD PLAYERS, 1890/95

*The Card Players* is one of Cézanne's best-known works. Card players are a common subject for artists and many versions of such a scene existed before Cézanne set up his canvas. He made five versions of the scene in all. Just as in his still-life pictures and paintings of Sainte-Victoire, he painted the subject again and again exploring variations of the theme. In one version only two players are depicted, facing each other. In another three players sit around the table while another has three players, a standing onlooker and a boy at the shoulder of the central card player.

### SOMBRE COLORS

We can tell from the simple clothes that the figures clearly belong in the Provençale countryside and their serious expressions suggest they have a hard life. This dark gloomy atmosphere is emphasized by the sombre colors used by the artist.

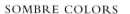

### ABSTRACT QUALITIES OF THE IMAG

The very symmetrical composition with ey focused down on the cards gives the pictur a stillness which recalls Cézanne's still-life paintings. Cézanne's arrangement of peopl and prop-like objects is organized in a manner which deliberately sets out to present a combination of shapes and color instead of telling the story of two men playing cards. The artist is more interested in the abstract qualities of the image than a representation of an event.

# FAMOUS IMAGES

After the death of his father in 1886, Cézanne inherited a large fortune and he could have led whatever life he chose. He decided on the simple life at Jas de Bouffan, the family house in Aix, painting the surrounding countryside and whatever was close at hand. Cézanne often found models for his portrait paintings among the laborers who worked on the estate at Jas de Bouffan. He could afford to pay these workers to sit for him for long periods of time, for Cézanne was as exacting with his studies of people as he was with the still life and landscape. He painted at Jas de Bouffan, living an increasingly secluded life with his sister as well as Hortense and Paul, until he set up a new studio on the road to Les Lauves which afforded views of his favorite motif, Mont Sainte-Victoire. It appeared that Cézanne increasingly shunned contact with people, sometimes positively ducking out of sight of acquaintances he might meet in the street.

### WOMAN WITH A COFFEE POT, 1890/5

It is likely that the subject for this painting was one of the servants at Jas de Bouffan, possibly the housekeeper. There is a feeling of massiveness about the form of the woman, a sense that the figure is as monumental as the mountain outside Aix that Cézanne loved to paint.

The vertical forms of the cafetière and standing spoon echo the erect pose of the woman who appears to be painted in a different plane to the table top, just as Cézanne painted conflicting perspectives in his still-life pictures.

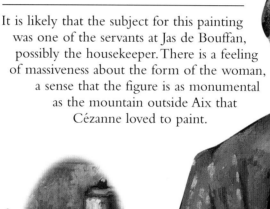

The blues and greens of the woman's dress against the orange and burnt brown of the wall paneling and tablecloth tend to accentuate her solidity and isolate her from the background.

BATHERS, 1875/77

This is one of the earliest examples of Cézanne's
paintings of bathers in the landscape.

# FAMOUS IMAGES
## THE BATHERS

*I*n 1899, the Jas de Bouffan was sold and Cézanne moved into an apartment in Aix with a housekeeper. His wife and son spent most of their time in Paris and Cézanne had a house built at Chemin des Lauves in the hills outside Aix. The house had a studio on the first floor with a ceiling some five meters high and a long narrow slit in the outer wall in order to move large canvases. Around 1900, Cézanne returned to a favorite subject, figures in the landscape. He had painted a number of paintings on this theme in the 1870s and 80s, but he now concentrated on making a number of large paintings including the biggest canvas at over 6 and a half feet by 8 feet.

### THE LARGE BATHERS, 1894-1905

This group of bathers comprises all female figures, like the other large bathers canvas. Cézanne did not mix male and female bathers together in his pictures, possibly for fear of creating a scene which would be considered inappropriate, and which would distract from his main purpose of using the figures as compositional devices, completely anonymous as human beings. However symbolic elements have been introduced into the picture and it is certain that Cézanne would have been aware of their meaning. The dog, curled up asleep at the foot of the picture, represents faithfulness.

The fruit on the ground and in the basket represent the loss of innocence. These symbols have been used for centuries, and Cézanne himself used similar references in earlier works including *The Modern Olympia* (see page 15) which was based on a painting by Manet.

**THE LARGE BATHERS, 1906**

Cézanne spent seven years working on this painting in his methodical manner, returning to the canvas on numerous occasions in order to change aspects, or to add a little, just as he did with all his paintings. The canvas, which is now in the Museum of Art in Philadelphia, was the largest Cézanne painted. It has a strong triangular-shaped center emphasized by the leaning figures and trees, and comprises a group of women—no men are present—who appear to be resting after bathing. The women are crudely depicted, and are more important for the structural shapes they present than for their individuality.

At the center of the triangle on the far side of the river are two figures and behind them a church tower. One of the figures standing on the far bank is a man with his arms folded, staring across at the women. It has been suggested that this is Cézanne himself, under the shadow of the church, looking across the river at the women, at a scene he can never reach. Several of the women are staring back towards the figure. Is this a comment on his relationship with women from whom he grew more distant as life progressed?

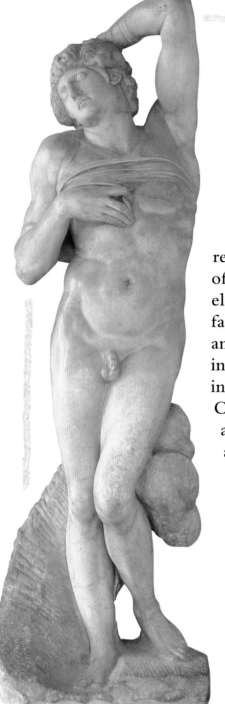

# HOW WERE THEY MADE?
## THE BATHERS

Cézanne would draw figures from life, although he became increasingly awkward with models, especially in unclothed poses. Instead, he started to rely upon memory and references taken from sketches and reproductions of paintings from the Old Masters in the Louvre and elsewhere, even sketches from illustrations in his sister's fashion magazines. One report mentions Cézanne using an album entitled *Le Nu au Musée du Louvre* (The nude in the Louvre Museum), which he bought from a shop in Paris as a reference for figure studies. Wherever Cézanne did make studies from life he would use and reuse the figure in many works, treating it as a stock item which could be called upon for a number of different purposes.

### A PHENOMENAL MEMORY

For his bathers series, Cézanne relied on his memory of the human form to help him create the figures. *"Painting is in here"* he said, tapping his head. Critics have found clear references in the Bathers series to known works such as Michelangelo's *Dying Slave* sculpture (above).

## BATHERS

n addition to the canvases painted in oils he produced a number of pencil and watercolor sketches dominated by blues and greys. These did not serve as preparatory sketches for the oil paintings but are independent versions in their own right. Some of the watercolor and oil paintings appear unfinished because Cézanne has left areas of the paper or canvas uncovered, so the base color shows through. It is almost as if he act of filling in the canvas would have unbalanced the picture, and that the spots of white are as important as the patches of color in creating an overall harmony. This painting demonstrates the "hatching" brushstrokes that Cézanne frequently used, going in different directions to provide movement across the picture surface.

*Cézanne in front of one of the Large Bathers*

### THE LARGE BATHERS—DETAIL

This detail from the sky of *The Large Bathers* (page 25) shows the way in which Cézanne applied the paint. Loose, large brushstrokes have been used to apply fairly thin coats of pigment in a very free style. The contra-angled strokes are clearly visible in this detail, and serve to animate the picture's surface when seen from a distance. The picture gives the appearance of being painted quickly although it is known that Cézanne spent literally years working on the canvas.

27

# THE AUDIENCE FOR THE PICTURES

C ézanne exhibited with the Impressionists during the 1870s and at small shows such as Les Vingt in Brussels but did not have his own exhibition until 1895, when his work was exhibited at the gallery of Paris art dealer, Ambroise Vollard. Cézanne did not need to sell his paintings to make a living as he was financially independent after the death of his father. His work was exhibited sporadically during the late 1890s, and an auction of Émile Zola's art collection on his death in 1902 saw Cézanne's paintings fetch an average of 1,500 francs. The first gallery to buy his work was the Nationalgalerie in Berlin. Shortly before his death in 1906, the art world was beginning to take notice of Cézanne's work, with 30 paintings being displayed in the 1904 Paris Salon and 10 paintings being exhibited at the Grafton Street gallery in London in 1905, thanks to the efforts of dealer Durand-Ruel. In 1907, the year after Cézanne's death, a major retrospective exhibition of his work featuring 56 paintings was held at the Paris Autumn Salon.

## PORTRAIT OF VICTOR CHOCQUET, 1876/7

Victor Chocquet was a civil servant in the Ministry of Finance who was not wealthy, but nevertheless became a collector of art after befriending the Impressionist painters. Cézanne painted his portrait many times. Chocquet built up an impressive collection of paintings including 35 works by Cézanne.

## DARK AND LEGENDARY

The art critic Gustave Geffroy (left) saw the exhibition organized by Ambroise Vollard and wrote the following: *"Passers-by walking into the Galerie Vollard, in rue Laffitte, will be faced with about 50 pictures: figures, landscapes, fruit, flowers, from which they can finally reach a verdict on one of the finest and greatest personalities of our time. Once that has happened, and it is high time it did happen, all that is dark and legendary about Cézanne's life will disappear, and what remains will be a rigorous and yet attractive, masterly and yet naive life's work... He will end up in the Louvre."*

## THE BATH, *c*.1881

*Mary Cassatt*

The American Impressionist painter Mary Cassatt met Cézanne in 1894 when they were both staying at Claude Monet's home town of Giverny. She describes her first encounter with Cézanne; *"When I first saw him, he looked like a cut-throat with large red eyeballs standing out from his head in a most ferocious manner, a rather fierce-looking pointed beard, quite grey, and an excited way of talking that positively made the dishes rattle…in spite of the total disregard for the dictionary of manners, he shows a politeness towards us which no other man here would have shown."*

## ORTRAIT OF AMBROISE VOLLARD *(left detail)*, 1889

A young art dealer named Ambroise Vollard who had made contact with Cézanne through his son Paul, decided to champion Cézanne's work. He arranged a one-man exhibition of Cézanne's paintings in his Paris gallery in 1895, exhibiting 50 works to a public who knew nothing of this painter from Aix.

## SELF-PORTRAIT *(detail)*, 1873/6

Cézanne painted the portraits of his wife, his son, friends such as Zola and Gasquet, and sometimes the servants and laborers around the family estate, but did not undertake commissions in the same way as his contemporaries, such as Renoir, did. Cézanne did not need the money from such commissions but also his very slow and methodical way of working did not lend itself to private sittings. The artist painted his own portrait repeatedly, one model he could guarantee would pose without problems, unlike his young son who could never stay still to the satisfaction of his father. This self-portrait was made around 1875. The critic Louis Vauxcelles described Cézanne in an article: *"Cézanne is a legendary figure with a coarse bristly face, a body wrapped in a haulier's rough woollen greatcoat. But this Cézanne is a master."*

# A LASTING IMPRESSION

**THE FATHER OF US ALL**

Cézanne was described by Picasso (shown left with Jaqueline Roque) as *"My one and only master... Cézanne was like the father of us all."*

Cézanne's art is considered today to be of profound importance to the development of Western art in the 20th century. Historians point to Cézanne's search for the underlying structure in his compositions as the foundation of modern art, from which Cubism and then Abstraction came. He has never been considered an Impressionist painter despite being one of that small group who first exhibited a new way of painting which was so shocking to its public. It is above all Cézanne's obsession with formal elements of composition and his use of color as tone, rather than the Impressionist pursuit of light on surface, that makes his art so important to those who followed. Cézanne's work made it possible for artists to start to question what they saw, the way in which they saw it, and how they interpreted and represented what was in front of them.

**HOMAGE TO CÉZANNE**

*Maurice Denis*

Many artists of different persuasion found something to admire in Cézanne. The Cubists such as Braque and also Picasso considered him the father of Cubism. Symbolist painters such as Gauguin and Maurice Denis looked to Cézanne's work as a source of inspiration even though Cézanne himself thought the Symbolist work too concerned with surface decoration. In 1900, Maurice Denis painted a homage to Cézanne. This painting shows a group of artists gathered round the Cézanne painting *Still Life with Compotier* which had once been owned by Paul Gauguin. Included in the picture are Maurice Denis and his wife, Odilon Redon, Pierre Bonnard, Édouard Vuillard, Paul Serusier, and the art dealer Ambroise Vollard.

## L'ESTAQUE

*Georges Braque*

In a letter to the artist Émile Bernard, Cézanne wrote: *"Treat nature by means of the cylinder, the sphere, the cone, with everything in its proper perspective so that each side of an object or plane is directed towards a central point. Lines parallel to the horizon give breadth, that is a section of nature… Lines perpendicular to this horizon give depth. But nature for us men is more depth than surface…"* This letter has become very famous because when Cézanne referred to seeing nature in terms of the basic shapes, it appeared that he was already looking at things in the Cubist's way. Cubist art first came to the public's attention in 1907 when Braque exhibited a painting at the Paris Salon and Matisse commented that he had reduced everything to little cubes. Cubism has been seen by art historians as the breaking point between representational art and abstract art that was to dominate the 20th century.

## MONT SAINTE-VICTOIRE, 1905/6

A few weeks before he died Cézanne wrote to his son in Paris: *"I must tell you that as a painter I am becoming more clear-sighted before Nature, but with me the realization of my senses is always painful. I cannot attain the intensity that is unfolded before my senses. I do not have the magnificent richness of coloring that animates Nature."*

## LES LAUVES

The studio that Cézanne had built at Les Lauves remains today as a small museum to the artist. Unfortunately it was not possible to preserve the view across to Sainte-Victoire which was so important to Cézanne—it is now obscured by apartment blocks.

# GLOSSARY

**Sandro Botticelli (1445-1510)**—An extremely influential painter who lived and worked in Florence at the end of the 15th century. His best-known works, such as *The Birth of Venus*, use both pagan and Christian imagery together, and are executed in a style which was soon to be displaced by the High Renaissance style of Michelangelo.

**Hatching**—This is shading by means of parallel lines on a drawing or painting. Cross-hatching is shading with two sets of parallel lines, one crossing the other. It is often used to depict shadows or dark tones rather than filling an area with solid color.

**Expressionism**—The Expressionist movement in art sought a way to express emotional force through exaggerated line and color. Expressionist painters turned from the naturalism found in Impressionist art and attempted to create emotional impact with strong colors and simplified forms such as those found in Van Gogh's work.

**Still life**—The still life usually depicts a collection of objects (jugs, plates, flowers, fruit, candles, etc.) which do not appear to be important in their own right but were usually chosen by the artist to symbolize more than their individual appearance. Items such as skulls, hour-glasses, candles or butterflies, were often depicted to represent the transient nature of life, for example, as were certain types of flowers known for their seasonality. The tradition started in about the 16th century.

**Motif**—This is a word which is used to describe a distinctive idea or theme which is continuously elaborated by the artist and applies to many kinds of art forms such as music, painting and literature. Cézanne's motif was Mont Sainte-Victoire, which he painted repeatedly during his lifetime.

**Oeuvre**—A French term which is used to describe the entire output of one artist. An Oeuvre catalogue, therefore, attempts to give a record of every work produced by the artist. The term can also apply to musicians and writers. Zola's book which caused a rift with Cézanne was entitled *L'Oeuvre*, and was a play on words.

## ACKNOWLEDGEMENTS

North American edition Copyright © 2009 *ticktock* Entertainment Ltd.,
First published in North America by *ticktock* Media Ltd.,
The Old Sawmill, 103 Goods Station Road, Tunbridge Wells, Kent, TN1 2DP, UK.
All rights reserved. No part of this publication may be reproduced, stored in a retrieval system, or transmitted in any form or by any means electronic, mechanical, photocopying, recording or otherwise, without prior written permission of the copyright owner.

ISBN 978 1 84696 970 6
Printed in China
9 8 7 6 5 4 3 2 1

Picture Credits  t=top, b=bottom, c=center, l=left, r=right, OFC=outside front cover, IFC=inside front cover, IBC=inside back cover, OBC=outside back cover.

AKG; 3r, 10r, 30tl. Bridgeman Art Library (London); 2tl, 8/9t, 22t & 22cr & 22bl & OBC, 26l, 28tl, 28bl, 28/29t, 30/31t. Giraudon; OFC (main pic), 2/3c & OFC, 4tl, 4/5b, 5t & 5br, 6tl, 6/7b, 6/7t, 8/9b, 10tl, 11r, 12cb & OBC, 12/13t, 13bl & 13br, 14bl & 14cl & 14/15t & 15br, 16bl, 16/17b, 17br, 17tr, 18tl, 19, 20tl, 20/21b & 21br & IFC, 21t, 23bl & 23c & 23br, 24tl, 24bl & 24/25b & 26br & 27bl, 25t & 25br, 28/29c, 29br, 30bl, 30/31c, 31br. Réunion des Musées Nationaux © RMN/R.G.Ojeda; 18cb, 27cr. Roger-Viollet © Harlingue-Viollet; 2cb. Roger-Viollet © Collection Viollet; 7br & 32ct. Tate Gallery (London); 9br,

Every effort has been made to trace the copyright holders and we apologize in advance for any unintentional omissions. We would be pleased to insert the appropriate acknowledgement in any subsequent edition of this publication.

# INDEX

## A

Abstract art 18, 30
Aix-en-Provence 2, 6, 8, 10-12, 16, 24
Aubert, Anne-Élisabeth 2, 8, 11, 12
Auvers-sur-Oise 6, 10

## B

Baille, Jean Baptiste 2, 8, 12
The bath (Cassatt) 29
Bernard, Émile 18, 31
The Birth of Venus (Botticelli) 32
Bonnard, Pierre 30
Botticelli, Sandro 3, 32
Braque, Georges 30, 31

## C

Café Guerbois 6
Caillebotte, Gustave 8
Cassatt, Mary 29
Cézanne, Louis-Auguste 2, 3, 8, 10-12, 23
Cézanne, Marie 11
Cézanne, Paul
  art exhibited 9, 10, 12, 15, 28
  influences 4-7
  interpretation 14-17
  techniques 4, 18-27
  works
    The Abduction 5
    Apotheosis of Delacroix 4
    The Artist's Father 10
    The Artist's Son 10
    The Autopsy 5
    Bathers 24, 26
    Bend in the Road 19
    The Card Players 22
    The Cutting 6
    Flowers and Fruits 20
    The House of Dr Gachet at Auvers 6
    The House of the Hanged Man 7
    Joachim Gasquet 13
    The Large Bathers 24, 25, 27
    Madame Cézanne in a Red Dress 11
    A Modern Olympia 15
    Mont Sainte-Victoire 16, 31
    Mont Sainte-Victoire Seen from Les Lauves 17, 18
    Mountains in Provence 18
    Murals in Jas de Bouffan 3
    The Murder 5
    Paul Alexis reading to Émile Zola 13
    Portrait of Ambroise Vollard 29
    Portrait of Victor Chocquet 28
    Self-Portrait 29
    Still Life with Compotier 30
    Still Life with Curtain 21
    The Strangled Woman 4, 5
    Vessels, Basket and Fruit 21
    Woman with a Coffee Pot 23
  family 2, 8, 10, 11, 12
  friends 2, 10-13
  photographs of 7, 18
Cézanne, Paul (son) 10, 11, 12, 23, 24, 29
Chocquet, Victor 28
Classicism 4, 5
Collège Bourbon 2, 8
Conil, Maxime 16
Courbet, Gustave 4, 6
Cubism 18, 30, 31

## D

Daumier, Honoré 4
The Death of Sardanapalus (Delacroix) 5
Degas, Edgar 9
Le Déjeuner sur l'Herbe (Manet) 6, 24
Delacroix, Eugène 4, 5
Denis, Maurice 30
Doria, Count Armand 7
Durand-Ruel, Paul 8, 12
Dying Slave (Michelangelo) 26

## E

École des Beaux-Arts 2
Emperaire, Achille 12
Expressionism 8, 32

## F

Fiquet, Hortense 6, 10-12, 23, 24, 29
The Floor Strippers (Caillebotte) 8
Four Girls on a Bridge (Munch) 8

## G

Gachet, Dr 6, 15
Gasquet, Joachim 13, 17, 29
Gauguin, Eugéne Henri Paul 8, 9, 30
Geffroy, Gustave 28
Geothem, Marie van 9
Germinal (Zola) 13
Gowing, Lawrence 30

## H

hatching 26, 32
Homage to Cézanne (Denis) 30

## I

Impressionism 7, 17, 18, 28
  exhibitions 7, 8, 9, 10, 15
Ingres, Jean Auguste Dominique 3, 4

## J

Jas de Bouffan 3, 12, 23, 24

## L

Les Lauves 12, 17, 23, 24, 31
L'Estaque 6, 11
L'Estaque (Braque) 30-31
The Little Dancer of Fourteen Years (Degas) 9
Louvre 4, 27, 28

## M

Manet, Édouard 6, 9, 14, 15, 24
Matisse, Henri 31
Michelangelo 26, 32
Monet, Claude 6, 7, 8, 9, 17
Mont Sainte-Victoire 6, 12, 16-17, 32
Montifaud, Marc de 15
motif 16, 32
Munch, Edvard 8

## N

Nana (Zola) 13
Nationalgalerie, Berlin 28
Lè Nu au Musée du Louvre 26

## O

L'Oeuvre (Zola) 12, 13, 14, 32
Olympia (Manet) 14, 15

## P

Picasso, Pablo 30
Pissarro, Camille 6, 7, 9, 10

## R

Realism 5
Redon, Odilon 30
Renoir, Pierre Auguste 6, 8
Romanticism 4
Roque, Jacqueline 30
Les Rougon-Macquart (Zola) 13

## S

Salon 4, 6, 8, 15, 31
  Cézanne exhibited 12, 28
Salon des Refusés 6
Serusier, Paul 30
Seurat, Georges 9
Sisley, Alfred 8
Solari, Emile 12
still life 20-1, 32
Symbolism 30

## T

Titian 14, 15

## V

Valabrègue, Antony 12
van Gogh, Vincent 8, 9, 32
Vauxcelles, Louis 29
Venus of Urbino (Titian) 14, 15
Les Vingt 28
Vollard, Ambroise 12, 30
Vuillard, Édouard 30

## W

Whistler, J.A.M. 9

## Z

Zola, Émile 2, 8, 12-14, 28, 29

# CÉZANNE

TICKTOCK ESSENTIAL ARTISTS

A comprehensive,
informative and highly
readable introduction
to the world of Cézanne.

Written by David Spence, an expert
in the field, this book is based
on the very latest research.

Over 100 beautiful col...
and illustrations bring the world
of Cézanne to life, and shed new
light on the masterpieces he created.

Cézanne   Degas   Gauguin

Manet   Monet   Renoir

ISBN 978-1846969706

50695

9 781846 969706

$6.95          Canada $7.95